Hitler's Vikings

Furious, the Bolsheviks threw themselves against us, the situation was hopeless but the boys fought formidably. While I helped Gebauer to feed the MG with new ammunition I could hear myself swearing non-stop, wishing them the worst possible tortures in hell. I let Gebauer handle the MG alone while I fired alternatively with the assault rifle and with my sub-machine gun. He forgot the danger, pushing his chest above the parapet in order to fire better. 'Down!' I screamed but he laughed, he was just 19 years old. Too late. Gebauer suddenly jerked backwards and sank to one side. I turned him around towards me. He was hit under the left eye, the bullet passing through his neck. He was still alive, blood flowing down from cheek and neck. He begged; 'Write to my mother ... just a few lines ...' and then
I was alone.

(Swedish SS-Unterscharführer Erik Wallin)

HITLER'S VIKINGS

THE HISTORY OF THE SCANDINAVIAN WAFFEN-SS: THE LEGIONS, THE SS-WIKING AND THE SS-NORDLAND

Jonathan Trigg

SPELLMOUNT

Front of jacket: Berlin 1945 – the end. Ragnar Johansson, probably the last Swedish Waffen-SS grenadier to die in World War II, lies next to the shattered Nordland Sdkfz 251 half-track he drove over the Weidendammer Bridge as he, Hans-Gösta Pehrsson and other Nordland survivors tried to escape the city after Hitler's suicide.

Back of jacket: Norwegian Waffen-SS recruiting poster – as with many other recruiting posters used by the Waffen-SS in Scandinavia this one was designed to appeal to the local population's stirring Viking past.

To Erik, a soldier and a gentleman, rest in peace.

First published in 2010
This paperback edition published in 2012 by
Spellmount, an imprint of

The History Press
The Mill, Brimscombe Port
Stroud, Gloucestershire, GL5 2QG
www.thehistorypress.co.uk

© Jonathan Trigg, 2010, 2012

The right of Jonathan Trigg to be identified as the Author
of this work has been asserted in accordance with the
Copyrights, Designs and Patents Act 1988.

British Library Cataloguing in Publication Data.
A catalogue record for this book is available from the British Library.

ISBN 978 0 7524 6729 0

Typesetting and origination by The History Press
Printed in Great Britain
Manufacturing managed by Jellyfish Print Solutions Ltd

Contents

Acknowledgements

This book was probably the first one I thought of writing when I set out on my journey, more than seven years ago now, to chronicle the various foreign volunteer contingents of the Waffen-SS. After all the SS-Wiking was far and away the most famous of the 'non-German' élite divisions and, as its deliberately evocative name suggests, Scandinavians were meant to be its mainstay. Yet I decided early on to delay it for later in the series, saving the best until last perhaps, who knows, that's for others to decide. One unexpected advantage of that decision was that along the way I was able to meet and make contact with a host of people from all over the world whose interest in and knowledge of the Scandinavian Waffen-SS is second to none.

Foremost among this cohort are of course the veterans themselves. Thousands of Norwegians, Danes, Swedes and Finns served in the Waffen-SS during the Second World War and although battle and old age has winnowed their numbers, there remains a relatively large community of men who were eyewitnesses to the greatest and most terrible conflict the world has ever seen. Their willingness to talk to me and share their memories and experiences are the very foundation stones of this book, and I am in their debt. In particular I would like to thank Bjørn Østring and his amazing wife Bergljot, Paul and Gertrude Hveger (as ever a soldier's wife is his most prized asset!), Bjarne Dramstad, Vagner Kristensen, Erwin Bartmann, and the utterly irrepressible Jan Munk. To all I say a huge thank you and I hope the book does you and your memories justice. And a very special thank you to Greta Brörup and her husband Erik, who passed away in January 2010; Greta, I am saddened by your loss.

Alongside these veterans stand a great many others who have been instrumental in making this book a reality. First among equals is James Macleod, historian, enthusiast and soldier. Knut Flovik Thoresen of the Norwegian Army and Jens Post of the Danish Army (good luck in

Afghanistan, Jens) have been a huge help. Not that wearing a uniform was a pre-requisite; a whole phalanx of civilian experts stepped forward too, such as the brilliant Lennart Westberg and Martin Mansson from Sweden, Olli Wikberg from Finland, from Australia Hugh Page-Taylor, from Florida Erik Wiborg (historian and shipping broker no less), and the ever-generous Paul Errington, Chris Hale and John Moore. Last but never least the captain of print and photo wizardry – Tim Shaw (and his eager apprentice Max). To those not named I apologise and offer my thanks.

In my first two volumes I followed the lives of volunteers from before the war, through their recruitment and service, and beyond. In my third instalment this was impossible given the almost total lack of surviving Muslim veterans. This time round there was an embarrassment of riches, and I decided it would be unfair to single out two or three veterans, which would have left the contributions of many others out in the cold. I hope readers agree this was the best approach.

Alongside the testimony of eyewitnesses, historians like nothing more than written primary sources, and in this context these usually consist of fading unit diaries, after-action reports, and citations. So many of these valuable records were lost at the end of the war but those that survived are looked after by some incredibly competent individuals who are seemingly always willing to help writers, so thank you again to Frau Carina Notzke at the Bundesarchiv in Freiburg, and to Frau Martina Caspers in Koblenz.

The work of other writers has of course been invaluable. Firstly, the incomparable Paul Carrell, whose pioneering work in the 1960s, *Hitler's War on Russia*, looking at the war with the Soviet Union from a German viewpoint, should be required reading for everyone studying the period. Secondly, Douglas E. Nash's book on the Battle of the Cherkassy Pocket, *Hell's Gate*, delivers that rare treat, an astounding work of history and a cracking read.

Beyond veterans and archives, and often linking the two, lies the growing power of the internet. As online communities become ever-more pervasive and well-connected they can act as invaluable research and information tools, and for this topic yet again Troy Tempest's www.feldpost.tv/forum and Jason Pipes' www.feldgrau.net were incredibly useful.

Thank you as well to everyone who has bought and read *Hitler's Gauls*, *Hitler's Flemish Lions* and *Hitler's Jihadis*; I hope that this fourth instalment doesn't disappoint. Several people helped me with proof reading and with the text, made suggestions and amendments and corrected mistakes to improve the writing and flow, for that I thank them, and whilst I have of course made every effort to achieve accuracy if there are any mistakes then they are entirely my own.

Lastly I have now officially given up trying to convert my wife Rachel into becoming a fan of military history. It was a valiant effort but I am big enough to admit defeat. But, as ever, she has supported me all the way, and if this is the last book in the series I owe her a huge thank you for all the support over the years. As for the ever-wonderful Maddy and Jack, as this is the only part of the book they will read I will say read on and you never know, you might like it!

Notes on the Text

Military ranks: Waffen-SS ranks are used throughout for Waffen-SS personnel. A conversion chart to comparative British Army ranks has been provided as Appendix B. For officers and soldiers of the German Army (*Heer*) their ranks are given firstly in their original German and then the British Army equivalents in brackets. Red Army ranks are given directly in British Army terms.

Military terminology: As far as possible the military terminology used is that of the time and the army involved, on occasion an attempt has been made to 'translate' that terminology into modern British Army parlance in order to aid understanding.

Unit designation: All German orders of battle use an English translation and then the original unit designation, e.g. Mountain Corps is followed by 'Gebirgs Korps' in brackets, and this is continued throughout except in certain circumstances where it is further simplified to improve the flow of the text or to establish authenticity, as in the relevant chapter titles. The only exceptions to this rule are for the national legions from Norway and Denmark. As so many veterans from those units have been extremely kind to me in researching this book I feel it only right that I repay that kindness by using their own names for their formations. So I use the Danish 'Frikorps Danmark' instead of the German 'Freikorps Danmark' and the Norwegian 'Den Norske Legion' (the DNL) instead of the German 'Legion Norwegen'. I hope this doesn't confuse readers. Again, to remain true to the time, Russian formations are numbered, while German formations at corps or army level are either written out or use the original Roman numerals. Smaller units such as divisions and regiments are numbered.

Foreign words: Where non-English words are used they are italicised unless in common usage and English translations are provided. If they are then used often in the text they are no longer italicised.

Measurements: Distances are given in miles but weapon calibres are given in their usual metric form.

Place names: Particularly with regard to places in the former Soviet Union I have stuck with one spelling if there are several, mostly the one in common usage at the time, but have also initially tried to include other derivations in brackets to aid the reader following the ebb and flow of campaigns on any modern maps they may have. However, I am aware that since the Ukraine achieved its independence many place names have rightly been 'ukrainian-ised'; I have tried to include them as well. French has its accents, German its umlaut, and the Scandinavian languages have their own intonations; I have tried to get this right, if I have failed I apologise.

Preface

Scans of every general-interest book on the Waffen-SS, and they are legion, constantly refer to Norwegians, Danes, Swedes and Finns serving in their ranks and fighting in some of the most famous battles of the war. In fact the first ever book I read on the Waffen-SS, Rupert Butler's *The Black Angels*, made enough references to these men to whet the appetite but not satisfy it. Like many others I was fascinated and wanted to know more. I dug deeper and found myself in a wholly unexpected world. A world not of dry history but of real people whose personalities began to emerge from the text: of a paranoid Adolf Hitler wanting a dedicated body of troops to protect him and his rule from overthrow, of Heinrich Himmler carrying out genocide for his master while dreaming of vast armies of blond, blue-eyed 'supermen' from every corner of the globe and all under his control. Suddenly the monsters weren't under the bed any more but on the page.

The Waffen-SS has gone through several permutations in the public mind. A tiny gang of strong-arm thugs became goose-stepping giants decked out in sinister black uniforms. War transformed the picture into one of a brand-new military élite winning plaudits in campaign after campaign. Yet the trophies were tarnished. The links to the concentration camps, the Holocaust and the utter barbarity of the regime they served lingered on. Then in a post-war world, to quote the title of Gerald Reitlinger's famous book, they became the 'alibi of a nation'. Even now the armed SS stir up waves of controversy. Perhaps it is too much to hope for sober reflection and examination of the men who won such tremendous victories against the odds as the capture of Belgrade, the storming of the Klissura Pass and the victory at Kharkov, while at the same time shooting unarmed prisoners-of-war at Le Paradis and Malmédy.

There were no Scandinavians at Le Paradis or Malmédy, but they wore the same uniform as the men who pulled the triggers at those massacres.

This book, the fourth in the Hitler's Legions series, seeks to uncover the reality behind the myth. Why was there a Scandinavian Waffen-SS and what did they and their recruiters hope to achieve? The men who went off to war, sometimes thousands of miles from their homes, often did not return. For those that fought it was an intensely personal experience, and while the history of the great battles of the Second World War has been written and re-written it is far too easy to get lost in the sweeping movements of vast armies and forget that those hosts were made up of individuals, each struggling to do his or her duty and survive. This book seeks in some small way to tell the story of those individual soldiers caught up in what is still, and hopefully will remain, the largest war ever fought. As one of the veterans said to me at the end of an interview:

Last but not least, make sure that you do your very best to stop anything like it from ever happening again. Make sure that you and future generations will not have to face an ordeal like the one mine had to. So much evil, so many tears, so much blood … never again.

Jon Trigg
Sheffield, UK

Introduction

Let thunder growl, you were louder than it.
Let the winds blow, you were swifter than they.
Let the water freeze, you were harder than ice.
Let the wolves ravage, you were fiercer than they.
You were a man, a warrior, a Viking,
and none was your master, until one day your day was done,
and you went into the darkness still laughing.

From the thirteenth century Icelandic Viking saga, *The Burning of Njal*

Vikings, Northmen, the Norse – the very names themselves conjure up romantic and bloody images of strident, horn-helmed warriors and dragon-prowed longboats, of adventure, glory and legendary discovery. For almost 500 years, from around AD 800, these raiders and sea pirates terrorised huge swathes of Europe and Asia. In their open boats they dominated the North and Baltic Seas, sailed down the Liffey, the Humber, the Seine, the Dnieper and the Volga, crossed the Atlantic to colonise Iceland and Greenland, and even reached the New World centuries before Christopher Columbus was born.

At first they would appear from nowhere to raid and pillage, and then just as quickly sail away home, then they began to come to conquer and to settle. Hundreds of thousands of Scandinavians left their beautiful but poor homelands to make new lives in Ireland, Britain, France, the Baltic lands and even the Ukraine. With a sword in one hand, and more often than not, a bag of trade goods in the other they turned the seas and rivers of Europe into highways for commerce as well as routes for raiding and savagery. They founded cities that are still with us today like Dublin and Limerick, as well as long-disappeared states such as Kiev Rus, the Duchy of Normandy and the Orkneys. Sailors, merchants and craftsmen, they were first and foremost warriors whose military prowess was recognised as far away as Constantinople, the fabled Great City of Viking storytelling, 'Miklagard'. In that city they formed the Emperor's bodyguard, his élite Varangians.

Then, like a powerful storm, they seemed to blow themselves out. Having changed the face of Europe they disappeared from it. Other nations and peoples came to the fore as the Scandinavians sank into the relative obscurity that enfolds them still. Where once they were central to Europe and its future, they became little more than its northern fringe, both geographically and politically. A brief resurgence of empire and power for royal Sweden came in the seventeenth century but was abruptly ended by Peter the Great in the bloody defeat at Poltava in 1709.

Christianised during their heyday of pillage and war, the Scandinavians then began to form into centralised kingdoms that became free and peaceful constitutional monarchies over the course of centuries, and all without the trauma of a revolution or civil war. Multi-party democracy has become the accepted norm, and the modern states of Denmark, Norway, Sweden and Finland were, and still are, prosperous and contented. Cultural traditions are strong and celebrated wholeheartedly, but the cult of the warrior (the dominant aspect of Viking life) has been firmly rejected; the national armies are small and poorly funded, and neutrality is the default position. When the horror of industrialised war enveloped Europe in 1914, the Scandinavians remained aloof and avoided the butchery of the trenches. Involvement in the Second World War was forced on them by invaders, but even then Sweden managed to remain neutral and free throughout.

As the populations of other European countries exploded with the advent of the Industrial Revolution and huge migrations swept across borders, the total number of Scandinavians stayed relatively low and the different populations remained ethnically homogenous. Even today, with pretty liberal asylum and immigration policies, the number of immigrants is remarkably low in comparison to elsewhere in Europe. On the eve of the Second World War the entire populations of Sweden (6.5 million), Denmark (4.5 million), Finland (4 million) and Norway (3.5 million) added up to less than a third of Great Britain's, and minorities tended to be very small and made up of other Scandinavians – Finland's biggest minority was ethnic Swedes.

Yet despite the passage of centuries the image of the Viking warrior has persisted, and was never more powerful than during the war that engulfed Europe from 1939 to 1945. It exerted a powerful pull on some members of the Nazi leadership, and found expression in the creation of six legions, battalions and divisions in the Nazis' own Varangian guard, an organisation that remains deeply controversial even now, more than 60 years later – the Waffen-SS. The numbers involved were significant as well, with between 10 and 20,000 Norwegians, Danes, Swedes and Finns joining during the war; the entire pre-war Danish armed forces numbered just 6,600 men.

At first the only Scandinavians in the Waffen-SS were a handful who joined before the war, and even then most of them were either ethnic Germans born the wrong side of a re-drawn border or of mixed German/Scandinavian parentage. But that didn't matter as the Waffen-SS was established as a German and not a multi-national force, intended to showcase the superiority of the so-called Aryan master race (*das Herrenvolk*). However, before a shot had been fired in anger their character was changing. Adolf Hitler may have caused the armed SS to be born, but the man who nurtured it, Heinrich Himmler, had a very different vision as to what the armed SS could and should be. Himmler foresaw legions of athletic, blond, blue-eyed giants standing guard over a German-dominated Europe stretching from the Atlantic right up to the Urals, and to achieve this he needed men, and lots of them. The *Wehrmacht* (the German armed forces comprising the army – *Heer*, navy – *Kriegsmarine*, and air force – *Luftwaffe*) jealously controlled the flow of German national recruits so Himmler had to look elsewhere. Suddenly the idea of recruiting tall, blond-haired, blue-eyed *Scandinavians* seemed a very good idea, and there were even rightwing pro-Nazi parties in the Nordic countries to act as ready-made recruiting pools. The only question was how to get hold of them; the answer was invasion.

The rise of the extreme Right in the 1930s was not a phenomenon restricted to Germany. All across Europe in the wake of Mussolini and Hitler a plethora of parties and movements had appeared. In Britain it was Mosley's BUF, in France it was Doriot's PPF and Déat's RNP, in Belgium Degrelle's Cristus Rex and De Clercq's VNV, and in Holland Mussert's NSB. In Norway it was Quisling's NS, in Denmark Clausen's DNSAP and in Sweden Lindholm's SSS, among others. Nowhere, outside Germany and Italy, did these parties seriously challenge for political power, and levels of support varied from the PPF's substantial quarter of a million members to the very low thousands for the Swedish parties. While elements of the French, Dutch and Flemish movements sometimes exhibited a semi-mainstream appeal, this was not the case in Scandinavia where they remained small, poorly-supported and prone to in-fighting. All this changed at midnight on 29 November 1939 with the following statement to his troops by General Kirill Afanasievich Meretskov of the Red Army:

The leader of the Danish neo-Nazis, Frits Clausen, strolls through crowds of saluting supporters.

> Comrades, soldiers of the Red Army, officers, commissars and political workers! To fulfil the Soviet Government's and our great Fatherland's will I hereby order: the troops in Leningrad Military District are to march over the frontier, crush the Finnish forces, and once and for all secure the Soviet Union's north-western borders and Lenin's city, the crib of the revolution of the proletariat.

This communication heralded the invasion of one of Europe's smallest countries by one of the world's largest. The Soviet first wave alone comprised more than 250,000 men, it outnumbered the Finns two-to-one, and was accompanied by fleets of tanks and aircraft and masses of artillery. Against them the Finns had little more than a handful of First World War anti-tank guns and obsolete planes.

The rest of Scandinavia, and indeed the world, looked on horrified as a supremely confident Red Army swept forward into Finland expecting an easy victory over the tiny nation. The resulting fight was anything but, as the courageous Finns held their ground and inflicted devastating reverses on the ill-prepared Soviets; nowhere more so than in the utter annihilation of the Red Army's 44th Division in the snow at Suomussalmi in late December. By the time hostilities ended on 13 March 1940 the Red Army had been forced to commit more than one million Soviet troops to the fighting and Stalin had been humiliated. As for the Swedes, Norwegians and Danes, they were both angry and fearful as they looked east and saw a brutal dictatorship seemingly willing to assault peaceful countries and bring death and destruction to their doorsteps. The Scandinavian Far-Right's answer was to look south to Nazi Germany for salvation.

When the Germans came to Scandinavia though, it was not in a spirit of brotherly love, but in the back of armoured personnel carriers as they invaded and occupied Denmark and Norway in the spring of 1940. Sweden remained neutral and inviolate. Himmler naively believed that the invasions would be the signal for thousands of locals to flock to the banners of the Waffen-SS. So recruiting offices were opened in Oslo and Copenhagen in 1940 to fill a new SS division of 'Germanics' – the term given to peoples Himmler considered to be on a racial par with Germans – the aptly-named *SS-Wiking*. The new division was to have three regiments; the veteran national German *Germania*, and the new Dutch *Westland* and the Scandinavian *Nordland*. The Finns were allowed to form an all-Finnish battalion (although many of the senior positions would be filled by Germans) – officially sanctioned by their government – in the new division.

Bjørn Østring in the trenches around Leningrad wearing a typically non-issue jumper from back home. For the Scandinavians comfort was more important than strictly adhering to the Germans' rigorous dress regulations. (Erik Wiborg)

Left: Danish recruiting poster for the Waffen-SS. The Viking image in the background was intended to evoke a glorious, martial tradition in the minds of would-be volunteers.

Right: Recruiting poster for the Norwegian SS-Ski Battalion Norge. The theme is very much one of defending hearth and home from the evils of communism.

However, even including the Finns, fewer than 3,000 Nordics came forward to join the Dutch and Flemish recruits, and the SS-Wiking had to rely on native and ethnic Germans to make up the numbers. Disappointed but not finished, the SS tried again in 1941 using the new war against the Soviet Union as its recruiting sergeant. They formed so-called 'national legions' in both Norway and Denmark, respectively the *Den Norske Legion* and *Frikorps Danmark* (the *Legion Norwegen* and *Freikorps Danmark* in German). Swedes were covertly encouraged to join as well and a slow trickle started to come in. The DNL and Frikorps never reached even regimental strength and were not given the best equipment or thorough training. Armed with little more than small-arms, the Norwegians were sent to man the siege lines facing Leningrad in the frozen north of Russia. There they spent a frustrating 18 months slogging it out with the Russians in almost First World War conditions as their strength dwindled and reinforcements dried up. The Danes fared even worse, being sent to reinforce the SS-Totenkopf Division in the horror of the Demyansk Pocket. They lost two commanders in a month and whole rafts of volunteers were swept away in the vicious fighting.

As the Scandinavian legions were training and preparing for the Front their countrymen in the Wiking were taking part in the largest military operation the world had ever seen – Operation Barbarossa, the invasion of the Soviet Union. The Wiking's Scandinavians drove across eastern Poland and into the Soviet Union proper, joining Army Group South in its advance through the Ukraine. Through the summer and autumn the Wiking distinguished itself in the 'battles of the frontier' and the subsequent capture of the Ukraine. The winter saw it reach the Don River before retreating back to the Mius River as the horrendous weather and ferocious resistance stopped the headlong advance in its tracks – Barbarossa had failed. In spring 1942 the Wehrmacht went on the offensive again, and the Wiking was in the forefront of the renewed push east to simultaneously reach the Volga River and occupy the oil-producing Caucasus region. Within touching distance of the fabled city of Astrakhan, on the shores of the Caspian Sea, the Scandinavians were stopped again and forced to retrace their steps north. By this time casualties had wreaked havoc in their ranks and their numbers were pitifully low; the division had become German in all but name. The new year of 1943 found the Wiking and its remaining Scandinavians back in the Ukraine on the defensive against growing Soviet pressure.

Far to the north that warm spring, both Nordic national legions were depleted, disgruntled and exhausted. Withdrawn back to Germany they were disbanded and the legionnaires offered the chance to sign on again to join yet another new SS division – the *SS-Nordland*.

The Norwegian Wiking NCO, Rottenführer Tord Bergstrand, fighting in Russia during Operation Barbarossa, 1941.

The Nordland, as its name suggests, was conceived as the pinnacle of the Nordic war effort for the Waffen-SS. The regiment of the same name from the Wiking was nominated as the cadre for the new division with the majority, but not all, of Wiking's Danes, Norwegians and Swedes transferred over. With this act the baton of the Scandinavian Waffen-SS was firmly passed from the veteran Wiking to the freshly-minted Nordland, and a new chapter begun for the Scandinavian Waffen-SS. That chapter would be written without the Finnish battalion, as its members were withdrawn home by their government and the unit replaced in the Wiking by an Estonian battalion. The Wiking old boys were joined in the Nordland by their countrymen from the national legions and a new tranche of volunteers. By this time the days of the Scandinavians being used mainly just to fill the ranks of the German-officered infantry companies were gone, and they occupied a lot of the technical posts as well as command appointments. The very best and latest equipment came along as well to complement their newly-recognised military competence, and the Nordland was designated as a powerful panzer-grenadier division (a mixed unit of infantry and tanks) with its own armour.

Forming and training in occupied Yugoslavia, the Nordland was intended as one of three élite divisions in the newly-created *III Germanic SS-Panzer Corps* under the command of the charismatic Felix Steiner. The other two were to be the Wiking (now a hugely-powerful panzer division) and a new Dutch division, the *SS-Nederland*. As it turned out the Wiking couldn't be spared from the Russian Front, and indeed never fought alongside its intended stable mates, while the Dutch could only form a large brigade rather than a full division. Regardless, the Corps was considered battle-worthy and sent more than 1,000 miles north to the Oranienbaum Pocket near Leningrad. But after more than two years of siege it was the Red Army that held the advantage and not the besiegers. As 1944 dawned the Soviet juggernaut burst out of the Pocket and sent the Germans reeling back towards the Baltic states. The Scandinavians in the Nordland fought doggedly as they were forced backwards, joined in their desperate defence by Estonian and Latvian Waffen-SS divisions fighting to protect their homes. By spring the Nordland was dug in around the ancient Estonian city of Narva and the river that runs through it of the same name. Massive Soviet attacks developed into what became popularly known as the 'Battle of the European SS', some of the most brutal and intense fighting seen in the entire Russo-German war. The fighting was immensely costly with thousands of Danes, Norwegians, Swedes, Dutch, Estonians and Flemings dying alongside their German comrades; but the Red Army was held, giving the Wehrmacht a rare success that summer.

Felix Steiner (centre, with peaked cap) as commander of the Wiking Division in Russia in 1941. He would become the guiding figure in the foreign Waffen-SS and a much-celebrated figure among veterans after the war. (Comm. Felix Steiner)

The Nordland Regiment advance through Russia during Operation Barbarossa, summer 1941. (Erik Wiborg)

Russia 1941 – some of the Wiking's Danes; Torkild Herman Nielsen is sitting on the bonnet in the middle, Ignatz '*Ine*' Schwab is second from right sitting on the fender. Schwab volunteered along with his two brothers Hugo and Niels. Niels was killed in action with the 1st SS-Brigade in February 1942. Ignatz was awarded the Iron Cross at Cherkassy before himself being killed in action. (Jens Post)

The German Army in the East (the *Ostheer*) might have held in the north, but it was not so fortunate in the south, where almost a quarter of its total strength was wiped out by the Soviets' gargantuan summer offensive, Operation Bagration. As the Red Army charged forward the Wiking was called north from the Ukraine to bolster the desperate defence. Despite the creation of the Nordland there were still a few hundred Nordics who had stayed in the old flagship Germanic division, and these men now found themselves rushed to join their Waffen-SS brethren from the Totenkopf in the shadows of Warsaw. On the Vistula the two SS panzer divisions again proved their worth, and in dramatic fashion managed to finally halt the Bagration offensive hundreds of miles from its start point.

At the same time the German's Army Group North was forced to send some of its best divisions south to try and plug the huge gap in the line left by Bagration, and was then hit by its own Red whirlwind and almost crushed. Estonia was lost and the Nordland, along with the rest of the Army Group, was bottled up in the Latvian province of Courland. With their backs to the sea and a 'no retreat' order from the Führer in their pocket, the newly-christened Army Group Courland fought a series of six epic battles that would finally end on 8 May 1945 with the exhausted survivors filing into Soviet captivity. The Nordland was saved from that uncertain fate by a withdrawal order that took it by sea back to Germany for one last throw of the dice defending the eastern German provinces of Pomerania and East Prussia.

For the Wiking, 1945 saw it sent with most of the remaining premier Waffen-SS divisions to the south of the Eastern Front in Hungary. So as a last irony, as the Red Army geared up for a final push across Germany to capture Berlin and destroy Nazism, the last and best of the Führer's 'fire-brigades' were deployed hundreds of miles away vainly trying to relieve the siege of Budapest and recapture the Hungarian oilfields. Wiking's Scandinavians would fight in three more desperate attacks on the Magyar plains before being bundled back into Austria.

Back in northern Germany a hugely depleted Nordland, along with its European stable mate divisions – the Dutch SS-Nederland and Belgian SS-Langemarck and SS-Wallonien – took part in one last offensive as they tried to blunt the Soviet advance towards the Oder River. Unsurprisingly, the flow of eager recruits from Denmark, Norway and Sweden had dried up and the Nordland's battalions were mere shadows of their former selves, the gaps filled with unemployed ground crew from the Luftwaffe and sailors from the Kriegsmarine. In a last hurrah, the besieged German town of Arnswalde was relieved, and the grateful garrison and local civilians flooded out to dubious safety in German-held territory. The Nordland was then forced to retreat yet again to defend the Oder River line at the river port of Altdamm opposite Berlin.

Like an old punch-drunk boxer the division reeled under blow after blow, but stubbornly refused to lie down. It was at the mercy of events. When it came the Soviet offensive across the mighty Oder splintered the division with hundreds of men surrounded, killed or forced to retreat north. Those that survived, including the command group, somehow regrouped and ended up in Berlin where they became the mainstay of the defence. Along with a French battlegroup (a *kampfgruppe*) from the SS-Charlemagne Division, a Latvian SS battalion, some Hitler Youth boys and the remnants of some Army formations, the Nordland fought on in the rubble of the Third Reich's capital. Hitler's suicide finally signalled a welcome end to the fighting in the city. Spurred on by dread of Soviet captivity many of the surviving Nordic volunteers joined their German comrades in attempting to break out west on the night of 1 May. Most of them, including their highly-decorated former divisional commander Joachim Ziegler, did not make it. A few did succeed and headed home. Those who did not die or escape joined the endless columns of prisoners being herded east to years of suffering in the Soviet Union's slave labour camps, the infamous *gulags*.

For the Danes and Norwegians still in the Wiking, the end of hostilities offered the same dangerous option, to head west and surrender to the Anglo-Americans and escape the vengeful Red Army. The Wiking men fared better than their comrades in the Nordland, and most reached safety. Those that didn't, joined their countrymen in Siberia.

As the volunteers were gradually released from POW camps, they headed home and were greeted less than warmly by their countrymen. Denmark and Norway in particular were convulsed with a need to cleanse themselves of the shadows of collaboration. Tens of thousands of people were investigated, tried and convicted of a variety of offences. Leading collaborators and political figures were executed and most of the volunteers went to prison. Even neutral Sweden punished some of its own ex-Wiking and Nordland men, few as they were. It was to be many years before all the former volunteers were free from jail or Soviet gulags. Still young, they sought to rebuild their lives, neither forgetting what they had done, nor dwelling on it either. Most worked hard, had careers, married and brought up families. Grandfathers and great-grandfathers now, their actions still provoke powerful reactions even today, with some celebrating them as heroes and the harbingers of a new 'European identity and army', while others utterly condemn them. The reality though is that while the vast majority of people, quite rightly, deplore the evil of Hitler and Nazism, they know nothing of the foreign volunteers who fought for that most controversial force, the Waffen-SS. If we are never to repeat the tragedy of the war and the Holocaust it is necessary to continually inform and educate people as to what really happened, and for people to make a judgement on the Scandinavian volunteers it is just as necessary to put the facts in front of them so they can make up their own minds. This book sets out those facts about the thousands of young Norwegians, Danes, Swedes and Finns who joined the Waffen-SS.

I

1940 – Occupation, the SS-Wiking and the Beginning of the Scandinavian Waffen-SS

A new man, the storm trooper, the élite of central Europe. A completely new race, cunning, strong, and packed with purpose … battle proven, merciless to himself and others.

Ernst Jünger, winner of Imperial Germany's highest bravery award, the Pour le Mérite (the 'Blue Max') at the age of 23 in the First World War and author of *Storm of Steel.*

The Waffen-SS

In the near-anarchy of Germany's Weimar Republic of the 1930s it was commonplace at political meetings for fights to break out and speakers to be physically attacked by thugs from opposing parties. This was especially true for Communist and Nazi events, and the parties organised their supporters into paramilitary groups to both protect themselves and attack opponents. The Nazis enshrined this activity in the brown-shirted *Sturmabteilung* (the SA – Storm Troop), but as the size of the SA ballooned it became harder to control. Under the increasingly strident leadership of the flamboyant ex-soldier Ernst Röhm, the SA began to demand revolutionary social change in Germany that was unacceptable both to Hitler and his backers in the German Army (the *Reichswehr*) and big business. Hitler needed a counter-balance to the SA and he found it in the concept of a small, élite, political police force answerable only to him – the SS.

Originally a tiny 20-man group of toughs recruited to protect Hitler personally as Nazi Party leader, the pre-war *Schützstaffel* (the SS – Protection Squad) was the brainchild of one of his subordinates, the bespectacled and unprepossessing Heinrich Himmler. Hitler bestowed upon him the rather grandiose title of Reichsführer-SS and encouraged a rivalry with the SA. Himmler was loyal but also possessed of vaulting ambition, and he used his talents as a ruthless political intriguer and administrator to take Hitler's original idea and, in less than a decade, create nothing less than a state within a state, and a multi-faceted organisation whose malign power and influence spread across Germany and all the occupied lands.

As the SS gradually became a byword for every aspect of Nazi activity, Himmler did not forget its original purpose; indeed it was central to his plans for the future. Sitting in his headquarters, in a former art school on the Prinz Albrecht Strasse in Berlin, or in the restored Gothic grandeur of the Schloss Wewelsburg in Westphalia, the strict vegetarian and one-time chicken farmer dreamed of an SS empire that stretched from the Atlantic to the Urals. That empire was to be created and safeguarded by a new force, not the existing German Army, but by a 'second army of the state', utterly loyal and dedicated to the ideology of National Socialism – the 'Armed' or *Waffen-SS*.

Political soldiers

For the new Waffen-SS, Himmler translated Hitler's vague concept into a fully-fledged programme encompassing everything from unbelievably strict entrance criteria, to exacting training standards, to views on religion and morality, even down to the minutiae of uniforms. As ever with Himmler the key was 'detail'. All nations' armed forces have entry standards, usually physical, educational and moral ones. Recruits must have the physical fitness and level of education that enables them to perform their duties, while being of good character and not a convicted felon. For the Waffen-SS these baseline requirements were taken to a hitherto unheard of extreme. Recruits had to be aged between 17 and 22, and a minimum of 5'9" tall (168cm – above the average for the time and also Himmler's height). They had to be physically fit and at least of secondary education standard, although university graduates were quite rare, unlike in the Army.

While these standards weren't unduly strict in themselves, they were overlaid with a 'racial and political' element that was exacting to say the least. From 1935 onwards Himmler instituted the requirement for every would-be SS recruit to prove their 'pure' Aryan genealogy, dating back to 1800 for enlisted men and 1750 for officer candidates –great-grandparents and beyond. Having to produce a family tree to enlist was unheard of in the rest of the Wehrmacht, and in any other army in the world for that matter. It was then, and remains still, a peculiarity of the Waffen-SS. But it wasn't even enough to *be* Aryan; you had to *look* Aryan. The Reichsführer himself used to boast of examining the photo of every prospective Waffen-SS officer to ensure they exhibited the required level of 'Nordic features', with blond hair and blue eyes being top of the list. But it didn't stop there; as the Waffen-SS was as much about the mind as the body, so applicants also had to demonstrate the requisite level of ideological commitment as outlined in 'The Soldiers' Friend' (*Der Soldatenfreund* – a handbook issued to every member of the armed forces):

> Every pure-blooded German in good health [can] become a member. He must be of excellent character, have no criminal record, and be an ardent adherent to all National Socialist doctrines. Members of the Hitler Youth will be given preference because their aptitudes and schooling are indicative that they have become acquainted with the ideology of the SS.

Even in supposedly 'Aryan' Germany these phenomenally high standards meant the rejection of a staggering 85 per cent of all applicants, and the rate was even higher for Hitler's personal bodyguard regiment, the *SS-Leibstandarte Adolf Hitler* (LSSAH – the SS Bodyguard Adolf Hitler), where a single dental filling was grounds for rejection. For those lucky few who passed selection, the terms of service were a minimum of four years for rankers, 12 years for NCOs (corporals and sergeants) and 25 years for officers. In contrast, soldiers of all ranks in the modern British Army sign up for a maximum of three years.

The *Leibstandarte*, *Verfügungstruppen* and the *Totenkopfverbände*

Once signed up, a recruit joined one of the three original premier Waffen-SS formations: a minority went into the *Leibstandarte*, commanded by Josef 'Sepp' Dietrich, based at the old Prussian Cadet School in the Lichterfelde Barracks in Berlin. There they were a law unto themselves, even amongst the Waffen-SS, with much more emphasis on ceremonial and parade ground duties than was good for their future military effectiveness. While this military neglect was true for the semi-independent Leibstandarte, it was most definitely not true for the men who joined the real cradle of Waffen-SS military excellence, the *Verfügungstruppen* (SS-VT – 'Special Purpose Troops'). Later famous as the *Das Reich* Division, the SS-VT was initially composed of two regiments, the *Deutschland* and *Germania*, who were then joined by a third, the Austrian-manned *Der Führer*, after the annexation of Austria in 1938 (the Anschluss). Unlike its sister formation the Leibstandarte, the SS-VT focused exclusively on becoming a first-rate military unit, and men from these three pre-war regiments would come to dominate the short-lived history of the Waffen-SS. If a recruit did not join Dietrich's men or the SS-VT, he ended up in the aptly named *Totenkopfverbände* ('Death's Head Units'), under the brutal leadership of Theodor Eicke. Organised on a regional basis with regiments (*Standarten*) in each major city in Germany their duties revolved around guarding Nazi Germany's concentration camps. While professional military training was not their forte, the Totenkopf regiments in effect became a major reserve pool for the Waffen-SS as it grew after the outbreak of war.

A new type of training

Initially military training in the Waffen-SS was pretty basic, but this changed dramatically after Himmler managed to persuade a number of professional ex-Army officers to join the new force. Lured with promises of rapid promotion and a blank page on which to make their mark, two men in particular joined up who would forge the Waffen-SS into the élite it would become – Paul Hausser and Felix Steiner. Both were decorated veterans from the First World War, had gone on to serve in the post-war fighting in eastern Germany against local Communists, Poles and Balts, and were also that rarest of beasts in any nation's military – original thinkers.

Felix Martin Julius Steiner, born in 1896 in East Prussia, served as an infantryman during the First World War, fighting at the Battles of Tannenberg and the Masurian Lakes in the east, and Flanders and Cambrai in the west. Appalled by the mass slaughter of huge conscript armies in the trenches, he became a strong advocate of using small, highly motivated, highly trained and well-equipped assault units. Much of the training programme the Waffen-SS came to use was written by this fairly short, slightly overweight figure, who seemed to have a smile and cheery word for everyone who served under him.

Paul 'Papa' Hausser was 16 years older than Felix Steiner, and also an eastern German, hailing from Brandenburg. Every inch the military patrician, Hausser was of slim build, with grey-white hair and a prominent, aquiline nose. Having retired from the army in 1932 as a Lieutenant-General after a distinguished career, he was personally invited to join the Waffen-SS in 1934 by Himmler himself. Made responsible for 'professionalising' the Waffen-SS, and ensuring it was a modern military force in every sense, he started his transformation at the two SS officer schools at Bad Tölz in Bavaria and Braunschweig in Lower Saxony. After turning them into premier military academies, he went on to become the overall inspector of the SS-VT.

Young Finnish Waffen-SS volunteers take cover in a trench during training.

Between them these two quite extraordinary men created something entirely new in the German armed forces. Training in the German Army was very effective but also very formal, with an emphasis on building teamwork through parade ground discipline and a strict adherence to the hierarchy of rank. Hausser and Steiner swept this approach away, with their priorities being threefold: firstly, supreme physical fitness and comradeship built particularly through sport; secondly excellent combat skills including the repeated use of exercises with live ammunition, and lastly, skill-at-arms focusing on superior marksmanship. SS recruits were taught how best to operate in small groups, the eight-man section and the 30-man platoon (*Gruppe* and *Zug* – see Appendix B for further description), the value of aggression and attack in defeating an enemy and keeping down casualties, and the benefits of a close and easy relationship between men, NCOs and officers. All officer candidates had to serve time in the ranks, they trained and ate with their men, and promotion was seen to be on merit rather than class and education. Off-duty Waffen-SS men even addressed each other as 'Comrade' (*Kamerad*) rather than by their formal ranks. Such things were unheard of in any European army of the time. The Waffen-SS wore different uniforms as well, in the field they were the first force to wear camouflage combat clothing, and in barracks they often wore an all-black uniform, giving rise to their nickname, 'the black guards'. Their entire theory of battle, their 'doctrine', was also different, insisting enthusiastically on an all-arms battle relying heavily on firepower and movement with tanks, artillery, aircraft and infantry all working together. These things are now standard practice in modern armies across the globe, but at the time they were ridiculed by the far more conservative German Army.

First Blood – the Night of the Long Knives

Despite its growing professionalism, the Waffen-SS was still viewed in 1934 as a political police force 'playing at soldiers'. The SA was by far the dominant force in Nazi politics with its three-million-strong membership swaggering across Germany loudly shouting for a 'brown revolution' that would sweep away the old conservative institutions like the army, and remove power from the big industrialists to usher in a new 'socialist' state (*Reich*). Needless to say Hitler was horrified by these ideas and decided to destroy the monster he had created, and the instrument of that destruction was to be none other than the armed soldiers of the SS.

On 30 June 1934, SS formations left their barracks to break the power of the SA once and for all in the infamous 'Night of the Long Knives'. The Leibstandarte was in the vanguard, and drove all the way south to the Bavarian spa resort town of Bad Wiessee, where Röhm had gathered many of his fellow SA leaders for a conference. The SS were given clear orders – round up the SA men and shoot them immediately. Röhm himself was arrested, put in a cell in Munich's nearby Stahlhelm prison, and offered the opportunity to blow his own brains out. In total shock at the situation he refused, and was instead shot dead by his erstwhile comrade and Totenkopf leader, Theodor Eicke. Most of the senior SA leadership nationwide were murdered, many of them shouting '*Heil Hitler*' as they faced the firing squads, believing they were actually victims of an SS plot to overthrow their beloved Führer. At a stroke the SA was decapitated and removed as a threat. Hitler was jubilant. His faith in the soldiers of the SS was vindicated, and as a direct result a grateful Führer elevated them into an independent arm of the Nazi Party, no longer subject to the control of the SA as they had been up until then.

Two months later in a state decree, Hitler outlined the main task of the newly-independent force. Trained on military lines, it was to stand ready to battle internal opponents of the Nazi regime should the need arise. Only 'in the event of general war' would it be employed outside Germany's borders for military operations, in which case only Hitler could decide how and when it would be used. The Army was not happy with the situation, but the Defence Minister, Field Marshal Blomberg, foolishly let himself be convinced by Hitler that the intention was to create an armed police force and not another army. This reassurance, like so many of Hitler's, proved entirely false.

Recruitment of 'foreigners' into the Waffen-SS before the war

Both Hitler and Himmler originally conceived the Waffen-SS as a purely German force. The belief was in a small, 'racially and ideologically pure' élite. However even from the very beginning a tiny number of recruits joined up who began to stretch the definition of 'German', and over time established a direction for the Waffen-SS that would lead to the multi-national army of 1945.

Back in 1919, the Versailles Treaty had not only emasculated Germany militarily, but had also annexed territory with ethnically German populations and handed it over to neighbouring states. The mixed Franco-German region of Alsace-Lorraine was given back to France (the future SS-Wiking panzer regiment commander Johannes-Rudolf 'Hans' Mühlenkamp was actually born a German in Lorraine, but 'became' French when he was nine), the 65,000 ethnic Germans in the Eupen area were handed over to Belgium, and Denmark got the 25,000 Germans living in agriculturally-rich north Schleswig-Holstein (called South Jutland by the Danes). Over in the east the creation of the Polish Corridor to the Baltic Sea had split Germany from its East Prussian province and left thousands of native Germans in newly-created Poland, where eventually of course they would become the *casus belli* for the Second World War.

As far as Hitler was concerned, all of these people were actually 'Germans' no matter what their passports said, and so from the start they were allowed to join the Waffen-SS. When they enlisted they were not officially recorded as Danish, Polish or whatever, but as native Germans and so their number is impossible to calculate accurately, but it was in the hundreds. Two such volunteers were Johann Thorius and Georg Erichsen, both ethnic Germans from Danish north Schleswig-Holstein. Thorius volunteered for the SS-VT in 1939 and served in the Germania Regiment. Recommended for a commission, he passed out from Bad Tölz and went on to command the 12th Company of SS-Panzer Grenadier Regiment 24 Danmark as an SS-Obersturmführer. Never classed as a Dane by the Waffen-SS, Thorius's war ended in 1944 when he lost an arm in combat in Estonia. Erichsen was another 'non-Dane' in SS eyes. Like Thorius he was recommended for a commission, and actually passed out as top student of Tölz's 9th Shortened Wartime Course, beating the Finnish volunteer Tauno Manni to the prize. Erichsen's reward was an instant promotion to SS-Untersturmführer, and appointment as Rudolf Saalbach's adjutant in the famed SS-Armoured Reconnaisance Battalion 11 (*SS-Aufklärungs Abteilung 11*). Retreating into Courland with his battalion in late 1944, he took part in vicious defensive fighting and was recommended for the prestigious Honour Roll Clasp bravery award during the Fourth Battle of Courland. He was killed in action in late January 1945 before the award was confirmed.

Muddying the waters further were the large and diverse ethnic German populations scattered all over eastern and south-eastern Europe, stretching right into the very heart of Stalin's Soviet Union. The blanket term used for these German-speaking peoples was *'volksdeutsche'* (ethnic Germans) – as opposed to *'reichsdeutsche'* which described those born within the 1939 frontiers of the Third Reich. The volksdeutsche were primarily a Hapsburg phenomenon, as the Austrian monarchy had encouraged a process of German migration into their ever-growing empire over the course of centuries, often to solidify their control of newly-acquired and distant provinces. So by the advent of Hitler's Reich hundreds of thousands of these volksdeutsche lived in German 'colonies' in Yugoslavia, Rumania, Hungary and Czechoslovakia. As for Russia, her volksdeutsche even had their own autonomous republic within the Union – the German Republic of Podvol'zhya, centred on the steppe lands of the Volga River region, with its capital the wholly German town of Engels. The two million or so Volga Germans, as they were known, were descendants of settlers invited by the Tsarina Catherine the Great after the end of the Seven Years War to colonise the under-populated area. Ironically, given later events in 1942, there were 24,656 of these volksdeustche living peaceably in Stalingrad of all places. Following the Wehrmacht invasion though, their centuries-old loyalty to Russia did not save them, and on Stalin's orders the Republic was liquidated in September 1941 and the entire population deported en masse to inhospitable zones of far-off Kazakhstan. Hundreds of thousands died of hunger and disease, and their community disappeared from the pages of history forever.

Back in the 1930s members of these volksdeutsche communities were not directly targeted by the Waffen-SS, but some made their way across Europe to Germany to join up. Erwin Bartmann, who served as an SS-Unterscharführer in the Leibstandarte from early 1941, remembers just such a volksdeutsche from Rumania in his own unit. This volunteer spoke excellent German, unlike many of his brethren, and had been in the Leibstandarte for several years before Bartmann enlisted prior to Barbarossa. Before the war they were just a trickle, a curiosity, but in time the recruiting restrictions placed on the Waffen-SS by the Wehrmacht authorities hugely increased the importance of the volksdeutsche to Himmler's dream of a new SS army.

However, outside of the 'lost' Germans of 1919 and the volksdeutsche, it was a third potential pool of recruits for the Waffen-SS that was to lead directly to the much-vaunted idea of the Waffen-SS as a 'European army' – the so-called 'Germanics'. The Germanics were not in any way German, but were peoples that the Nazis considered to be their ethnic cousins, part of the Nazi legend of the greater 'Aryan' people of pre-history that had spread out over north-western Europe. Included on the list of 'acceptable' populations and ethnic groups were the Dutch, the Flemish Belgians (initially the Walloon Belgians were seen as ethnically beyond the Pale), the Anglo-Saxon English (but not the Celtic Scots, Welsh or Irish), the Swiss, and the Nordics of Denmark, Norway, Sweden and Finland. Even Americans of northern European descent were seen by Himmler as potential future recruits. Bruno Friesen, born in Canada to German-speaking Mennonite Ukrainians, was in this category; he ended up serving as a tank gunner in the Army's Panzer Regiment 25. Again, as with the volksdeutsche, there was no concerted recruitment effort to attract Germanics before the war started, but individuals were allowed to join. They were given no special dispensation by the Waffen-SS authorities, and had to pass the normal selection criteria and training programmes. By the invasion of Poland there were more than a hundred of these Germanics in the Waffen-SS.

This meant that by the summer of 1939 the Waffen-SS consisted of a handful of units, with no more than a small percentage of men who were not born within Germany's existing frontiers. This only changed as a result of a direct clash between Himmler's mounting ambition for his new force and traditional Wehrmacht manpower policy. From the perspective of the Scandinavians and the other Germanics, what changed was that cherished policeman's phrase – motive and opportunity.

Five years after the SA was crushed, Himmler presided over a military arm consisting of four élite regiments –a German regiment was usually of 2–3,000 men, roughly equivalent to a British brigade – of the Leibstandarte, Deutschland, Germania and Der Führer, along with a further four of Totenkopf (Oberbayern, Brandenburg, Thüringen and Ostmark), and another couple of thousand men in various training, depot and administrative roles. Impressive as this was, Himmler was hungry for more. While Hitler was still convinced the Waffen-SS should remain small, his loyal lieutenant was increasingly thinking of huge legions of racially defined supermen. To achieve this Himmler needed far more than the 25–28,000 men he already possessed. Standing in his way was official Wehrmacht policy.

In 1940 the German Armed Forces High Command (the *OberKommando der Wehrmacht* – OKW for short) decreed a manpower ratio split of each year's available draft at 66 per cent for the Army, 25 per cent for the Luftwaffe and just 9 per cent for the Kriegsmarine – Nazi Germany always saw itself as a land-based power. The Waffen-SS had no quota, and even if a recruit expressed the desire to join the black guards he was rarely allowed to, as the Wehrmacht usually just took the recruit's wish 'under advisement'. Begrudgingly, to accommodate Hitler's wishes, a framework was put in place that allowed the Waffen-SS to take in men on a formation by formation basis only. Therefore Himmler could enlist men into the Germania Regiment for instance, but when it was full it was full, and no further volunteers could be put on the books.

Under such a system the SS-Main Office (*SS-Hauptamt* responsible for recruitment) forecast that at best they would get two per cent of the available draft in any given year. That was 12,000 men per annum, when the existing units alone needed 3–4,000 men a year just to stay at full strength. At that rate of growth Himmler would need the Reich to last its vaunted 'Thousand Years' in order to achieve the size he saw as essential to fulfilling his dream of a Germanic empire.

Ingenuity, administrative flair and a certain amount of deviousness were required given the situation, and as the Reichsführer-SS pondered his dilemma, the solution came from a 44-year-old ex-gymnastics instructor from Swabia with iron-grey hair and a bristling moustache – SS-Gruppenführer Gottlob Berger. Berger was a fanatic, whose life had been shaped by war. One of four brothers, he was the only one to have survived the horrors of the First World War. Two died in the trenches and the third was executed in the US as a spy. An early convert to Nazism, he joined the SS and rose through the ranks. Not one of Himmler's favourites, he nevertheless headed up the SS main office. A practically-minded administrator, he had little time for Himmler's more wild flights of racial fantasy, but regarding existing Waffen-SS recruitment he saw a large-scale solution to the manpower problem. For some time he had been investigating the enlistment potential of what the SS called, 'similarly-related lands (*artverwandten Ländern*), such as Norway, Denmark, Sweden, Holland and Flanders, as well as the volksdeutsche communities. Berger had even gone as far as becoming the chairman of both the German-Croatian Society (*die Deutsch-Kroatischen Gesellschaft*), and the German-Flemish Studies Group (*die Deutsch-Flämischen Studiengruppe*) in order to build relationships with ethnic German groups and pro-Nazis abroad. So the plan he took to Himmler was a simple one; in essence it was to bypass the OKW rules and recruit from abroad. Himmler was delighted with the idea and backed it wholeheartedly; there would be thousands more like Johann Thorius in the future ranks of the Waffen-SS.

The Far Right in Scandinavia

In Italy, back in 1922, the march of the Right had swept Mussolini into power to become Europe's first fascist dictator, and eleven years later the convulsions emanating from the Great Depression helped propel Hitler's

National Socialists into government in Germany. In the 1930s all four Nordic countries – Norway, Denmark, Sweden and Finland – were functioning multi-party democracies, and all except Finland were also constitutional monarchies. Politically, Social Democrats of various persuasions formed the mainstream of political life across them all, but they were not immune to the rise of the extreme Right. At first inspired by Italian fascists, and then increasingly by Hitler's Nazis, a plethora of extremist parties mushroomed all over Scandinavia and the wider Continent. In Norway there were two such parties, in Sweden another two, but in Denmark there were no less than 21 separate Far Right parties. None commanded widespread popular support, or success, at the ballot box, but all were to play a prominent role in the future history of the Scandinavian Waffen-SS.

Norway and Quisling

Vidkun Abraham Lauritz Jonsson Quisling was born in 1887 in the small village of Fyresdal in southwest Norway, and into solid respectability as the son of a Lutheran pastor. He would go on to found and lead the largest pro-Nazi party in Norway and achieve immortality, his surname becoming synonymous with treachery and collaboration. His adult life started brightly. He joined the Norwegian Army and attained the highest ever marks achieved by an officer cadet, and he then went on to rise rapidly through the ranks doing various high profile jobs including stints as the Military Attaché in both Leningrad and Helsinki. Asked for by name by the famous Norwegian explorer and then League of Nations European Famine Relief Director, Fridtjof Nansen, Quisling helped save thousands of Ukrainians from starvation in the early 1920s by distributing food aid to the stricken populace. Returning to Norway in triumph, Quisling was next sent to Moscow as Secretary to the Norwegian Legation, where he also represented Great Britain's interests and earned himself a CBE from His Majesty's Government for his trouble. Well-known and respected, the 44 year-old Major Quisling was asked in May 1931 by Prime Minister Kolstad to join his Cabinet as Norway's Defence Minister. Quisling looked destined for the role. A tall, powerful man, he was used to wearing a uniform and being obeyed, and was very much at home in the conservative upper echelons of Norwegian society. A future as a powerful politician beckoned. He then proceeded to make a total pig's ear of the whole thing. Often haughty and arrogant before, becoming a minister hugely increased Quisling's feelings of self-importance. Within months he was making enemies of everyone and friends of no-one. He alienated industrial workers and the Socialists by calling them 'communist lackeys' (this was

The head of the SS (Heinrich Himmler fourth from left with raised right arm) and the Norwegian collaborationist leader Vidkun Quisling (bareheaded to the right of Himmler) at a recruiting rally in Oslo. Despite all the extravagant effort, recruiting among Norwegians was always a hard task and there was never huge popular support for either Quisling's NS Party or the Norwegian SS. (Erik Wiborg)

Recruiting rally for the NS and the Waffen-SS at the Oslo hippodrome. (Erik Wiborg)

based on documentary evidence of Moscow secretly funding the Socialists), while at the same time being incredibly thin-skinned and unable to take any criticism at all. Becoming increasingly rightwing, he was drawn towards Mussolini and, closer to home, the neo-fascist Norwegian Greyshirts under their leader, Terje Ballsrud. After two painful years, Kolstad's government was voted out, and with it went Quisling with his reputation in tatters.

Desperate to salvage something from the wreckage of his career, and still insistent on his own brilliance, Quisling formed his own party, National Unity (*Nasjonal Samling*, the NS) on 17 May 1933, Norway's National Day. Based on an appeal to nationalist, conservative Norwegians the NS deliberately tried to ape the recent success of the German Nazis by having its own SA-type paramilitary body the *Hird* (named after the ancient household troops of Viking kings), and even calling Quisling the 'Leader' (*Fører*). A youth wing was also established, designed partly to emulate the German Hitler Youth. The NS Youth Front (NS *Ungdomsfylking* – NSUF) would be a major source of future Waffen-SS volunteers and was under the leadership of the young Bjørn Østring.

Born in Gjøvik in 1917, the young Bjørn went to live with his grandparents after his father died and his mother remarried. There, like many of his friends, he became interested in nationalist politics and the NS. He joined the new party, met Quisling himself and formed an attachment to him that would last his entire adult life. The two men became close friends, and Østring would go on to become one of the leading NS figures. He cut an imposing figure, being of a slim but muscular build and just under six feet tall with dark blond hair and piercing blue eyes. Like many of Quisling's most fervent supporters, Østring was a serving soldier, carrying out his national service as a private in The King's Guard Regiment in 1940. He was, and is, strongly nationalist and anti-communist rather than pro-German, and along with many other NS members he would end up fighting against the Germans during their subsequent invasion.

Above: Bjørn and Bergljot Østring's wedding in Oslo. Quisling is sitting on the far right. (Erik Wiborg)

Left: Finnish War veteran and Danish Waffen-SS officer, the aristocratic Christian von Schalburg, surrounded by local peasant women while serving in the Ukraine with the Wiking in 1941.

Back in 1933 initial support for the NS was small but vociferous, and it was clear that although not possessing a common touch, Quisling did inspire total devotion in his 15,000 or so party members. He drew up a 30-point political programme outlining his plans for an authoritarian government, and took it to the country in the October General Election. After only being in existence for six months, the NS polled a low but respectable 27,847 votes (about 2% of the votes cast), not enough for a seat in parliament. Quisling was at least consoled by knowing he resoundingly beat the only other neo-fascist Norwegian party, the Norwegian National Socialist Workers Party (the *Norges Nasjonal-Socialistiske Arbeiderparti* – NNSAP). But three years later at the next General Election, after masses of work and propaganda and with high hopes, the NS's vote actually fell slightly to 26,577 and the party was consigned to electoral obscurity.

Undeterred, Quisling sought to build alliances abroad, and the NS joined the Italian-sponsored, pan-European Action Committees for Rome Universality (*Comitati d'azione per l'Univeralita di Roma* – CAUR). Here he met and mingled with other fascist leaders such as France's Marcel Bucard, the Irish General Eoin O'Duffy and Frits Clausen, leader of Denmark's own National-Socialist Workers Party (*Danmarks National-Socialistiske Arbejder Parti* – DNSAP).

Denmark and Clausen

Clausen himself was actually born a German citizen in disputed Schleswig-Holstein. He served in the Imperial German Army in World War One, went to Heidelberg University and qualified as a doctor before turning to Danish Far-Right politics. Joining the DNSAP in 1931, he became its leader in 1933, adopting the same title as his Norwegian counterpart, Fører, and founding a Hird-type militia, the Storm Troopers (*Storm Afdelinger* – SA), as well as a youth wing, the National-Socialist Youth (*National-Socialistiske Ungdom* – NSU) led by the aristocratic Count Christian Fredrik von Schalburg. The DNSAP and its youth wing were strongest in Clausen's home province of Schleswig-Holstein, and they would prove fertile ground for future Waffen-SS recruitment. In many ways the polar opposite of his fellow Scandinavian fascist leader, Clausen was a loud-mouthed heavy drinker running to fat; Quisling was a fastidious intellectual who neither drank nor smoked. But Clausen made a far better fist of democracy than Quisling did, increasing his party's polling from a tiny 757 votes in 1932, to 16,257 in 1935 and a very respectable 31,032 in 1939, a total which gave his party three seats in the Danish parliament. While succeeding in making the DNSAP acceptable to at least a proportion of the electorate, he signally failed to unite all of Denmark's neo-Nazis under his leadership. Among the almost two dozen fascist parties were large outfits such as Wilfred Petersen's Danish Socialist Party (*Dansk Socialistisk Parti* – DSP) and tiny ones like K. Wendelin's National Cooperation (*Nationalt Samvirke*). Hosts of groups formed, splintered, disbanded and then reappeared under another guise, many of them with a membership that would fit into a room.

Sweden and Lindholm

In its pre-war, neo-Nazi politics, Sweden resembled Denmark more than Norway, with no overarching movement like Quisling's NS. Instead there were many minor parties that enjoyed moderate, small-scale, electoral success. The tall, blond ex-Swedish Army Sergeant, Sven-Olov Lindholm, was the most influential neo-fascist leader in the country, first establishing the Swedish Fascist People's Party (*Sveriges Fascistiska Folkparti* – SFF) with Konrad Hallgren, before moving on to form his own movement, the Swedish Socialist Union (*Svensk Socialistisk Samling* – SSS) in 1938. Membership peaked at about 5,000, and the high water mark was the 6% of voters who plumped for Lindholm in the 1932 Gothenburg municipal poll. Thereafter, as with Quisling's NS, support bumped around at the 2% mark. The SSS party-faithful would prove the mainstay of the Swedish contribution to the Scandinavian Waffen-SS.

Finland

The Finns are racially distinct from their Nordic cousins and had been part of the Russian Tsarist Empire for over a century, only achieving independence (with German help) after the collapse of the Romanov dynasty in 1917. Unlike so many other breakaway parts of the former Russian Empire, such as the Ukraine, Georgia, Kazakhstan and so on, the Finns managed to hold on to their freedom after Russia's Civil War, and by the 1930s were an accepted member of the international community. Finland had emerged from its War of Independence from Russia with a functioning democracy solidly embedded in the mainstream, but as one might expect some quite powerful extremes on both the political Left and Right. The Finnish Communist Party was an active force, supported by Moscow, but banned by the state. At the other end of the scale was the Patriotic People's Party (the IKL), which, although not neo-Nazi was still in the fascist camp. Much to the chagrin of the Finnish Communists, the IKL was legal, and it held 14 seats out of the 200 in the national parliament giving it a fairly influential voice in the political life of the country. Having said that, the IKL did not become a major recruiting source for the Waffen-SS.

The Far-Right parties supplied many clues to what a future Scandinavian Waffen-SS would look like, and the biggest clue was about numbers. It was clear that neo-Nazism and fascist ideology was very much a minority interest in Scandinavia.

The Winter War

As the storm clouds gathered over the Continent in the 1930s and the international League of Nations faltered, all four Nordic countries sought to remain aloof from the looming conflict. The United States' President Roosevelt urged them all to come to terms with Nazi Germany to safe-guard their freedom, but in the end only Denmark did so, signing a Non-Aggression Pact with Hitler on 31 May 1939. In the end it was not Nazi Germany that struck the first blow but that other brutal dictatorship, Joseph Stalin's Soviet Union.

The 1917 Bolshevik Revolution was the signal for many of Tsarist Russia's minorities to break away and claim independence. True to Russian tradition, the revolutionary Communist government that seized power did not accept these erstwhile cries of freedom and set out to crush the infant states and reincorporate them into the new Soviet empire by force. This determination meant the 1920s were to be some of the bloodiest years in Russian history as the Civil War raged and Red armies brutally snuffed out all opposition.

Finland was one of those nations that reached for its independence in the chaos of 1917. Led by a six-foot-two aristocrat and former Tsarist general, Baron Carl Gustaf Emil Mannerheim, the Finns fought for their freedom and won it. A civil war swiftly followed as home-grown Finnish communists sought to take over the country, but after several horrendous years the fighting finally ended and an independent, democratic Finland began to rebuild. What followed was almost two decades of extraordinary national effort, so by the summer of 1939 the country had somehow managed to repay most of its crippling foreign debt, broken up and redistributed the giant, old landed estates to 300,000 small holding farmers and was prepar-ing to host the 1940 Olympic Games in Helsinki – the stadium was almost finished! Unfortunately, down in the Kremlin the decision had been taken to invade Finland and make it part of the Russian empire once again.

After the usual propaganda assault, diplomatic strong-arming and political double-dealing so characteristic of both Stalin and Hitler's approach to foreign affairs, the Red Army's tanks rolled across the border on 30 November 1939 – the Winter War had begun. Expecting little resistance (and even the support of a pro-Soviet workers uprising) the Red Army drove into Finnish Karelia. Simultaneously more Soviet troops attempted to cut the country in two by invading much farther north along the incredibly long 800-mile border between the two states. What followed has become military legend, a series of events reminiscent of the Spartans at Thermopylae, as the massively outnumbered, poorly-equipped but superbly led and motivated Finnish Army not only stopped the Soviet behemoth, but came within an ace of defeating it outright.

The Red Army was reeling from Stalin's Purges at the time, robbed of the majority of its experienced officer corps as they were marched to the firing squad or the gulag, and astoundingly unprepared for a war in the snowy wastes of Finland. The result was thousands of Soviet soldiers herded onto the Finnish defence lines and mowed down in heaps. As one Red Army officer wrote:

> Of the more than 100 men of my company who went into the first attack, only 38 returned after the second one had failed … The rest I remember through a fog. One of the wounded, among whom we advanced, grabbed at my leg and I pushed him away. When I noticed I was ahead of my men, I lay down in the snow and waited for the line to catch up with me. There was no fear … this time the Finns let us approach to within 100 feet of their positions before opening fire.

Forced by circumstance to improvise, the Finns invented the 'Molotov cocktail' to take on Russian tanks, silently skiing through the wintry forests to ambush the road-bound Soviet infantry. As the world watched in amazement, the vaunted Red Army was beaten again and again with whole divisions being swallowed up in the dark, primeval Nordic landscape.

Fighting for her survival, Finland appealed for help, but no national government was prepared to come to her aid. People themselves were very sympathetic, and across Scandinavia in particular, feelings were running high at what was viewed as naked Communist aggression. Official aid might not have been forthcoming, but on an individual level an avalanche of intrepid volunteers, many of them serving soldiers in their own armies, made their way to Finland and took up arms against the invader. One thousand two hundred Danes came together to serve as a complete battalion under the command of two regular Danish Army officers, Paul

Rantzau-Engelhardt and V. Tretow-Loof. From Norway came 727 volunteers, and they joined up with no less than 8,260 Swedes. All had answered the recruiting call of 'For the honour of Sweden and the freedom of the North', to form the Swedish Volunteer Corps as it became known (the *Svenska Friviligkoren*). A further 500 Swedes enlisted directly into the Finnish Army. Welcome though these reinforcements were, they were not going to be enough to change the outcome. The chastened Soviets regrouped, massively reinforced their troops, changed their tactics and commanders, and launched a second huge offensive in the New Year. The exhausted Finns and their Scandinavian allies fought them every inch of the way, but the result was a foregone conclusion. In March 1940 the Finns sued for peace having lost 25,000 men killed and many more injured. Exact Soviet casualties are unknown, but it is reasonable to assume that at least 200,000 Red Army soldiers died in the snows of Finland. The resulting peace settlement stripped Finland of 11% of its land and 30% of its economic base, but none of its population. In an amazing migration every single Finn who found themselves in newly-acquired Soviet territory abandoned his or her home and trekked over the new border to Finland proper.

The effect of the war on many in Europe, especially parts of the Danish, Norwegian and Swedish populations, was to radicalise them and reinforce their existing view of the threat posed by Soviet communism. Just as the invasions of Afghanistan in 1979 by the Soviets and of Iraq in 2003 by the Coalition acted as recruiting sergeants for radical Islam, so did the Winter War act as a future recruiter for the Waffen-SS's fight against communism. The Dutch SS-Wiking volunteer, Jan Munk, said of the attack on Finland: 'I thought it foul, it just strengthened my anti-communist thoughts. I was also very surprised that no country went to Finland's aid.'

Most of the Scandinavian volunteers agreed with this view, and disgust at the Soviet invasion of their close neighbour was probably the Waffen-SS's best recruiting asset. The Norwegian Nasjonal Samling members like Bjørn Østring definitely thought so: 'I was already an anti-communist, but the Soviet attack on Finland strengthened my existing political convictions. Without doubt I feared a Soviet takeover of Europe and I volunteered at the very start to stand side by side with the Finns.' Bjarne Dramstad agreed:

This is the key point of why I ended up in the Waffen-SS. My elder brother Rolf served as a volunteer in a Swedish company in the Winter War, and he was awarded a medal for bravery for saving his wounded company commander. I wanted to go to, but I didn't because of my mother who already had one son away in the war. My elder brother Rolf was my idol from my

The young Dutch volunteer Jan Munk's platoon from the Wiking's SS-Westland Regiment just before it was sent to the Russian Front. Munk is kneeling in the front rank on the extreme right wearing glasses. All the grenadiers were foreign volunteers with only the platoon's NCOs being Germans. Almost none survived the war. (Jan Munk)

Above left: Danes served in many Waffen-SS units. This is a gun crew from the Germania Regiment's 13th Company in Russia during Barbarossa, on the far right with the glasses is the Danish volunteer Henry Doose Nielsen. (Jens Post)

Above right: The amateur boxer and Swedish Army soldier, Erik 'Jerka' Wallin. Like many of his fellow Swedish Waffen-SS volunteers Wallin was a pre-war member of Sven-Olov Lindholm's neo-Nazi SSS Party.

childhood. I mean we had our own problems in Norway in the 30s before the war, with the communists and the Labour Party creating 'red guards' at the factories, and I can't remember if I was impressed by Germany at that point, but I was definitely afraid of the communist threat from the Soviet Union, especially after the attack on Finland, and I wanted revenge. I also wanted to participate in crushing the terrible system they had over there.

The very shortness of the war meant that many of the Scandinavian volunteers were still in training when hostilities ended, but dozens were still killed in the fighting. Those that survived went back home fired with a determination to combat communism whenever they could, and spread the word to anyone who would listen. Many of them rejoined their own armies and, though few in number, would become some of the hard wood of the future Scandinavian Waffen-SS. Among them were Danes, such as the handsome and debonair Christian von Schalburg and the youthful and idealistic Johannes-Just Nielsen; and Swedes like the tall amateur boxer Erik 'Jerka' Wallin and the intelligent and charismatic Gösta Borg.

Invasion!

Finland was not the first European state to suffer an attack from a totalitarian dictatorship. Poland had that unfortunate honour. Back in September 1939 the Wehrmacht had swept over the border and annihilated the Polish armed forces using a new kind of warfare – blitzkrieg. Final defeat for Poland was assured when the Red Army joined in and invaded the eastern half of the country, as agreed under the secret terms of the Nazi-Soviet Non-Aggression Pact. That invasion had begun the Second World War, as France and Great Britain honoured their treaty with Poland and declared war on Hitler's Germany, although not with the Soviet Union as it happened. The next seven months became known in the West as the 'sitzkrieg', as neither the Germans nor the French and British did anything much other than scowl at each other over the border. None of the Nordic countries had mutual assistance treaties with Poland and so none had declared war on either Nazi Germany or the Soviet Union. Denmark, of course, already had its Non-Aggression Pact with Germany. They all went about their everyday business much as before and studiously ignored the warring sides. Militarily they posed no threat to Germany, with their armies being mainly made up of poorly-equipped conscripts and reservists around cadres of professionals, with little modern airpower or equipment to speak of. In the end that would not matter.

On the morning of 9 April 1940 Denmark became the first country in history to be attacked by parachute. Operation Weser Exercise (*Unternehmen Weserübung*) began with a small unit of Danish-speaking Brandenburger commandos (in Danish Army uniforms) capturing the Padborg bridge in a daring attack, to allow German ground troops to flood north. Airfields and strategic locations were seized and it was all over by breakfast. It had been so quick that King Christian X and the Danish government had no time to flee to safety. The Wehrmacht had lost two planes shot down and a few armoured cars damaged. Thirteen members of the Royal Danish forces were killed and 23 wounded.

Norway, attacked on the same day, was an altogether different scenario. The German cruiser *Blücher* appeared in Oslo fjord carrying most of the German command staff and called on the garrison to surrender. On hearing of the invasion, Quisling sent out an instruction to all his supporters telling them not to resist. The Norwegian Army officer in charge of Oslo's shore batteries at Oscarsborg, Lieutenant August Bonsak, was an NS member but without a moment's hesitation he ordered his guns to open fire and sent the *Blücher* and its surprised crew to the bottom of the sea. The future Waffen-SS volunteer Bjarne Dramstad recalled the invasion:

My elder brother [Rolf, the Winter War veteran] participated in the fighting and the shameful retreat of the Norwegian Army in Østfold. He had just returned from Finland and ended up manning a machine-gun at the fighting for Sørmoen bridge. When the Germans attacked the bridge he was left alone with his machine-gun firing at the Germans, as his friends had deserted, taking with them all of Rolf's personal belongings. Somehow Rolf managed to escape German captivity.

Unable to help Denmark, the French and British were determined to go to Norway's aid and sent a joint Expeditionary Force to land in the north at Narvik to try and throw the Germans out. What should have been a lightning campaign almost became Nazi Germany's first ever military defeat. Edouard Dietl's élite mountain troops (the famed Austro-German *gebirgsjäger*) facing the Anglo-French force were so close to destruction they were given permission by Hitler to march into internment across the Swedish border if necessary. In the end they fought it out and hung on. Fighting was still going on when the Germans launched their invasion of France and the Low Countries in May, and only then was the Allied Expeditionary Force hurriedly withdrawn on 8 June to continue the battle in France. In the meantime, King Haakon VII, a relation of the British Royal Family, had escaped to London along with his government. They joined the Poles as the second government-in-exile resident in London. When the fighting finally ceased in Norway on 10 June the campaign had lasted 62 days (the Battle of France would last only 46) and both the Wehrmacht and the defenders had suffered about 5,000 casualties each, with 527 Norwegian soldiers and about 300 civilians killed. The Kriegsmarine was badly mauled, losing the *Blücher* and no less than 10 destroyers to the Royal Navy.

Unlike Norway and Denmark, Sweden's neutrality was observed and no German troops landed on her shores. As long as Swedish iron ore, so important for Germany's industries, kept flowing south, then Berlin was happy to leave the Swedes well alone.

Occupation

Heavy-handed occupations were not the German intent following their invasions. In Denmark the existing state institutions were left in place; the police, the judiciary, the monarchy and even the armed forces. No attempt was made either to foist Danish neo-Nazi parties on the government, much to Clausen's chagrin. There was no Reich's Commissar or Military Governor imposed, the senior Nazi official in the country was still the Ambassador, Cecil von Renthe-Fink acting as a Plenipotentiary (a *Reichsbewollmachtiger*). General Kurt Lüdtke was appointed as commander of the occupying forces, but had no role in the administration of the country. The elected Prime Minister, Thorvald Stauning, was pretty much pro-German anyway, as was his Foreign Minister Erik Scavenius, who signed Denmark up to Hitler's Anti-Comintern Pact.

While Denmark became a model occupation in many ways, Norway was a different kettle of fish all together. Quisling seized his chance and appointed himself as the head of a new government, broadcasting to the nation his assumption of power. Everyone was taken aback. The Nazis had no forewarning and neither did any of Quisling's NS colleagues. It became clear in no time at all that there was no popular support for Quisling, and his pretensions to leadership were actually hurting Germany's cause in the country. After just six days he was removed from office by Hitler himself, and the bespectacled Josef Terboven was appointed as Reich's Commissar for Norway. Terboven and Quisling took an instant dislike to each other and the struggle between the two of them was to blight the German occupation for the next five years.

Away from the salons of power in Oslo, the occupation on the whole mirrored Denmark's in its focus on establishing good relations with the local people. By a matter of months Bjarne Dramstad had missed out on doing his national service alongside Bjørn Østring in The Kings Guard Regiment, and thus facing the Germans in uniform, and instead was limited to lending his bicycle to an older friend to enable him to reach his mobilisation point on time. Dramstad was angry at the invasion, and resented the Germans, but said of their occupation: 'The Germans were very correct in their behaviour, they treated the Norwegian POWs well, and were friendly towards us civilians. If they had behaved worse then maybe I wouldn't have joined, but my war and motivation were for Finland in any case and not for Germany.'

Bjørn Østring served in his regiment during the invasion, had been captured during the fighting and was then quickly released. He thought the Germans behaved extremely well and that this influenced his decision to join-up: 'My home town had about 5,000 inhabitants and the German General Engelbrecht quartered as many soldiers there. Relations between them and the population were correct and friendly. Most of my friends held the same views as I did.'

The Scandinavian Waffen-SS is born

Just 11 days after German paras spilled out over Denmark, and the *Blücher* was sent to the bottom of Oslo harbour, the order went out from Berlin to establish a new Scandinavian SS regiment, the *SS-Nordland*. No longer were foreigners to be just an adjunct to Waffen-SS expansion, this was the very first direct attempt to appeal to, recruit, train and arm a specific formation of volunteers from outside the borders of the Third Reich. Nothing like it had been done before and it set a clear precedent. The SS-Nordland was nothing less than a revolution, and the first step on a path that would lead to an armed SS in 1945 that was mostly non-native German, and where Scandinavians, Frenchmen and Latvians would be among the last and most dogged defenders of Hitler's burning capital.

The regiment itself was to be composed of volunteers from all over Scandinavia, and it needed a lot – the best part of 2,000 men all up. Despite the optimism of the SS authorities, recruitment was frustratingly slow. By the end of June only about 200 Norwegians, 112 Danes and a handful of Swedes had come forward. One of the earliest was Dane Paul Vilhelm Hveger, a 22-year-old from Nyborg. Hveger had watched his sister Ragnild win a silver medal for swimming at the 1936 Berlin Olympics before he joined the army as a Royal Life Guard. Demobilised after the invasion, he was deeply impressed by German military power and efficiency: 'I volunteered for the Nordland Regiment in 1940. After some initial training that spring, me and the others were sent home. Called back in the summer, I first went to Klagenfurt, then Vienna and finally Heuberg, where I joined the 7th Company as a rifleman.'

The Danish SS-Nordland Regiment volunteer, Paul Vilhelm Hveger. Hveger was an ex-Danish Army Royal Life Guard before joining the Nordland's 7th Company as a grenadier. (Jens Post)

Denmark was still adjusting to the shock of occupation, fighting was still going on in Norway, and with no war against the Soviet Union, anti-communism wasn't a driver for recruitment either. Little wonder that few men were willing to step forward. Politics played its part as well, with many would-be volunteers seeing the new regiment as lacking a Scandinavian character. The Norwegian Bjarne Dramstad definitely though so: 'The Nordland Regiment didn't appeal to me, it was too "German" in my eyes.'

In contrast farther south the Waffen-SS had more luck in the Low Countries following their invasion in May. The *SS-Westland* Regiment, established on 15 June as the Dutch/Flemish equivalent of the Scandinavian Nordland, attracted more than a thousand volunteers in its first two months of existence.

Undeterred, the indefatigable Gottlob Berger officially opened recruiting offices in Oslo and Copenhagen and Himmler persuaded Hitler to sanction the establishment of a new, fifth, Waffen-SS division to serve alongside the Leibstandarte (a brigade at the time), the Verfügungs, Totenkopf and SS-Polizei. The SS-Polizei Division had been established in 1940 and was composed, as the name suggests, of ex-policemen transferred to the SS.

The new formation was to be named the *SS-Division Germania*. Field-Marshal Keitel, Chief of the OKW, sent the following order to establish the new formation: 'The Führer and Supreme Commander of the Wehrmacht has ordered the establishment within the framework of the Army, of a new SS division which shall utilise the manpower becoming available from those countries inhabited by people of related stock (Norway, Denmark, Holland).'

Hans Jüttner's SS-Leadership Main Office (*SS-Führungshauptamt* – responsible for training, equipping and organising Waffen-SS field units) sprang into action, and on 3 December 1940 the veteran SS-Germania Regiment from the SS-VT became the cadre unit of the new division (the Verfügungs Division was given a Totenkopf unit, SS Infantry Regiment 11, as a replacement). The SS-Nordland and SS-Westland were brought in as the centrepiece, and a new German-manned artillery regiment added as the last piece of the puzzle. Confusion reigned, with the division having the same name as one of its own regiments, so by the end of the month Berlin had decided to change the divisions title to '*Wiking*,' to reflect its intended Nordic make-up, as it began to form at the Heuberg training ground in southern Germany.

This was a momentous day for the Scandinavian Waffen-SS. The Wiking was to become the forerunner and torch-bearer of all the SS foreign volunteer formations, and especially the Scandinavians. Over time the new division would become an acknowledged élite, able to stand comparison with the very best of its Waffen-SS and Army brethren, and a powerful totem for all foreign volunteers.

SS-Wiking and SS-Nordland first commanders

With so much riding on the success of the Wiking, the choice of divisional commander and other key leadership appointments was crucial. And here Himmler had a moment of true inspiration. After working hand in glove with Paul Hausser to turn the SS-VT into a mould breaking force, Felix Steiner had been rewarded with the field command of the SS-Deutschland Regiment (SS Regiment Number 1 no less). He had led it well in the invasions of Poland, the Low Countries and France, and earned the Knight's Cross in August for its performance. He was now further rewarded by being given his own division – the Wiking. From day one Steiner completely understood the nature of his assignment and its difficulty. He did not seek to impose German norms on the foreign volunteers, nor did he mollycoddle them, but instead sought to foster an ésprit de corps that would pay off handsomely at the front and lead to four years of martial glory and an enviable military reputation.

For regimental commanders, Steiner had the Bavarian, Carl Ritter von Oberkamp, in charge of the experienced Germania (von Oberkamp had just succeeded his fellow Bavarian Carl-Maria Demelhuber in the role), and the Dutch/Flemish Westland was to be led by Hilmar Wäckerle. As for the Scandinavians of the Nordland the choice fell on the son of an Austro-Hungarian artillery general – Friedrich Max Karl von Scholz – always known simply as 'Fritz' von Scholz. Von Scholz was no 'Aryan superman', that's for sure. Of slight build and medium height he was almost bald at only 44 years old. He didn't have Steiner's charisma or Hausser's presence, but he was an attentive and experienced commander and a perfect choice for the fledgling unit. He had already commanded a battalion of the Der Führer Regiment during the campaign in the West in 1940, and had been awarded both classes of the Iron Cross. His promotion to head the Nordland was the beginning of a three-and-a-half year relationship with Nordic volunteers that would see him earn their respect and admiration as well as the Knight's Cross with Oak Leaves and Swords, and would only end with his death in combat on the banks of the River Narva in Estonia. All three Nordland battalions were commanded by Germans; Harry Polewacz, Arnold Stoffers and Walter Plöw. Both Polewacz and Stoffers would win the Knight's Cross and the German Cross in Gold while serving in the Wiking.

The Nordland Division's first and most influential commander, the Austro-Hungarian aristocrat Friedrich Max Karl von Scholz, affectionately known by all as 'Fritz' von Scholz. He would lead the division until his death in action at the Narva in 1944.

The Wiking itself was organised as a standard Waffen-SS infantry division of the time, with its three infantry regiments having three battalions each, and its heavy weapons concentrated in an artillery regiment of four battalions. Three of these latter battalions were equipped with 10.5cm light field howitzers, and one with the far bigger 15cm heavy howitzers capable of hitting targets 13 kilometres away. There was also a single light armoured car company of SdKfz 222s, each armed with a machine-gun and a 20mm cannon. The entire division, including its all-important artillery, was motorised with trucks, motorcycles and *Kubelwagen* – the German version of the American Jeep and British Land Rover – for the infantry and supporting elements, and prime mover vehicles for the artillery. At a time when the vast majority of the Wehrmacht was no more motorised than in the First World War, this was a huge advantage and set the division apart as a spearhead formation.

Why did Danes and Norwegians join the Wiking?

Unsurprisingly this is the most common question about the volunteers. Was it unemployment, the lure of money and higher living standards? Were they all fanatical Nazis and anti-Semites? Was the Waffen-SS somehow 'attractive', or were they just bored young men looking for adventure? The Dutch psychologist, Dr A.F.G. van Hoesel, carried out the first study of its kind in 1948 of fellow-countrymen convicted of political crimes, of whom some 264 were former SS volunteers. He came to few conclusions other than that a lot of them had been unemployed at the time, and many had few skills. A far more useful piece of work, on the background and situation of the volunteers, was carried out by the Danish sociologist K.O. Christiansen in 1955. Of the 13,000 or so Danes who were sentenced for collaboration after the war, he studied 3,718 who were former members of the Waffen-SS or Luftwaffe anti-aircraft troops, and interviewed no less than 654 of them. The resulting profile revealed that the majority were from cities and larger towns, and unlike van Hoesel's study, indicated that many were pretty well-educated and from the middle class. Naturally enough, a high percentage were also members of neo-Nazi parties and were strongly anti-communist.

Ex-SS-Sturmbannführer Oluf von Krabbe, a Danish veteran and latterly commander of the 1st Battalion SS-Grenadier Regiment 68 of the *SS-Langemarck Division*, echoed the same view as Christiansen in a similar study a few years later.

One thing that was abundantly clear from all the different investigations was that whatever the Scandinavians joined for, it seemed pay and reward were not a major factor. One of the earliest Danish volunteers was the serving army officer Erik Brörup. Born in 1917 into a solid Copenhagen middle-class background (his father was in the furniture business), young Erik was one of three children, well-educated and with good prospects. Despite all of this young Erik was a rebel at heart. A fit young man with light brown hair and blue-eyes he was passionate about outdoor pursuits, enjoying horse riding and cross-country skiing especially. Never willing to toe the line, he would later have an enormously varied career in the Waffen-SS, serving in no less than three different divisions, the Wiking, the *Florian Geyer* (an SS cavalry division) and the Nordland, as well as the *Frikorps Danmark* and the specialist *SS Para Battalion 500*. His reasons for joining up seem to speak for many of his countrymen at the time:

At school in Denmark in 1934, I served in a militia unit named the Konigens Livjäger Korps, which roughly translated would be something like King's Own Rifles. It had been raised in 1801 to fight the English! [The Royal Navy bombarded Brörup's hometown of Copenhagen during the Napoleonic Wars.] When I was called up for national service I chose the cavalry, after seeing the movie *The Bengal Lancers*. I started recruit training as an officer-candidate on 22 October 1937 in the Gardehusar Regiment. They were household cavalry and a real bunch of snobs. I must have pissed them off somewhat, because at the outbreak of war in September 1939 I didn't get the usual automatic promotion to Second Lieutenant. This was despite my coming fifth out of 35 candidates in military proficiency tests. They said it was because I had 'fascist sympathies' and was therefore 'politically unreliable'.

Then my service was cut short by the arrival of the Germans in April 1940. Our Captain and old tactics instructor explained to us just exactly what the SS-Verfügungstruppe and Waffen-SS were, and what they did in the West in 1940. [As an exemplar of Waffen-SS combat behaviour the instructor read out the Knight's Cross-winning exploits of Fritz Vogt who Brörup would later serve under on the Eastern Front.]

I also learned there was a sub-office of the recruiting department of the Waffen-SS in Copenhagen; and they were hiring soldiers for the SS-Regiment Nordland. Having done nothing but soldiering I figured it wouldn't hurt to ask, so I went in Sam Browne belt and spurs. They checked me out, found out that I wasn't such a bad soldier after all and offered me, for starters, my equivalent rank – SS-Standartenjunker – and a chance to join the next officers' training course at the SS Officers School at Bad Tölz in Bavaria due to start on the 15th of July 1941. I had to get permission from the Danish government to enlist, which I did, and by the 25th of April 1941 I had signed my contract.

So much for motivation. Basically I went to Germany because they treated soldiers right. I was a professional soldier and I am damned proud of the fact that as a foreigner I became an officer in one of the best divisions ever, and I have never rued or regretted what I did.

The influence of family and friends was also hugely important to these impressionable young men. Another Danish volunteer, Emil Staal, had joined Clausen's DNSAP as a 16-year-old in 1937, three years later when several of his friends from the Party enlisted in the Nordland, so did he, at the tender age of 19. While Bent Lemboe was encouraged to join by his father, a member of the DNSAP since 1933. Both young men felt supported by their family and friends in volunteering. They were also strongly anti-communist and thought war between Germany and the Soviet Union was inevitable. When that war did come, they fought with the Wiking in Russia. Both survived, although Staal was invalided out in 1942 after being seriously wounded in the Caucasus when just 22 years old.

Over in Norway, Bjørn Østring's decision to enlist was heartily endorsed by his grandparents. It was not the same for Bjarne Dramstad:

Above left: The Danish Waffen-SS officer volunteer Erik Brörup. His amazing career in the Waffen-SS would see him serve in the Frikorps Danmark, three separate SS divisions and the élite SS Parachute Battalion 500. (Erik Brörup)

Above right: Before the war Brörup served in the aristocratic Danish Gardehusar Cavalry Regiment. (Erik Brörup)

I didn't tell anyone except my brother Rolf, some in my family were quite negative about the Germans, and after all I had two brothers on the other side; one in the US Army's 99th Battalion [the 99th was almost entirely recruited from Norwegian Americans] and one sailing convoys with the Allies who was sunk by German U-Boats and later joined the Norwegian Navy in Canada.

The post-war Norwegian Army officer, Svein Blindheim – later the author of *Vi sloss for Norge* (*We fought for Norway*) with Bjørn Østring – came to the same conclusions as his Danish contemporaries when he studied former Norwegian volunteers. He found NS party membership and volunteering tended to run in families, so making signing up a positive thing to do for the young men involved, but at the same time severely limiting the pool of potential recruits. Anti-communism and sympathy for the Finns were strong motivators too. The two Norwegian Nordland volunteers, Ole Brunaes and Leif Kristiansen, were shocked at Norway's easy defeat in 1940 and felt that only Germany could protect Norway against the Soviet Union:

I [Leif Kristiansen] didn't know what Quisling stood for and what he thought, but I could see the British plot developing: provoke German occupation of Scandinavia in order to produce a German-Russian War.

Though I [Ole Brunaes] doubted we would come into action in time – England, Germany's only opponent left, was nearly beaten – we accepted the aim of Norwegian independence, later on from 22 June 1941 the motivation of volunteers was plain enough: to fight the Soviet communism threatening Europe and thereby Norway.

There was a huge range of reasons for joining up. The Dutch SS-Westland volunteer, Jan Munk, was typical of many of these young men and his rationale could have as easily come from a Dane or a Norwegian.

There was a lot of friction at home with my very anti-Nazi father, one year we went by car into Germany to a favourite restaurant for a delicious trout dish. In the town there was a festival or celebration or something. There were flags flying, garlands everywhere and I saw groups of Hitler Jugend boys and girls marching and singing and they looked so happy and I thought it was wonderful, my father said 'Look at all those Nazi children, isn't it terrible, they will all grow up to be no good.' I just couldn't understand this, that was the moment that I think I became pro-Nazi. I also spent a lot of time talking politics with an aunt, my mother's sister, and uncle who were active members of the NSB [Anton Mussert's Dutch pro-Nazi party]

Jan Munk in front of his section hut at Ellwangen. Wounded in action on the Russian Front he would end the war leading Hitler Youth teenagers against the advancing Americans. Unwilling to sacrifice their lives for a hopeless cause, Munk sent the boys home. (Jan Munk)

and very pro-Nazi. My grandmother was also pro-German by the way. These political discussions carried over into my final year at the HBS [secondary school] when one day someone said; 'If you admire them so much why don't you join them?' Well that was it, and that is really how I joined.

Training and equipment

Recruits were not the only thing the Waffen-SS struggled to squeeze out of the Wehrmacht High Command, the other was land. To train properly, a soldier needs an enormous amount of the stuff, he and his comrades need it to practise on, march and drive over, and most importantly to fire their weapons in. In 1940 a tank round could travel a mile before exploding, a bullet from a rifle two miles or more, while an artillery round could go more than ten. Add in safety distances so you don't end up killing and maiming your own men, plus the need to manoeuvre, and you're talking about a good-sized training area for a single battalion being 20 square miles. The SS-Wiking Division had more than fifteen battalions. Naturally not all an army's divisions are in the training areas at the same time, but overall the availability of suitable ground is a key pinch point in preparing a field force for war. The British Army has always been short of this vital commodity, hence training is carried out today in countries such as Germany, Canada, Poland and Kenya. In the Third Reich the German Army was unwilling, and unable, to release adequate training zones to the SS. The advent of war radically altered this situation as newly-conquered countries were exploited, and that is why almost all Waffen-SS training took place outside the borders of pre-war Germany. For example, in Poland the old cavalry barracks at Debica was seized and the surrounding countryside forcibly emptied of civilians, and voilà, an SS depot was created. For the Danish and Norwegian volunteers, the former French Army camp at Sennheim in Alsace (following the fall of France the region was annexed by Germany) became their destination as recruits and also the de facto home of the western European SS.

All military training is hard. War is such a frightening and incredibly violent environment that preparation for it must be immensely tough and uncompromising. For a civilian it is a culture shock of epic proportions. My own time at the Royal Military Academy Sandhurst was hard enough, and I had spent five years in the Cadet Force and three years in the Territorials in my University Officer Training Corps beforehand. Most of my intake had done the same, but for the minority who had not, the Sandhurst experience was of an altogether different magnitude. How some of them stuck with it I will never know. The same in essence went for the Scandinavian volunteers, those with prior service tended to adapt quickly, while complete novices struggled. Having already been a soldier for several years, Erik Brörup, settled in well:

How hard was it? I can state quite categorically that the training I went through in the Danish cavalry was tougher than anything I later encountered in the Waffen-SS. Manoeuvres were very realistic, with live ammunition being used on certain exercises, but not before every man knew his weapon and how to take cover. By the way, similar 'shoots' were also used in the Danish forces.

Others found it more difficult, such as Ole Brunaes.

The training was, of course, no Sunday school. Our German instructors were no real deep psychologists, but, like us, ordinary healthy German youth, from all parts of the people and from all professions. They had self-confidence, were well-skilled with a dynamic efficiency and were remarkably proud of their famous German military traditions. We Norwegians, coming from a country where national defence had been neglected, the military professions ridiculed and any tradition nearly ruined, had a lesson to learn with regard to accuracy, toughness, discipline and cleanliness – physically as well as morally – fingernails being examined before eating, the locking of wardrobes strictly forbidden, thefts from comrades punished hard.

The Danes and Norwegians seemed to be similar in many ways, but there were differences according to German Wiking officer SS-Obersturmführer Peter Strassner:

> The Danes were more robust and less sensitive than the Norwegians, loved good food and drink, but now and then were obstinate and tended to be strongly critical. The Norwegians, on the other hand, worked harder and were more serious and contemplative ... In their military achievements they developed an almost totally instinctive awareness which led them to be somewhat careless with regard to their own safety.

As for the Swedes, the tall and hook-nosed Erik Wallin described their natural approach to training as 'mostly our Swedish style, a little bit slow and not too strenuous, not like the double-quick speed of the Waffen-SS.' Bjørn Østring echoed this view. 'The training was hard, and our German instructors used their own language. Some of them we liked, others not. My company commander said: "When you go into action it will be easier than being here"; and he was right!'

Official reports to Berlin from Sennheim confirmed the Scandinavian volunteers as 'independently minded and strongly inclined to criticism'. This was not what the Waffen-SS was used to.

Mistreatment of the volunteers

Himmler, Berger and Steiner may have seen the Scandinavians and other foreign volunteers as brothers-in-arms, but most of the German Waffen-SS training apparatus either did not care about the nationality of its recent recruits, or far worse, thought them inferior to native Germans. This problem festered within the foreign Waffen-SS right up to the end of 1942, by which time the dissatisfaction in the ranks had reduced the flow of volunteers to a trickle. The Reichsführer himself was then forced to act or see his dream of a pan-Nordic SS turn to dust. Back at Sennheim in 1940 that did not necessarily mean Scandinavian recruits were discriminated against. Erik Brörup said of his time:

> I wasn't personally subjected to any form of demeaning or degrading treatment because I was a Dane. I went through officers' school where there was respect for every individual, not like the usual senseless bullshit you normally find – the US Military Academy at West Point being a case in point ... An absolute no-no was to curse or call anyone by insulting names and the

like. The honour and dignity of any man, officer or other rank, was not to be violated. This had a lot to do with the great sense of comradeship which was instilled into the Waffen-SS. A mutual respect existed. Many commanders radiated a certain charisma and their troops would follow them to hell and back.

While the overall picture seems to be mixed, perhaps maltreatment can sometimes be in the eye of the beholder. According to Bjarne Dramstad it was not always Germans who were the guilty parties:

I was in Fallingbostel near Hamburg, we had instructors from the Braunschweig Officer School, but it was the Norwegian NCOs we had who were real bullies. I remember a couple of brothers in my Company who became Unterscharführers and thus instructors. These two clowns tried to be harder than their German masters all the time, giving us punishments for just about everything. The training was hard and I really learned to hate the German military mentality at that point. One time I opposed an unfair treatment of my friend and ended up having to clean all the toilets in the barracks. When any NCO came along I had to salute him and report; 'Schütze Dramstad, the biggest idiot in 14 Company at your service.' Many of us hoped these idiots would show up at the Front so we could settle the score with them. The language of command may have been German but we spoke Norwegian, a lot of us didn't learn to speak German well at all.

Above left: Brörup never lost his love of horses and spent part of his Waffen-SS service in the 8th SS Cavalry Division Florian Geyer. (Erik Brörup)

Above right: Erik Brörup poses for a photo in his officer's uniform. (James Macleod)

II

1941: First Blood – the Den Norske Legion, the Frikorps Danmark and the Wiking in Barbarossa

In this year terrible portents appeared over Northumbria, and miserably frightened the inhabitants: these were exceptional flashes of lightning, and fiery dragons were seen flying in the air. A great famine soon followed these signs; and a little after that in the same year in January the harrying of the heathen Northmen miserably destroyed God's church in Lindisfarne by rapine and slaughter.

The Vikings raid on Lindisfarne in AD 793 – *The Anglo-Saxon Chronicle*

On 18 December 1940 Adolf Hitler issued the following directive for Number 21 Case Barbarossa, named after the medieval German Holy Roman Emperor Frederick Barbarossa: 'The German Armed Forces must be prepared, even before the conclusion of the war against England, to crush Soviet Russia in a rapid campaign ... Preparations will be concluded by 15 May 1941.'

With that pronouncement the wheels were set in motion for what would become the biggest ever conflict between two enemies – the Russo-German war of 1941-1945. In its scale and scope it would come to dwarf every struggle before or since, its savagery would plumb the depths of infamy, its human cost almost defy belief and its aftermath would shape the history of the world for more than half a century after it ended. It would also define the armed SS. For the remainder of its short life the vast part of its combat strength would be deployed in the East, only one of its final 38 divisions never served there. Ideologically it became a totem against Soviet Communism, and increasingly it drew its manpower from the Soviet Union as well. Come the end in 1945, no less than six Waffen-SS divisions were manned for the most part by Slavic easterners and thousands more were officially and unofficially serving in the other divisions as so-called 'Willing Helpers' (*Hilfswillige – Hiwis* for short).

A very rare photograph of the SS-Nordland grenadier Sverri Djurhuus, one of the only positively identified volunteers from the remote Scandinavian Faroe Islands. (James Macleod)

The SS-Wiking prepares for battle

From its inauguration in late December 1940, the SS-Wiking had just six months to prepare for the invasion of Soviet Russia. With Steiner's appointment, the command structure and divisional elements began to come into being. The SS-Germania was, of course, a veteran unit and the new SS Artillery Regiment 5 was being assembled quickly (initially almost totally German-manned, the composition would change in the future as Scandinavians joined this highly technical arm). But it was the formation and training of the two new infantry regiments – SS-Nordland and SS-Westland – that was proving problematic. With Scandinavian volunteers in particular coming in their hundreds rather than the thousands, it became necessary to draft in large numbers of native Germans to bring the infantry companies up to strength. This was less than ideal but meant by early June, on the very eve of Barbarossa, the SS-Wiking stood at an impressive total of 19,377 men; however, less than 10 per cent of that complement were 'Germanics'. Of the 1,564 foreign volunteers only 932 were Nordics; 421 Finns, 294 Norwegians, 216 Danes and 1 Swede (this was the Winter War veteran Gösta Borg who was serving in the Westland). The rest were mainly Dutchmen, with a small number of Flemings and Swiss. Overwhelmingly, the Scandinavians were pooled in the infantry companies under German NCOs and officers, very few were either in technical arms or command positions. The largest Nordic contingent was then Finnish, and – as you would expect – their story was different from everyone else's.

Finns in the Wiking

Nazi Germany had not supported Finland in the Winter War, but as Hitler moved inexorably towards conflict with Stalin's Soviet Union, both countries instinctively drew closer together against a common enemy. The Finns were never going to be a particularly powerful ally though, given their still-small army and lack of modern military equipment. They had also lost a large number of their best troops in the fighting in 1939–1940. Those that were left were experienced, highly skilled soldiers, but they were few. Nevertheless, the Nordland was opened up to Finnish volunteers on 13 February 1941 and the first 116, all combat veterans, arrived in Germany in the second week of May and were sent straight to the Wiking. A further three hundred or so arrived in the next couple of months, so that by June there were seven officers and 200 men in the Nordland, five officers and 76 men in the Westland, nine officers in the Germania, and the remainder of the contingent was spread around the rest of the division.

The Germans were so pleased with them that they planned to recruit as many as possible, preferably another whole battalion. The Finnish Government, informed in late January of the impending invasion of the Soviet Union, made two stipulations about Germany's recruiting ambitions; firstly that ethnic Swedes (who comprised about 15 per cent of the total Finnish population) should not predominate in the unit, and secondly that the new intake had to be organised into a separate battalion within the division with Finnish officers and NCOs using their native language to command. German liaison was welcome but in effect this was to be a national Finnish unit, which was why Helsinki was keen for ethnic Finns to form the bulk of recruits. Berger, desperate for more Nordic recruits, agreed, and thus was born the SS-Volunteer Battalion Nordost. However the Nordost name was quickly dropped, and the battalion rechristened the Finnish Volunteer Battalion of the Waffen-SS (*die Finnisches Freiwilligen Bataillon der Waffen-SS*). Berger may have been happy to go along with most of the Finnish government's conditions but he also had one of his own, which was was that the overall battalion commander be a German. The man he chose for this extremely delicate task was Hans Collani. Prior to joining the Waffen-SS, Collani had been a merchant seaman plying his trade in the Baltic, and as

An SS-Leibstandarte ball in 1939. The Leibstandarte's commander Sepp Dietrich is on the left and he is laughing with his then-Adjutant, Hans Collani. Collani would go on to command the Finnish SS for its entire lifetime before dying in action at the Narva in 1944. Badly wounded and surrounded, Collani shot himself rather than be captured by the Soviets.

such, had had frequent dealings with all manner of Scandinavians before giving up the sea and joining the Leibstandarte back in 1933. He was a conciliatory character and no German supremacist, this made him an ideal choice and his Finnish troops took to him well. The men themselves arrived in two separate batches and were sent south to train near Vienna. In a matter of weeks the battalion was up to its full strength of just over 800 men, and hard at it under its SS instructors. But it would not take its place in the Nordland Regiment until early 1942 as unlike the Finns already in the division, many of these new recruits had no prior military experience. The Wiking would have to go into action in Barbarossa without them.

Excellent news as this infusion of new blood was for the SS authorities, it did little to hide the fact that the concept of the Nordland as a mainly Scandinavian-manned regiment had failed. Even a state-wide radio broadcast in Norway on 12 January by Quisling himself, for the first time publicly supporting the Nordland and calling for thousands of volunteers, only elicited a few hundred new recruits, and they would still be in training come invasion day. Naturally, the overall number of Scandinavian volunteers in the division would fluctuate over time, but the reality was that for the whole of its brief but glorious life the Wiking would always be manned mostly by Germans rather than non-Germans.

The most powerful force the world had ever seen

The Wiking was also in a race against time to be ready for the fateful day. Barbarossa was not going to be delayed because a brand new SS division with less than two thousand foreigners in its ranks was still in training. This was planned to be nothing less than the military event of the millennium, a demonstration of sheer brute force that in Hitler's own words would 'make the world hold its breath'. And truly the statistics of Barbarossa were mind-boggling. The Wehrmacht invasion force totalled 3,400,000 men grouped in 11 separate Armies, of which four were hugely powerful Panzer Groups (*Panzergruppe 1–4*) equipped with 3,332 tanks and armoured vehicles. A further 600,000 vehicles and 600,000 horses would provide the transport. Overhead the Luftwaffe, still fighting in North Africa and across the English Channel, readied three entire Airfleets (*Luftflotten*) of 2,770 modern aircraft.

The plan was to invade the Soviet Union with three sharp prongs, designated C in the north, B in the centre and A in the south.

Army Group C (*Heeresgruppe* C) in the north was commanded by the aristocratic Field Marshal Ritter von Leeb. His forces were ordered to advance from East Prussia, take the Baltic countries of Lithuania, Latvia and Estonia, and capture Russia's second city of Leningrad, while finally linking up with the Finns. This was not the primary axis of the invasion so Leeb's forces were the weakest of the three groups, comprising the Sixteenth and Eighteenth Armies and Panzer Group 4 (under Hoeppner) totalling 26 divisions – three of them motorised, three of them panzer and the rest being infantry on foot.

To the south, set to strike out from German-occupied Poland, was Field Marshal Fedor von Bock's Army Group B. Later renamed Army Group Centre (as C was renamed North and A changed to South), this formation was to be the fulcrum of the entire German war effort in the East throughout the war. When it succeeded Nazi Germany succeeded, and vice versa, so its utter annihilation in the summer of 1944 would herald the end of the state that created it. Von Bock's punch was the strongest of the three, comprising the Fourth and Ninth Armies and Panzer Groups 2 and 3 (under Guderian and Hoth respectively) with 35 infantry divisions, three security divisions, one cavalry division, five motorised divisions and nine panzer divisions, plus the premier motorised regiment in the Army, the *Grossdeutschland*. Its objectives were the destruction of the main Red Army formations in Belarus. The capture of Moscow was not explicitly stated.

On von Bock's right flank, and stretching down through Germany's allies in the Balkans, Rumania, Hungary and Bulgaria, lay Army Group A under the venerable Field Marshal Gerd von Runstedt. His German force of the Sixth, Eleventh and Seventeenth Armies and Panzer Group 1 (under von Kleist) totalled 22 infantry divisions, six mountain divisions, three security divisions, four motorised divisions and five panzer divisions. It was augmented by a further 15 Romanian divisions (their Third and Fourth Armies), two Hungarian divisions and two Italian divisions. Von Runstedt's objectives for Barbarossa were to cut off and destroy the Red Army west of the River Dnieper, take Kiev as the capital of the Ukraine, Kharkov (*Kharkiv* in Ukrainian) as Russia's fourth largest city, occupy the Crimea (including the massive Black Sea naval base at Sevastopol) and then push east to the River Volga and the city of Stalingrad. Just in case they got bored they were then to wheel south, invade the Caucasus and take its oilfields intact.

The invasion was to be faced by 12,000,000 Red Army soldiers grouped in 230 divisions, equipped with 20,000 tanks and 8,000 aircraft. Weakened though they were by Stalin's Purges, this was still a formidable force.

The Waffen-SS formations were spread over the three Army Groups, with the Wiking and Leibstandarte serving together as part of General Ewald von Kleist's Panzer Group 1 down in the south in Army Group A. Opposing the Scandinavians of the Wiking were the 69 infantry, 28 armoured and 11 cavalry divisions of Colonel-General Mikhail Kirponos's Southwest Front. At the time the overall strength of the Wiking (19,377) made it the most powerful formation in the armed SS, with the renamed Das Reich (formerly the Verfügungs) having 19,021 men, the Totenkopf 18,754, the SS-Polizei 17,347, the Leibstandarte (still in effect a very large brigade rather than a division) at 10,796 and the new Battlegroup Nord (*Kampfgruppe*) just 10,573, which was formed in 1941 from two Totenkopf regiments and would serve in Finland.

The Eastern Front opens

As the Wiking continued to form up back in Germany, the Wehrmacht moved its war machine to its jumping-off points in the east. The invasions of Yugoslavia and Greece in the spring forced a delay to Barbarossa, but finally the date was set and preparations completed. In the summer haze millions of men anxiously waited in the suddenly-crowded forests and meadows of Poland, east Germany and Rumania for the order to advance. At precisely a quarter past three on the morning of 22 June 1941 the massed ranks of German artillery opened fire, and it began. After a short barrage, and with armadas of aircraft flying overhead to destroy the Red air force on the ground, the armoured fists of Nazi Germany started their engines and roared towards their first objectives. Behind them, seemingly endless lines of dust-covered German infantrymen slogged along the roads and tracks trying to keep contact with their compatriots in the vanguard. Despite endless warnings, the Red Army was totally unprepared for the avalanche of steel and high explosive that engulfed its forward lines. The lack of preparedness was entirely down to Stalin personally, and his utter refusal to countenance a German invasion. The reasoning behind this has mystified historians ever since, and will probably never be completely explained, but it does seem that the Soviet dictator's overwhelming paranoia led him to believe that the only real threat to his rule was from inside the Soviet Union and not from without – how wrong he was.

The Wiking did not go into action on invasion day, but instead was rushed forward to join in the fighting as Army Group A's panzer troops pushed eastwards against the surprised Red Army troopers. Taking up position on the northern wing of the Army Group, the Wiking fired its first shots in anger on 29 June 1941, led by the SS-Westland Regiment, in what became known as 'the Battle of the Frontiers'. Along with the rest of von Runstedt's forces it was heading southeast across the Ukraine from its start point, pushing over the Dniester and Bug Rivers, through Zhitomir, Kiev and Uman, aiming to hit the mighty Dnieper River at Cherkassy. The intent was then to carry on to the Donets River at Izyum, and the Don and the Sea of Azov at Rostov. But first it crossed the former demarcation line between the German and Soviet forces in occupied Poland, and advanced into battle at the Galician border city of Lvov. Called 'Lemberg' in the old Austro-Hungarian days and 'Lviv' by the regions Ukrainians, Lvov was a metropolis with a past rich in history and dispute. The advancing Wiking barged straight into the defending Soviet 32nd Infantry Division and was held in vicious fighting until the armoured vehicles of the division's reconnaissance battalion arrived and swung the battle. Pressing on, the Westland's 1st Battalion, led by SS-Hauptsturmführer Hajo von Hadeln, forced a crossing by night of the steep-banked River Slucz at Husyantin, and prepared to break through the fortified Stalin Line in front of Zhitomir. The fighting was fierce and confused. A six-man reconnaissance patrol from the 17th Company, commanded by the German officer candidate SS-Oberjunker Vogel, was returning to its own lines when it found itself in the middle of a Soviet attack. Vogel did not hesitate and led his men into action to help their hard-pressed comrades. In the hand-to-hand fighting that followed the entire patrol was killed; three were Germans, two were Dutchmen and one was Danish. This man was the first ethnic Dane to be killed in action in the Wiking, his name was Gunnar Christiansen. He would be the first of many.

Fritz Ihle, a member of the Nordland's Recce Battalion, was one of many Danish North Schleswig ethnic German volunteers in the Waffen-SS. (James Macleod)

Here also, just two days after the Westland went into combat for the very first time, its inaugural commander was killed in action. Wäckerle had stopped his staff car to look over an abandoned Soviet tank, and was promptly shot dead by a surviving crewman hiding in the wreckage. He was immediately replaced by the Rumanian ethnic German, Artur Martin Phleps, who would go on to form and lead the 7th SS-Mountain Division Prinz Eugen before being killed in action himself in late 1944.

A week later, on 8 July the Wiking was hit by a torrential downpour while driving towards the town of Kozmin, and as the roads turned to seas of mud the division's pace reduced to a crawl. The Soviets took the opportunity to counter-attack and flung themselves at the strung-out unit. The Germania, Westland and Nordland were all pinned down in bitter fighting, while Steiner's Divisional Headquarters at Toratscha was all but overrun. In constant combat, the division held on and counter-attacked, seeing off the Soviet assaults. The Danish Winter War veteran, Heinrich Husen, became the second ethnic Dane to die at the Front during this fighting as he led a Nordland patrol on 2 August.

Change of plan

With Galicia overrun and the Dniester River secured, much to the delight of the Wehrmacht's Rumanian allies who had now liberated their previously lost lands, von Runstedt planned to swing north and seize Kiev as the Ukraine's capital and probable centre of Soviet resistance.

However, it had become clear over the last month to the elderly Prussian officer that in this huge land, with such an under-developed road network, railways were the key to all military movement. Kiev was indeed a rail hub, but it was not as important as the track junction at the city of Uman to the south on the far side of the River Bug. The Soviets confirmed von Runstedt's view when his opponent, the flamboyant Semyon Budenny, Stalin's handlebar-moustached crony from the Civil War, concentrated a big chunk of his forces there to defend it.

So began the first of the huge encirclement battles of 1941. Panzer units streamed south and east, bypassing resistance and searching out space into which they could then drive at full speed. Budenny, a personally brave and previously dashing cavalry commander, was no tactical mastermind. He swiftly lost the initiative and was left grasping at shadows, reacting to German thrusts and unable to fully understand what was happening. But this encirclement was not an easy operation, the panzers could cut off the Red Army formations from their rear and form the 'sack', but a mass of infantry was then needed to secure the catch or it would simply slip out of the trap, or even worse, destroy the isolated panzers. The orders went out to von Runstedt's foot-sore infantry – head for Uman as fast as possible. The Wiking was in the area and, being motorised, was able to react quickly to the situation. The Westland was detached and first sent to Talnoje to help close the pocket itself, while the rest of the division headed east and fought alongside the Luftwaffe's élite Hermann Goering Regiment around Korsun and Shanderovka. In a twist of fate the Wiking's volunteers would be fighting in exactly the same place three-and-a-half years later, but in far more dire circumstances, during the battle of the Cherkassy Pocket.

The Wiking's regiments successfully held the line against increasingly desperate attacks from the trapped Soviets, and by 10 August it was all over. 107,000 Red Army soldiers marched wearily into captivity. Von Runstedt's victorious troops also captured 1,000 guns and 300 tanks.

With the mass of Army Group South (all three Army Groups had now been officially re-titled) now grouped between Uman and the city of Nikolayev on the Black Sea to the south, Hitler took the momentous decision to halt Army Group Centre's relentless drive on Moscow and instead aim it south at Kiev and Budenny's remaining forces. After the disaster at Uman all of the Red

Army's southern forces were in disarray, and Hitler reckoned a cataclysm was imminent. The result was the gigantic encirclement battle of Kiev, the largest military victory of all time up to that point. A staggering 665,000 Soviet soldiers were captured, along with 884 tanks – to put that in context the entire population of Estonia was just 900,000 at the time, so winning at Kiev was almost like capturing an entire nation. Following this modern-day Cannae, the SS-Wiking was pushing ever-eastwards across the Ukraine, aiming to cross the great bend of the Dnieper River at the city of Dnepropetrovsk.

Dnepropetrovsk and the crossing of the Dnieper

August was slipping away as the men of the Wiking reached the mighty Dnieper. Still full of drive after two months of combat, a surprise thrust took the Nordland and its Scandinavians across the river to form a tenu-ous bridgehead on the eastern bank. It was a toehold the Red Army was determined to wipe out. A Nordland veteran wrote of the fighting:

> Every morning the Russians rushed the bridgehead and tried to crush it. A weight of artillery fire never before experienced rained down on the defend-ers' positions. They fought bitterly, refusing to yield a metre of ground. In these days, the Germans, Danes, Norwegians and Finns grew together into an exem-plary combat team. Morning after morning with great bravery, they fought off repeated Russian assaults. They were recognised by their Wehrmacht com-rades as the bridgehead's strong supporting pillar in the uneven battle.

One of the reasons for the power of the Soviet resistance was that the area was a pre-war training area for the Red Army's excellent artillery arm, and they knew every inch of it. The result was sheets of deadly accurate high explosive and razor sharp shrapnel. The defenders had even blown up the enormous hydro-electric dam on the river, a showpiece of Stalin's peace-time central planning, and flooded surrounding low-lying land. As ever, the Soviets were not going to give up easily, but neither was the Wiking. On 6 September the Westland and Germania stormed across the river to reinforce their beleaguered Nordland comrades. Passing through them, they then seized the nearby heights at Kamenka and smashed Red Army resistance. Eight entire Russian divisions were shattered in the fighting, and more than 5,000 Russians surrendered. The bridgehead was now secure and the advance could continue. Von Scholz was awarded the German Cross in Gold for the Nordland's achievements during the battle, and Felix Steiner wrote an Order of the Day that smacked as much of relief as of victory:

The division has become a symbol for the firm bonds uniting all the volunteers within its ranks, whether of German, Dutch, Danish, Norwegian or Finnish nationality. Division Wiking is for us all an expression of our unity and common fate, and we are worthy to take our place in the history of German soldiery.

More than a little flowery, but you get the idea.

East to the Don

With the Dnieper breached, it was another leap of almost 300 miles to the Donets and its junction with the Don east of Rostov. Mobility was now all, and on 10 October the Wiking was transferred to the IV Panzer Corps to help lead its surge eastwards. Moving northeast, the weary volunteers advanced along the Melitopol to Stalino railway line towards the town of Wolnowacha to try and cut-off fleeing Red Army units. Nature again played a hand, with torrential rain slowing the advance as it did in early July. This went on for a fortnight as the SS men slogged their way forward through the sheeting rain and vast seas of glutinous mud – the infamous *rasputitsa*. Engines broke down, vehicles sank up to their axles in the mud and horses' hearts gave out pulling wagons, but somehow by early November the city of Rostov-on-Don was in sight. The Danes, Norwegians and Finns now found themselves in the ancient land of the Cossacks, the rolling plains of the legendary freebooting steppe warriors. A totem for the Tsars for centuries, the strangely anarchic Cossack communities, living hundreds of miles away from Moscow, had chosen the losing side in the Civil War and been massively persecuted following the White defeat. Since then they had periodically risen in rebellion, the last one being in the spring of 1941 in the Schachty area north of Rostov. The Wehrmacht invasion would split their loyalties again with many joining the Germans, but at this time tens of thousands were also doing their duty in the Red Army. The first time the Nordland came across them the consequences were horrific, as recounted by one veteran:

I happened quite by chance to look towards the range of hills two to three kilometres north of our position. At first I couldn't believe my eyes. In the name of heaven what is that? A closed front of horsemen burst out of the hills and stormed towards us. I nudged SS-Untersturmführer Lindner who yelled: 'Alarm, Cossacks!' For a few seconds everyone was paralysed. Seconds seemed like an eternity. But then the spell was broken. Untersturmführer

Lindner and I each ran to a gun and finally the first shots roared out in direct fire. Meanwhile both of the anti-aircraft vehicles' machine-guns began to hammer. The range decreased – 700, 600, 500 metres. Now all guns were firing. A terrible sight. Horses and riders plunged to the ground, yet the cavalcade continues to storm ceaselessly towards us. By the time they are 100 metres away, the attack has been so decimated that it no longer poses a serious danger. Still some 70–80 Cossacks reach our firing positions swinging their saschkas [Cossack sabres] above their heads. The majority break through and disappear beyond the next hill, the rest have fallen in battle.

We are still quite numbed when the apparition has passed. Of approximately 600 Cossacks, more than 300 lay dead on the battlefield. Interrogation of the survivors revealed that the Russian commander thought that the troops in front of him were his own. By the time he recognised them as Germans it was too late to turn round, so he decided to try and ride over us.

The Nordland pushed on, ironically heading for the centre of the last Cossack rebellion at Schachty. By now Barbarossa was coming inexorably to a halt. Every mile the advance went east, meant another mile in the Wehrmacht's ridiculously long supply lines, while the Soviets' grew correspondingly shorter. Every bullet, every shell, every gallon of fuel and loaf of bread was now having to travel thousands of miles to reach the Front. Tens of thousands of vehicles had either been destroyed or had broken down and were littering the steppes. Those still going had been mended a dozen times already and were held together by bits of string more often than not. The panzers were in the same condition, with tracks and guns worn thin with use. The horses, which still provided the mainstay of Wehrmacht transport, were in even worse condition with tens of thousands dead (and supplementing the soldiers' rations) while those that lived were in a pitiable state. All the men had lost weight and their faces were gaunt, eyes sunken. Boots were paper-thin, rifles and machine-guns were worn out with use. The advance was literally exhausted. All along the Eastern Front the temperature gauge was now plummeting, and the troops were also beginning to feel the effects of what would become Russia's worst winter in a century. While the volunteers were struggling to stay warm, at least the cold had hardened the roads so the Wiking's vehicles could move again.

Like a drunk man staggering on and refusing to sleep, the Germans pushed forward into Russia's never-ending space. The Wiking arrived at yet another river, this time the Mius, which it crossed to reach the road to Astoahowo – another milestone on the way to Schachty. A sudden thaw then turned the roads to mud all over again. Along with the 14th and 16th Panzer Divisions, the Wiking somehow drove on, but all the units were worn down, and the Russians threw in counter-attack after counter-attack at the dangerously overstretched SS and Army men. The volunteers were amazed, how could the Red Army still be resisting after experiencing such catastrophic defeats? Perhaps they would have been wise to read Casanova's words regarding the Russian Army written during his first visit to Russia in 1764:

> All were struck by the brutality in the Russian army. This rested on an assumption that words have no power to inspire, and that leading by example is impossible; only a beating has the perverse effect of persuading wives, girlfriends, peasants and soldiers that they were truly loved.

Stalin and his Communist Party had taken this doctrine to an altogether different level, but it was not enough to save the city of Rostov from falling to the Leibstandarte and its Army comrades, along with another 10,000 Red Army prisoners. The Scandinavians of the Nordland had simultaneously headed for Alexandrovka and reached the River Tuslow, it was their last gasp and they could not hold it, they just were not strong enough anymore. With frostbite now adding to the mounting casualty list and the men at the end of their tether, Steiner bowed to the inevitable and led his weary division in retreat back west to the Mius, at Amurosjewka, to dig in for the winter. Some indication of the severity of the fighting the division endured can be read in Artur Phelps's citation for the German Cross in Gold, awarded for his leadership during the battles around the Mius:

The Mius River line, spring 1942; a very heavily armed Finnish SS shock troop. The section has two machine-guns, lots of extra ammo and stick grenades tucked into belts. (Olli Wikberg)

From November 17–20 1941, SS-Oberführer Phleps ... conducted the defensive battle of his combat group, reinforced by III./SS-Germania, in Darjewka. He managed to repulse the massive Russian attack. Through the mobile engagement of the weak reserves at his disposal, he held for two days with his regiment against three infantry brigades, one cavalry division and one tank brigade reinforced by a large artillery unit. Under the most difficult conditions he led an orderly withdrawal to Tuslow.

Phleps was not the only Wiking commander to be commended for his men's actions during the fighting from 17–20 November. Von Scholz's Scandinavians had again fought well and the regiment's conduct was recognised by the award of the coveted Knight's Cross to the 46-year-old Nordland leader, to accompany the German Cross in Gold won on the Dnieper back in August. His citation, personally written by Felix Steiner, read:

SS-Oberführer von Scholz again has deeply influenced, through his personal ruthless action, the development of the action in the multiple assignments given to his combat group. In the battles north of Rostov from November 17–20 1941 Battlegroup von Scholz had to cover the flanks of the First Panzer Army in decisive positions and to resist heavy enemy attacks.

From midday 17 November until the evening of 20 November, five Russian divisions supported by a tank brigade, tried to overrun Battlegroup von Scholz. They had to face these systematically prepared and operatively significant assaults in focal points along a 24 km-wide front, absorbing uninterrupted massive attacks in consecutive waves. The enemy had the constant support of heavy artillery and this increased daily with rocket-firing bombers and low-level attack aircraft. This sole Battlegroup halted massive attacks by forces of the 37th Russian Army Corps, which attempted to destroy the advance towards Rostov by attacking in depth against the flank of First Panzer Army.

The feat of the Battlegroup of SS-Oberführer von Scholz to resist the attacks of such a hugely superior force for four days would have been unthinkable without the personal intervention of von Scholz. He stayed day and night in the most dangerous positions. On November 18 he led the combat in Dobropolje, with his own weapon in hand, against massive attacks while enemy tanks broke through the infantry positions to his rear.

He was standing in the front line when his III Battalion met the furious attacks of the Caucasian 99th and 235th Divisions in the village of Tuslow. The tanks could not be stopped and they drove into the village, but the Russian infantry could not overcome the men of SS-Regiment Nordland.

Through his personal intervention he cleared up every crisis during those days. Every night he could report to the division that in his front all the tank attacks had been thrown back, and all the opposing infantry attacks had been repelled, with the enemy suffering heavy casualties.

Also on the evening of November 20, in spite of the repeated actions of the rocket launchers and the uninterrupted tank and infantry attacks lasting several days, the Front was restored. The disengagement from the enemy, as per higher orders, could be carried out according to plan and without disturbance from the enemy facing them.

On November 21 the Division, in an intermediate position, could repel new enemy attacks carried out during the night. He took advantage of the assault on Balabanow, by the Army's Panzer Regiment 2, to capture 400 prisoners in a surprise thrust that he personally led with weak elements from his Battlegroup.

Gratifying though it was to have the division's courage and skill acknowledged, there was no getting away from the fact that this was the first time the SS-Wiking had had to retreat in the war. For the surviving Danes, Norwegians, Swedes and Finns it was a salutary lesson. The war would not be won in 1941, and come 1942 they would have to fight again. Some uncertainty about the future began to creep into the minds of the volunteers as they sat on the Mius in their snow-covered bunkers and waited for spring.

Hundreds of miles north, the Germans were making one last belated lunge at Moscow to try and end the war before the year was out, Operation Typhoon.

Roll call of the Scandinavian Waffen-SS

By the launch of Typhoon, some 11% of the total original Barbarossa invasion force had become casualties – that's 410,000 men with only 217,000 replacements sent forward, and almost a third of the 3,332 panzers that had rolled over the border back in June had been lost. To try and keep the three Army Groups up to strength, a full 21 of the total OKW Strategic Reserve of 24 divisions had already been committed to battle. The onset of a horrendous winter, the bloody failure of Typhoon, and the Red Army's subsequent counter-offensives, sent the casualty figures soaring towards the one million mark as 1941 ended. The Wiking had shouldered its fair share of those casualties, with hundreds of men buried along the way from Lvov to the Dnieper to the Mius. The division's Scandinavians, concentrated as they were in the frontline infantry companies, had suffered badly. Of their invasion complement of 932, several hundred were dead, wounded or missing (including the first Swedish fatality – the 17-year-old SS-Sturmmann Hans Linden killed in action on 27 December). The Danes had lost 65 of their original contingent of 216 troopers. It was true that the attack on the Soviet Union had presaged a surge in volunteers back home as young men with anti-communist views had streamed through the doors of the recruitment centres in Oslo and Copenhagen, but most signed up for new national legions and not the Wiking, so overall numbers stayed relatively low. By the end of September there were still only 291 Norwegians, 251 Danes and eight Swedes in the division, almost exactly the same number as six months previously. There were concerns raised about the standard of the new boys and the inadequate training they had received back in Germany. Fritz von Scholz told his divisional staff in December that the 275 Danish and Norwegian replacements he had received had initially created a good impression but were 'much too soft; and 'cry like babies' when compared to the earlier volunteers. He demanded far better basic training and a strict ratio of 2:1 for Germans to non-Germans in the regiment to maintain combat efficiency.

The Scandinavian SS national legions

As hundreds of Scandinavian Waffen-SS men underwent their baptism of fire with the Wiking in the opening days of Barbarossa, across Europe a wave of pent-up anti-communism swept the Continent. Among the Far-Right parties, and especially their already-radicalised youth wings, the invasion struck a real chord and from Oslo to Brussels to Paris there was a rising clamour to join in. But for Hitler the battle was still just between Nazi Germany and the Soviet Union, the concept of a 'European crusade against bolshevism' had little traction at this stage. This was not the case in the SS. Both Himmler and Berger saw another opportunity to tap into fresh blood. The issue for them was how best to appeal to this cohort of potential volunteers. The European Waffen-SS, as embodied by the Wiking, was not benefiting substantially from the upsurge in enthusiasm, so it was clear another approach was needed.

The answer in every occupied country, and beyond, was the same – a national legion. It's not clear who first came up with the 'legion' idea, but what does seem clear is that it was not part of a preconceived 'master plan', but was totally ad hoc. The evidence seems to point at different collaborationist leaders in different countries more or less simultaneously coming to the same conclusion. Many of these men were well networked anyway through pre-war umbrella organisations, such as the Italian fascist-sponsored CAUR, and these relationships would doubtless have helped 'spread the word'. Whatever the circumstances, the net result was a rash of new units set up under SS and Army auspices (dependent on their perceived 'Aryan' credentials), with the intent of recruiting, training and sending into battle bodies of men representing their native countries.

The Army was made responsible for the legions from France, Walloon Belgium (Léon Degrelle and his fellows), Anté Pavelic's Croatia and Franco's Spain. Berger and the SS got Norway, Denmark, Flemish Belgium and Holland.

The Norwegian Legion – Den Norske Legion (DNL)

On the very day that the Norwegians in Wiking were getting their first taste of combat on the new Eastern Front, back in Oslo the Reich's Commissar, Josef Terboven, announced the formation of *Den Norske Legion* (DNL – in German *Legion Norwegen*). Quisling, despite his antipathy for Terboven, publicly supported the new formation and urged Norwegians to join. The initial impression given by the German authorities was that this new formation was not only destined to fight the Communists, but would probably do so in conjunction with the Finns, a very popular cause indeed. Quisling went further. Bjarne Dramstad:

> Quisling proclaimed that this was to be the base of the new Norwegian Army and was going to defend Finland. My brother Rolf thought this was a good idea, he did not join, he had done his share in the Winter War, now it was my turn.

A recruiting rally was held in Oslo on 4 July with an appearance from the Finnish Consul, and the reaction was immediate. Some 400 of the army's entire pre-war professional officer corps of 1,500 expressed an interest, along with contingents from the NS's paramilitary Hird and a new organisation, the Norwegian branch of the SS.

The Norwegian SS and Jonas Lie

As elsewhere, in what the Nazis viewed as the racially-acceptable parts of occupied-Europe, Himmler sought to establish a parallel home-grown SS structure to mirror that of Germany. It would then act as the Nazi vanguard in its own land and, come the successful conclusion of the war, would act

Above left: The ex-Leibstandarte war correspondent and Norwegian Minister for Police Jonas Lie (left), and the head of the entire SS machine, the Reichsführer-SS Heinrich Himmler. (Erik Wiborg)

Above right: The DNL recruiting office in Oslo. (Erik Wiborg)

Above left: Early recruiting poster for the Norwegian DNL; the uniform is Norwegian Army and there is no reference either to the Germans or the Waffen-SS. (Erik Wiborg)

Above right: One of the leading Norwegian volunteers, Olaf Lindvig, in his NS political uniform before he joined the DNL. (James Macleod) as the basis for a New European Order – with Himmler presiding over it all of course. In Norway the Reichsführer turned to Jonas Lie, a 42 year-old professional police officer, part-time detective novelist and grandson of a famous Norwegian author, to command the new force. From a well respected Norwegian family, Lie was friendly with Terboven, having previously met him when he was Essen's Gauleiter (Nazi-appointed local governor), and had then fought against the invading Germans before joining the Waffen-SS and serving in the Balkans with the Leibstandarte as a war correspondent. Having won the Iron Cross 2nd Class during the campaign, Lie then returned to Norway as an SS favourite and was appointed to lead the new 130-strong Norwegian SS – the Norges SS – on 21 May 1941.

Joint membership of the NS and the Norwegian SS (rechristened the next year as the *Germanic SS Norway* – *Germanske SS Norge* – GSSN) was common, but that did not mean the two organisations got on well, in fact quite the contrary. Never a member of the NS, Lie shared Terboven's dislike of Quisling, and was determined to undermine him and usurp his authority. A famous story about the antipathy between the two men describes how Lie was called to an initial meeting with Quisling and was kept waiting for a full five hours before being ushered in to see him. On entering his office Lie said: 'I have come to pay my respects.' Quisling's only response was 'Good.' Lie then about turned and left.

Early recruits to the DNL parade in Ulleval Stadium in Oslo in 1941; they are wearing Norwegian Army uniforms and are armed with Norwegian Army-issue rifles. (Erik Wiborg)

The SS-DNL – recruits and training

The SS hoped to recruit enough men to form a German-style infantry regiment of three full battalions, each with historic Norse names. The first was to be mainly recruited from the Oslo area and called *Viken* (its title was meant to be a nod of respect to the Oslo-based Hird Regiment of the same name but ended up just being a little confusing), the second would be *Gula* and the third *Frosta*. As it turned out the two latter battalions were never formed through lack of volunteers, but at least initially there was a certain amount of enthusiasm, especially among the Norwegian SS. Led by Lie himself, over a hundred of its members signed up immediately including the former Norwegian army officers Olaf Lindvig and Ragnar Berg. (The latter was also a founding member of the NS and very close to Quisling.) Leading NS luminaries, who were not in the Norwegian SS, signed up too, among them the leader of the NS Youth Front – Bjørn Østring, the Hird's Chief of Staff – Orvar Saether, and the ex-army officers Charles Westberg

Above left: One of the DNL's few German liaison officers, Dieter Radbruch. Radbruch was hugely popular with the Norwegians and eventually became a company commander, before being killed in action towards the end of the war. (Erik Wiborg)

Above right: The DNL's second boss and ex-NS Viken Battalion commander, Jörgen Bakke, (on the left). He lasted just two weeks before resigning in disgust at what he saw as undue German interference. (Erik Wiborg)

Above left: The Norwegian ex-Cavalry officer, Artur Qvist, who brought much-needed stability to the DNL after initial problems over its leadership. (Erik Wiborg)

Above right: Bjørn Østring, a leading member of the Norwegian Nasjonal Samling Party and close friend of its leader, Vidkun Quisling. Østring would go on to serve with distinction on the Russian Front before returning home when the DNL was disbanded. (Bjørn Østring)

and Artur Qvist (Østring was ex-army too of course). Indeed, so many men with command experience signed up that unlike other volunteer units, such as the Flemish SS-Legion Flandern, the DNL was from the start a very Norwegian unit with only a handful of Germans involved as liaison staff. According to Bjørn Østring:

> Our officers and NCOs were all Norwegians, but German advisors were detailed to our units. They had no command authority, but some of them tried to acquire some. Most of them were unpopular with us, the one brilliant exception being Dieter Radbruch, who then became an instructor for the Hird in Norway. He was also a guest at my wedding in Oslo. He later served in the Baltic States and was killed in action there.
>
> The Legion received its basic training as a unit at Fallingbostel [Lower Saxony]. Those destined to some sort of technical service received their specialist training in other military establishments. As an officer cadet I got my special training as a pioneer in Celle [now a British Army barrack].

The DNL parade through Oslo before heading off to Russia. (Erik Wiborg)

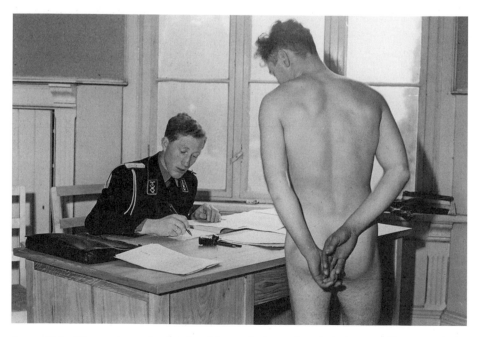

A would-be Norwegian volunteer has his particulars taken down – would he prove to be every inch an Aryan? (Erik Wiborg)

Above left: A Norwegian officer candidate from the DNL at Bad Tölz (he wears the *Bad Tölz* cuff title alongside his '*Legion Norwegen*' one) shows it's not all work and no play as he stands arm-in-arm with a Norwegian Red Cross nurse volunteer sporting typically 'non-standard issue' woolly mittens.

Above right: An early DNL volunteer with '*Legion Norwegen*' cuff title and field cap.

The DNL's rosy beginnings were soon brought up short by a series of German decisions that were to dominate its existence for the next two years. Firstly, it soon became clear to the volunteers, all enlisted on a three-month trial basis, that the Legion was to be a formal part of the Waffen-SS and not a Norwegian Army formation as hoped, and so German uniform was to be worn, albeit with a Norwegian flag shoulder shield, cuff title and lion collar tab. But far worse than this in Norwegian eyes was the OKW decision not to ship the Legion north to fight alongside their erstwhile Finnish Army brethren, but instead to place them under German command to fight on the Leningrad front. Bjarne Dramstad remembers the volunteers' reactions on hearing the news:

> We were transferred to the Front in Ju-52s, and it was just before the planes took off we were told that the destination was Leningrad and not Finland. I remember we were furious, but it was accepted. We were soldiers and soldiers followed orders, but many of us felt betrayed by the Germans.

To top it all, the Germans thought the war in the East would be over by Christmas, and therefore saw the value of the Legion more in propaganda terms than as a military asset. This meant training was not as thorough as it could have been and equipment was often second-hand from captured stocks rather than first-rate German arms. The result was inevitable; enthusiasm from the volunteers evaporated rapidly, especially among the ex-Norwegian Army officer cohort, and the grand plan for an entire regiment came to nothing. Hundreds of men left as soon as their initial three-month term was up, including their first commander, the Norwegian Army Colonel Finn Hannibal Kjelstrup (his son Sverre though remained). Kjelstrup's place was taken by the Viken battalion commander, Jørgen Bakke, but within two weeks he too resigned in disgust. Leaderless, poorly-equipped and lacking thorough training, the DNL was in trouble. Exasperated, the SS authorities cast around for a leader able to take the job on, and settled on the ex-Norwegian Army cavalry captain, Arthur Qvist. A tall, taciturn man in early middle-age, Qvist was a pretty unlikely appointee to head the Norwegian contribution to the Waffen-SS 'crusade in the East'. Like a good many of his conservative fellow-officers Qvist supported the traditional nationalism espoused by Quisling, and the two men were pretty close. Overall though, his politics were more of the old-fashioned patrician variety rather than anything more radical. After the brief reigns of Kjelstrup and Bakke, the Legion now enjoyed a period of stability under Qvist's command and began to remedy some of its training deficiencies at least. But by early 1942 it was clear that the 1,218 men still in the unit were trained and equipped as second-line infantry – the vanguard of a new European élite they were not.

But they were ready to be deployed at last, so a full eight months after Terboven announced its formation, the DNL flew out from Fallingbostel in February 1942, headed northeast through the occupied Baltic States and finally took up positions at the front in the concentric trench lines snaking around most of Russia's second city, Leningrad.

The Danish Free Corps – Frikorps Danmark

Back in Denmark a very different scenario was playing out as the Wehrmacht rolled eastwards. The apparatus of the State was still very much intact and so while the idea of Denmark becoming a 'co-belligerent' alongside Nazi Germany (as Finland did) was never seriously considered, the Germans were happy to work differently with the Danes than with any other country they occupied. A number of Danes, men like Erik Brörup, were already signing up to join the Waffen-SS, but as everywhere else in Europe the advent of Barbarossa acted like a shot of adrenalin to the system. Naturally enough, the members of the multitudinous Danish neo-Nazi parties were at the forefront, however the Germans were keen that support came not only from Clausen and his compatriots but from the political mainstream as well. A certain amount of diplomatic arm-twisting was employed behind closed doors and in no time at all, at the beginning of July 1941, the sitting Danish government announced the establishment of a national legion to fight in the East – the *Frikorps Danmark* (Danish Free Corps or *Freikorps Danmark* in German). The unit was entitled 'Free' rather than a Legion as the Germans were still projecting an image of Denmark as a sovereign state rather than an occupied country.

Danish citizens, including serving soldiers, were allowed to enlist and keep their state pension rights and Royal Danish Army seniority if applicable. The result was an initial draft of 480 men, many still in Danish Army uniforms. A few Swedes also found their way into the Frikorps having travelled south to join up. One such volunteer was Hans-Gösta Pehrsson. Like his fellow Swede, and SS-Westland volunteer Gösta Borg, the short and wiry Pehrsson was a member of Sven-Olov Lindholm's far-Right Swedish Socialist Union. Pehrsson would, over time, effectively come to

The Danish SS Knight's Cross winner Obersturmführer Johannes Hellmers. He won his award while serving with the Dutch Waffen-SS De Ruyter Regiment during the Fourth Battle of Courland.

lead the Swedish Waffen-SS. Most of the Danish Nazis coming forward had no military experience, so the Germans decided to shuffle the pack and transfer over to the new unit a number of volunteers already in the system, especially those with backgrounds as officers or NCOs. This was not to everyone's liking. Erik Brörup had already signed on the dotted line and was on his way to Bad Tölz when his orders were changed:

> When Operation Barbarossa, the invasion of the Soviet Union, started, all the Danish Nazis wanted to join the glory trail, and they started up the Frikorps Danmark. I had already received my marching orders for Bad Tölz, but at the last minute they were changed and I found myself in the Frikorps Danmark. I didn't mind that so much, but these Danish Nazis really pissed me off. I have never liked politicians – together with pimps and preachers I thought they were the lowest form of life. Whenever I voted, I went for the party which supported the military, otherwise I had no use for them.

Brörup's opinion of the new entrants was shared by a number of the volunteers and led to problems for the Frikorps from the start. Influenced by the Government and the King, a number of conservative Danish Army officers joined the Frikorps; this included well-regarded professional officers and NCOs such as Tage Petersen, Thor Jörgensen, Johannes Hellmers (who would go on to win the German Cross in Gold and the coveted Knight's Cross as an SS-Obersturmführer in March 1945), and the Frikorp's first commander – the aristocratic artillery officer Lieutenant-Colonel Christian Peder Kryssing. The tall, moustached Kryssing was no Nazi. Rather, this reserved, reticent man was a deeply conservative Danish nationalist. He had watched the Soviet invasion of Finland with horror, ever mindful of his own country's military weakness. Close to the Royal Family, he was keen to establish the Frikorps as an official Danish military force and not a Nazi tool. He made a public appeal for support on 5 July, a mere two days after taking up command:

> Men of Denmark, with the approval of the government, I have been placed in command of the Frikorps Danmark. This corps will fight against the bolshevik world enemy who has several times endangered the security of the north and thereby the freedom and way of life of our homeland. Men of Denmark, I call upon you to join the ranks of the Frikorps Danmark so that we may make a combined contribution against bolshevism. For the honour of Denmark, for the liberty of our people and for the future of our native land, we are united in the brotherhood of arms with those nations that have already entered the fight against the enemy of Europe and consequently of our homeland.

The Frikorps Danmark, from top left, left to right.

The Frikorps Danmark's four commanders: the aristocratic Danish artillery officer Christian Peder Kryssing, the totemic Christian von Schalburg, the exceedingly short-lived Hans Albert von Lettow-Vorbeck, and Knud Börge Martinsen, who would actually command the Frikorps twice. All were Danish bar von Lettow-Vorbeck.

The Frikorps Danmark commander and ex-Wiking officer, Count Christian Fredrik von Schalburg (left) with his son Alex; von Schalburg is shaking hands with one of his protégés, Sören Kam, who would go on to win the Knight's Cross.

Frikorps Danmark grenadiers advance during fighting in Russia, 1942.

Von Schalburg (left) shows a united front with Clausen (right). Clausen's heavy drinking would eventually contribute to his mental breakdown.

Extremely rare photograph of Frikorps Danmark volunteers ready to fly into the Demyansk Pocket in the ever-reliable Junkers Ju-52 transport planes, the revered 'Auntie Ju's'.

The Frikorps was now officially sanctioned, but this was not a rallying call designed to appeal to Clausen's cohorts. For the several hundred Danish Nazis who had already stepped forward to enlist, Kryssing's appointment was deeply unpopular and fuelled widespread anger. The men were moved from their initial base, at Hamburg Langenhorn, out east to Posen-Treskau in Silesia, but the move did nothing to lessen tensions and within a few months training had virtually stopped. The 1,164-man Frikorps was at war with itself. Graffiti began to appear on barrack walls reading 'Away with the democrat Kryssing', and the situation worsened when Kryssing had a young Danish volunteer arrested for spreading neo-Nazi propaganda. The Germans looked on with growing alarm and when it became clear that Kryssing had lost the confidence of many of his men, they acted. Along with a number of his fellow officers, Kryssing was removed from the Frikorps on 8 February 1942 and assigned elsewhere. Most of the deposed officers went to the SS-Wiking and ended up serving with distinction on the Eastern Front. As for Kryssing himself, he served in the Totenkopf, then the Wiking and ended up becoming the first non-German to attain general rank in the Wehrmacht when he was appointed to lead the 9,000 strong 'Coastal Battlegroup' at Oranienbaum in August 1943. Many of his former men were then in the new Scandinavian SS-Nordland Division right next door.

Christian Fredrik von Schalburg

With Kryssing's departure a new commander was needed, and one was found from among the Danish ranks in the SS-Wiking – Count Christian Fredrik von Schalburg. Born in 1906 in Poltava, southern Russia, to a Danish father and aristocratic Russian mother, when still a boy his family fled Lenin's new Bolshevik Soviet Union to Denmark where he was raised as a member of his class and commissioned into the social élite of the Danish Royal Life Guards Regiment. Handsome, popular and a good officer, the young Count rose to the rank of Captain and married into the German nobility (which allowed him to adopt the 'von' title). However his personal politics landed him in trouble. Von Schalburg was not a conservative like other members of his class such as Kryssing, he was a confirmed neo-Nazi. Not only did he join Clausen's DNSAP, he became the head of its youth wing – the NSU. Not a man given to subtlety or quiet diplomacy, von Schalburg trumpeted his involvement in the DNSAP, leading youth marches and giving public speeches in his Life Guards uniform. This was all too much for his military superiors, who consequently demanded his resignation. Leaving the army, he signed up as one of Tretow-Loof's company commanders in the Danish battalion being formed to fight the Russians in the Winter War, following which he came home to find the Germans ensconced in his homeland. Quickly reconciling himself to the new order, he joined the fledgling SS-Nordland as an officer and went with the Wiking as it advanced into the Soviet Union. Von Schalburg led his men from the front and earned both classes of the Iron Cross for his bravery during the summer's fighting. Promoted to the rank of SS-Sturmbannführer, he took command of the Nordland's 1st Battalion during the heavy autumn battles, and was part of a coterie of middle-ranking Danish officers in the Wiking – which included the anglophile artilleryman Johannes Brennecke, his old Winter War comrade Paul Rantzau-Engelhardt and his fellow Sturmbannführer, Svend Wodschow. His subsequent appointment to lead the Frikorps was an inspired decision. He was well-known in Denmark and was acceptable both to the Danish Nazis and to the conservatives. At last the bickering could stop and real training begin.

The new year of 1942 had ushered in a new commander and a new spirit in the unit, in a few months time it would be confirmed as ready for combat and sent east. Unlike every other national legion, that journey would not end in the siege lines around Leningrad but in the cauldron of the Demyansk Pocket, where it would fight alongside the SS-Totenkopf Division for its very life.

III

1942: Nazi Germany's High Water Mark – Leningrad, Demyansk and the Caucasus

The violent cursed host came rushing through, threatening cruel perils, and after slaying with mad savagery the rest of the brothers they approached the holy father to compel him to give up the shrine, but the saint remained with unarmed hand and was torn limb from limb.

The Viking raid on St Columba's shrine on Iona in ad 825. A.O. Anderson, *Early Sources of Scottish History* 1922.

Scandinavians across the Waffen-SS

The failure of Typhoon at the very gates of Moscow signalled a series of Red Army winter counter-offensives that left tens of thousands of men dead in the snow. The majority were Soviet, but enough were German to leave the Wehrmacht chastened and weakened as 1942's spring thaw arrived. At that time the Wehrmacht drew up a secret report, for OKW-eyes only, that stated that of their 162 combat divisions on the Russian Front, only eight were capable of offensive operations, and that the total armoured might of the German Army's 16 panzer divisions was a miserable 140 tanks out of the original 3,332. The Red Army had also taken an unimaginable bludgeoning in the previous eight months or so, and had effectively lost its entire pre-war strength with more than 4,500,000 men either dead, wounded or in German Prisoner-of-War camps slowly starving to death. The Soviet Supreme Command, the STAVKA, had responded energetically and millions of men were called to the colours, but it would take time to equip and train them to face the Wehrmacht. Time was a problem for the Soviets but a killer for the Germans now that the United States and its awesome military potential was in the war. So OKW drew

A signpost put up by DNL members to remind themselves just how very far they are from home as they besiege Leningrad. (Erik Wiborg)

up plans to launch yet another massive strike in the summer and finish off the Soviets for good.

The Scandinavian Waffen-SS would play their part in the coming campaign at both ends of the extraorinarily long Eastern Front. In the north, the now combat-ready Norwegian DNL, 1,218 men strong, was moving up to the trench lines surrounding Leningrad, while the 1,164 Danes of the Frikorps Danmark were nearing their baptism of fire in the inferno of the Demyansk Pocket hundreds of miles to the south. Farther south still, the SS-Wiking Division was licking its wounds from the winter fighting on the Mius River, while absorbing fresh intakes from the training depots. Having proved itself the previous year, the Wiking was to have a starring role in the coming German offensive.

Recruitment disaster

Not all was well with the Scandinavian Waffen-SS however, far from it. The advent of Barbarossa had indeed swelled the ranks of volunteers, but mainly in the two new national legions. Straight recruitment into the Wiking in particular was hard going. The SS authorities had hoped that a wave of anti-communist feeling in Scandinavia would see this number rocket and these fresh drafts would then swell the ranks of the Wiking over the winter. In reality, the numbers were relatively modest, so that by the beginning of February 1942 there were still only 947 Norwegians and 630 Danes in the ranks of the Wiking, while the 39 Swedes who had volunteered were spread across almost half a dozen Waffen-SS divisions (there was also one Swede in the Army's 3rd Panzer Division and another in the Luftwaffe's 8th Field Division). Unsurprisingly, the Swedish government was far happier to see their citizens enlist in the Finnish Army, so much so that the Finns formed an all-Swede unit, the Hangö Battalion, as part of the Finnish 13th Infantry Regiment that fought the Red Army on the Svir Front.

You did not have to look far to find the reasons why recruitment was so meagre. Gottlob Berger made the point crystal clear in a letter he wrote to Himmler on 9 February 1942. Berger outlined the problem, emphasising just how bad the situation was, and then laid the blame squarely at the feet of his rival, SS-Obergruppenführer Hans Jüttner. Berger pointed out that while his recruiters were responsible for drumming up the volunteers in the occupied lands, as soon as they signed on the dotted line they became the responsibility of Jüttner's massive SS-Leadership Office (SS-FHA – 45,000 men strong no less). Jüttner would then train and equip them and allocate them to field units to maintain manning. This division of responsibility was, according to Berger, the root of the problem. While his staff made arrangements with volunteers around retention of any rank they had previously held, preference of unit to serve in, and other basic terms and conditions, all of this was blown out of the water by the heavy-handed methods and lack of sensitivity displayed by Jüttner's organisation. The Swedish Army, for instance, was interested in seconding a number of officers to serve with the Germans to gain valuable frontline experience but despite Berger's enthusiasm for the project, it came to nothing. Berger outlined the action of the SS-FHA that caused the venture to fail in a personal letter to Himmler: 'The unceremonious discharge of one [Swedish] officer resulted in the closing off to us of the previously friendly Swedish officer corps and the destruction of a new and promising recruiting effort.'

The situation was even worse in Denmark after an incredible foul-up. In one disastrous incident, nine young Danish volunteers were sent to Das Reich after receiving only four weeks basic training and were all killed in action within days. Back in Denmark the news spread like wildfire and caused outrage. Recruitment fell like a stone as disgust mounted at what Danes saw as a lack of care and a breach of faith by the Waffen-SS. It also left Gottlob Berger privately ranting against what he rightly viewed as gross incompetence by the office of his arch-rival.

The result was widespread disillusionment among those willing to come forward. If he wanted to, Berger could also have quoted other examples from reports sent to him from the field, including the views of the controversial pre-war Norwegian writer, Winter War veteran, and now Waffen-SS DNL volunteer, Nils Per Immerslund:

Every tie, every connection, between Germany and Norway is lacking. The Germans think the volunteers will accept whatever treatment is meted out, and that Germany is hugely superior, but this was before they knew it for what it really is and by now even the old Norwegian Nazis could no longer deny it.

This was an important opinion given how high profile Immerslund was, both back home in Norway and within the Scandinavian Waffen-SS as a whole. The 31-year-old had already made a name for himself before the war through both his writing and his fighting, which saw him serve in Röhm's SA in Germany and Franco's Falange during the Spanish Civil War. His blond hair, blue eyes, film star looks and extreme views led him to be nicknamed 'the Aryan idol' ('det ariske idol' in Norwegian) in his homeland, but his self-loathing triggered by his homosexuality led him to seek out danger and take terrible risks. He ended up leaving the DNL, and became a correspondent in the SS's own regiment of war reporters, the Kurt Eggers. Serving with the SS-Nord in Finland he was wounded in action and died on 7 December 1943 in an Oslo hospital.

The anger of many of the volunteers at the treatment they received did not only manifest itself in words. In time-honoured military fashion some voted with their feet. Volunteers went home on leave and then fled to Sweden to avoid having to go back to their units, and on 12 March 1942 Felix Steiner reported back to SS headquarters in Berlin that, for the very first time in the war, the Waffen-SS had suffered from desertion at the front. Two Scandinavian privates serving in the SS-Nordland Regiment's 1st Company had gone over to the Russians from their advanced outpost in the frontline. The resulting uproar was loud. Himmler wrote to Berger on 14 April about the incident:

> The Missing in Action report from SS Division Wiking on Privates Asbjørn Beckstrøm and Ludwig Kuta, a Norwegian and a Dane who both shamefully deserted, once again reinforces my opinion that the ideological and military training of Germanic volunteers must be increased to obtain real success or our earlier efforts will be jeopardised.

In the Reichsführer's mind, the application of National Socialist principles may have been the key to success, but the problems he was trying to address were often of great personal significance. Himmler himself admitted that up to a third of volunteers had been disowned by their families as a result of their enlistment, and some wives had even left their husbands over the issue. The Norwegian volunteer, Leo Larsen, expressed the problem succinctly when he wrote from the Front to a friend in 1942: 'My father has very little sympathy with my political beliefs. So little, that when I tried to visit him on Christmas Eve while on leave (I hadn't seen him for 7–8 months) he threw me out.'

Left: A group of Finnish SS officers conferring in the endless spaces of Russia, autumn 1942. (Olli Wikberg)

Below: The newly-formed Finnish SS Battalion parades in front of Colonel Horn (officer saluting), the Finnish Military Attaché to Germany, and their new commander Hans Collani (far right) at Gross-Born on 15 October 1941. Horn presented the Battalion with a new unit flag at this ceremony. The flag was lost during the retreats of spring 1943. (Olli Wikberg)

This quote was included in an SS censor's report sent direct to Himmler. Larsen was not alone, the Dutch Westland volunteer Jan Munk said of his own family's reaction to his decision to volunteer: 'I became the "black sheep" of my family. The great majority of Dutch people were strongly ant-Nazi. Certainly my parents were, my younger brother joined the Resistance, as did my elder sister's husband.' But Munk was also one of the lucky ones: 'My parents never let me down though. My mother kept writing to me regularly as did my brother and two sisters. Fortunately mother kept all the letters that I sent to her and also photos and items that I left with her when on leave.'

The Finnish Waffen-SS Volunteer Battalion

What of the Finns? Well over a thousand had volunteered during 1941, and more than four hundred (those with combat experience) had spent the year fighting in the ranks of the Wiking. Eighty-one were killed in action in Barbarossa, with many more wounded, having fought the Red Army before they knew what to expect. The second tranche of 800 or so had spent all of summer and autumn being put through their paces on the training grounds of Vienna, Stralsund and Gross-Born. Apart from their battalion commander, Hans Collani, German involvement was not stifling, and to all intents and purposes the unit was an extension of the Finnish Army that just happened to wear Waffen-SS uniform. Receiving their Finnish-style battle standard in a ceremony on 15 October from Colonel Horn, the Finnish Military Attaché, the battalion was declared combat-ready on 3 December and dispatched east to join the Wiking in southern Russia in the New Year. It would prove a very welcome reinforcement to the depleted ranks of the Scandinavian Waffen-SS.

The SS-Wiking – there and back again to the Caucasus

1942 was set by both sides to be the decisive year of the war in the East. Hitler was determined finally to crush the Bolshevik threat, while Stalin was equally determined to see the Wehrmacht thrown out of Russia altogether. From the opening days of Barbarossa the previous summer, the Soviets had viewed Army Group Centre as the very fulcrum of the German war effort, and they assumed that the Germans shared this opinion. Accordingly STAVKA's expectation was for an offensive under Field Marshal Hans Günther von Kluge – in a play on the German word for

A group of Nordland Regiment grenadiers during the Wiking's advance into the Caucasus in the summer of 1942. It is a lull in the fighting, hence they are wearing caps and not helmets.

'clever', *klug*, he was known as 'clever Hans' – who had replaced the ill von Bock on 19 December, in the centre, aimed at capturing Moscow. They were to be mistaken. While taking the capital of the Soviet Union and destroying the huge array of forces grouped around it might have seemed an obvious target, the Soviets had misread Hitler's growing obsession with raw materials and the economics of war. The clue had been given the previous summer when, instead of thrusting forward and taking the capital in the autumn, Army Group Centre's precious panzers had been diverted south for the encirclement battles in the Ukraine. Hitler ranted on about taking the Soviet Union's 'breadbasket' and its industrial heartland in the Donets basin, and come 1942 he had the opportunity again to follow his own compulsion.

Hitler was clear to his generals; the main offensive would be launched by Army Group South and *not* Centre, and its objectives were the capture and securing of the oilfields in the Caucasus. With the Red Army growing stronger every day, and with Moscow and Leningrad still free, Nazi Germany's military might would be aimed at one of the most mountainous and turbulent regions in all of the Soviet Union, with few major cities and no strategic significance. Ultimately, this momentous decision would lead to the turning point of the whole war, when the most powerful field army the Wehrmacht possessed died in the snow and rubble of Stalingrad.

Case Blue (*Fall Blau*) was the codename given to the Wehrmacht's southern offensive in 1942. Outlined in Führer Directive No. 21, of 5 April, the situation was described thus:

The winter battle in Russia is drawing to its close. The enemy has suffered very heavy losses in men and materiel. In his anxiety to exploit what seemed like initial successes he has spent, during this winter, the bulk of his reserves earmarked for later operations … The aim is to destroy what manpower the Soviets have left for resistance and to deprive them as far as possible of their vital military-economic potential.

This was strategic planning in cloud cuckoo land. Not only was the Red Army mobilising millions more men from its unconquered Russian heartland, but more than 1,500 factories, dismantled in 1941 and shipped eastwards, were now in full production and pumping equipment through the Soviet system. The scale of munitions production alone had quadrupled from the 1940 level of 63 million tonnes to over 250 million tonnes in the spring of 1942. On top of this, vast reservoirs of vital supplies from Britain and the USA were pouring through the port of Murmansk in the far north, as the Germans were punished for their inability to take the city that winter. On board those Allied convoys were boots, coats, tanks and aircraft, and thousands of sturdy American-made trucks, which were slowly but steadily transforming the Red Army from a foot and horse-borne force to an army superior in mechanisation to its supposedly more advanced German enemy. Time was running out for the Reich, but it had another chance to win that spring.

Fedor von Bock, recovered from his illness, was once again put in charge of an Army Group, this time South – its previous commander von Reichenau had taken over from von Runstedt, suffered a heart attack and then died when the plane flying him to hospital had crashed. He was pitted against some of the rising stars of the reborn Red Army; men like Konstantin Rokossovsky, Nikolai Vatutin and Andrei Yeremenko. Together these three men commanded some 20 Soviet Armies spread in a huge arc from the Taman peninsula in the west, through the recaptured ruins of Rostov and up to the industrial city of Voronezh. Against them von Bock had two newly-reorganised mini-Army Groups; B in the north commanded by the bespectacled aristocrat and magnificently named General Maximilian Maria Joseph Karl Gabriel Lamoral Reichsfreiherr von Weichs zu Glon, comprising Friedrich von Paulus's enormous Sixth Army and Hoth's excellent Fourth Panzer Army (the renamed Panzer Group 3), along with the Rumanian Third and Fourth Armies and the Italian Eighth Army. Army Group A in the south was led by Field Marshal Wilhelm List and had the wholly-German Eleventh and Seventeenth Armies, and Ewald von Kleist's First Panzer Army (the old Panzer Group 1). In principle, the plan was simple. Drive east, and annihilate the Soviet armies between the Don and

Donets rivers in a huge pincer movement, then turn south and capture the Caucasus. While it looked straightforward Case Blue was built on a foundation of sand. The distances that had to be covered were vast and casualties had been so enormous the previous year that massive responsibility was being placed on the ill-equipped, poorly-led and undermanned armies of Germany's allies (the Hungarian Second Army would also be involved later on). The old campaigner Field Marshal von Runstedt described the force as an 'absolute League of Nations army', in which the Rumanian officers and NCOs were 'beyond description', the Italians 'terrible people' and the Hungarians 'only wanted to get home quickly'. Regardless, the Wehrmacht was committed, and preparations went ahead for the attack.

The SS-Wiking upgraded

Along with all the other Waffen-SS field formations, the Wiking had been fully motorised since its inception. This already marked it out amongst the largely horse-drawn German Army, but the decision was taken in 1942 to upgrade the division further to 'panzer grenadier' status. Before the war this designation meant nothing in terms of extra equipment or capability, it was more of an honorary title. However, from 1941 onwards it became accepted practice to equip panzer grenadier units with an armoured battalion of their own. This utterly transformed their effectiveness. For the Wiking this meant the addition of three entire companies of Panzer IIIs with long-barrelled 50mm guns, some 66 tanks in all, along with one company (20 vehicles) of Marder IIs (the powerful 75mm anti-tank gun mounted on an old Panzer II chassis). Some of the Wiking's artillery was made self-propelled as well. In effect, the division now had an armoured punch of close on a hundred vehicles.

The Wiking did not only receive a boost in its equipment table, but also among its ranks – the Finns had arrived in force. Supplied with French trucks from captured war stocks when they detrained at Vinnitsa in the Ukraine, Collani had led his men east during the winter months to join up with the Wiking in its defensive positions on the River Mius. The journey was truly awful, with more than 60 per cent of the trucks breaking down on the way, unsuited as they were to the rigours of a Russian winter. With no transport the majority of the Finns had had to march hundreds of kilometres through the snow and so did not arrive until early January – but at least they were there and in one piece. The division itself was reorganising and the Finns arrival meant that Fritz von Scholz could bring his Nordland Regiment back up to strength by disbanding his old third battalion, by distributing the men to the remaining two and making the newly-arrived Finns his new third battalion. This was not all done safely in the rear but in the frontline, with the Finns taking up positions facing the Red Army's 31st Guards Rifle Division. The 'Guards' designation indicated an exemplary unit and had been resurrected from Tsarist days to help motivate the men and it meant the Finns were facing a top notch outfit. In terms of bald numbers, a Red Army division was roughly equivalent to a Wehrmacht regiment – so the Finns were outnumbered almost three to one from the start. A few days after moving into the line, a Guards sniper shot dead the Finnish volunteer Onni Martkainen on 23 January 1942. He was the battalion's first fatality of the war. Back up to complement, and with all the new kit, the SS-Wiking was earmarked as a spearhead unit in Kleist's assault force.

The offensive would take the 2000 and more Scandinavian Waffen-SS men in the Wiking's ranks to places few outsiders had ever seen. They would begin in the steppes of southern Russia, before sweeping south through more Cossack country, until finally reaching the snow-capped fastnesses of the high Caucasus mountains and the fiercely independent Muslim tribes that lived there. Where they reached would become the high water mark of the Third Reich's empire, before they were sent tumbling back north in what the troops involved would disparagingly come to call the 'Caucasus there and back offensive' (*Kaukasus hin und zurück*).

The SS-Wiking drives to the south

Case Blue opened on 28 June, with von Weichs's Army Group striking at the city of Voronezh, several hundred miles north of Rostov and east of Kursk. Two days later, Paulus's Sixth Army initiated the next phase and thrust eastwards towards the far-off Volga River at Stalingrad. The Soviet response was to trade space for time and Timoshenko's forces retreated east to avoid destruction. All of this though was a precursor to the main event, when on 13 July the long-awaited Wehrmacht offensive began in earnest with the 73rd, 125th and 298th Infantry Divisions crashing into their opposite numbers on the Rostov front. The STAVKA was caught off-guard, as it still believed that the main German effort would come from Army Group Centre. Unwilling to accept they had got it wrong, the southern Red Army formations were left unreinforced and at the mercy of the assaulting German divisions.

Backed up by strong artillery, the experienced German infantry soon began to tear holes in the Russian lines through which the armoured and motorised formations could pour. Through one such gap charged the Wiking's panzer grenadiers along with the Slovak Fast Division, plus the

13th and 22nd Panzer Divisions. Riding hard, they entered Rostov itself on 23 July and surged towards the river. The Wiking's new panzer battalion overran the city's airfield, while the panzer grenadiers did the dirty work of street and house clearing. The fighting in the city was brutal, especially around the headquarters of the Soviet secret police, the dreaded NKVD, who were in Rostov in strength. The centre of the city had been turned into a deadly assault course, with strongpoints, mines, booby-traps, hidden bunkers and firing points. It took several days of savage hand-to-hand fighting to clear the city centre. Then a daring coup de main by a troop from the specially-trained Brandenburg Regiment secured the all-important road bridge over the Don to Bataysk. It cost the majority of the Brandenburgers their lives, but the way to the Caucasus was now open.

In recognition of the Wiking panzer battalion's outstanding performance and his own bravery during the assault on the city, their 34-year-old Lorrainian commander Hans Mühlenkamp (already a German Cross in Gold holder from his time in the Das Reich) was awarded the Knight's Cross on Felix Steiner's personal recommendation. His citation read:

> SS-Sturmbannführer Mühlenkamp, commander of SS-Panzer Battalion 5, as leader of an advanced detachment of the Division on July 22-23 1942, overran in a bold sudden attack after a hard fight, three lines of anti-tank ditches before Rostov. By 1430 hrs on July 23, he had broken into the western part of the city of Rostov. He cleared and occupied it, then pushed forward in a wide front up to the bank of the River Don. In the course of these battles Mühlenkamp destroyed 19 enemy cannons, 12 anti-tank guns and captured a large number of prisoners.
>
> Through his daring and prudent handling of the unit he has contributed decisively to the breaching of the west and northwest fronts of the deeply-set anti-tank ditch positions before Rostov, forcing our enemy to flee in confusion back across the Don. With that he has freed the way to Rostov and the Don for the infantry divisions advancing from the north and northwest. He has taken a decisive part in the capture of Rostov and created the conditions necessary for the crossing of the Don by the pursuing 73rd and 125th Infantry Divisions.

Oil, mountains and the Kuban steppe

With the crossing of the Don the Scandinavians of the SS-Wiking entered territory unlike any other in Europe. Before them stretched over 300 miles of the Kuban and Kalmyk steppes, criss-crossed by innumerable minor water courses, as well as the wide and deep Manych River. Beyond the plains were the Caucasus mountains themselves, the largest peaks in Europe, crowned by the eternally snow-covered summit of the 18,480-foot Mount Elbrus. The region was dirt poor but rich in oil; from Maikop in the west to Grozny in the east, the black gold flowed to Stalin's war machine. Maikop alone produced two and a half million tons of oil annually (the Wehrmacht consumed 7,305,000 tons in 1942). If captured intact, the Caucasus fields would feed Hitler's fuel-hungry armies all across Europe. The other major feature of the region was its military highways. The warlike hill peoples who inhabited the area, the Chechens, Ossetians, Dagestanis and others, had only been conquered by the Tsars in the previous century and had resented Russian rule ever since. The Russians had built two huge roads through the mountain passes so troops could move quickly to snuff out any trouble: the Ossetian Military Highway in the west from Kutaisi to Pyatigorsk in the north, and the Georgian Military Highway in the east shadowing the Caspian Sea from Grozny all the way south to Tiflis. These roads would be vital in the summer's fighting.

Under the baking Caucasus sun, the Wiking forged ahead with the rest of von Kleist's panzer force. It was the Berliners of General Breith's 3rd Panzer Division who first got across the Manych River on 1 August, and in their wake came the Wiking. Striking ever south, Maikop fell to Major-General Herr's 13th Panzer Division on 13 August, but they found the huge oil storage tanks ablaze and the oilfields themselves stripped of equipment and the wells capped with tonnes of concrete. Accompanying them down the western Caucasus, the grenadiers of the SS-Nordland took the railway junction of Kropotkin and surged across the Kuban River to establish a bridgehead on the southern side. They then turned southwest to try and take Tuapse on the Black Sea coast.

As impressive as the endless advance seemed, it was failing to achieve its objectives. Hitler had expressly set out in his Directive for Case Blue that the offensive wasn't only about capturing the Caucasus and its oilfields, but crucially it also had to encircle and annihilate the large Red Army formations facing it. The Führer wanted another Kiev. The only problem was that the Soviets were learning. Stalin's 'hold and fight' dogma of the previous year had been abandoned for the madness it clearly was. The STAVKA was now using Russia's age-old strategy of trading space for time, luring an invader ever deeper into its endless interior and then, when they were at the very end of their supply lines, hit them hard. It was working. German infantry divisions were marching 30–40 miles a day, with the panzers doing even more, but the horizon was never reached. The Soviets would simply sit on a river line, force the Wehrmacht to deploy and carry out an attack. As soon as the pressure got too much, the Russians would just disengage and drive away, leaving the Germans and their allies to punch into thin air. Cities, towns and villages were not fought over; Krasnodar the Kuban Cossack capital with its 200,000 inhabitants fell on 11 August, followed the next day by the Kalmyk's major town, Elista. But nowhere did the Wehrmacht fulfil its task and surround vast numbers of Soviet troops. They were always there, withdrawing in front of the Germans and heading ever closer to the mountains.

Elbrus 'conquered', but no more

Two months into the campaign though, and victory seemed in sight. If the Germans could sweep down the coast and take the ports of the Black Sea Fleet, they would turn the Sea into a 'German lake'. Turkey would almost certainly come into the war on Nazi Germany's side and could threaten the whole Middle East. Rommel, standing at El Alamein, could regroup and charge forward again as the British would be faced with a battle in their rear as well as to their front. In the East, if the Germans took the fabled city of Astrakhan on the shores of the Caspian Sea, they would cut off all Red Army forces in the Caucasus. They could be supplied by boat of course, but the reality would be half a dozen Soviet Armies stranded in the high mountains. But these were big 'ifs'. The Wehrmacht's soldiers had already covered almost 500 miles, men and machines were weary and battered, and the under-strength invasion force was dangerously spread out.

They were not finished yet though, and as if to prove it, on 21 August a party of alpine jägers from the 1st and 4th Mountain Divisions, led by Captains' Groth and Gämmerler, planted the swastika on the summit of Mount Elbrus. The Wehrmacht had conquered the highest peak in all of Europe. It was an incredible feat of mountaineering.

The steam was running out of Case Blue. Everywhere the Germans lacked the strength to reach their final objectives. They were 30 miles from Tuapse, 25 miles from the coast at Klydzh, and only 12 miles from Sukhumi, but it might as well have been the far side of the moon. The Red Army was fighting hard everywhere now, and the Wehrmacht had simply run out of aircraft, panzers, guns and men.

The SS-Wiking in the eastern Caucasus

As ever, Hitler blamed his generals and not himself for the failure. Field Marshal Wilhelm List was relieved of command at the beginning of September, as was Franz Halder, the Chief of the General Staff. From his headquarters at Vinnitsa in the Ukraine, hundreds of miles away from the fighting, an exasperated Führer ordered the offensive to be renewed and Grozny taken. By now it was late September and autumn had arrived, but obedient as ever the First Panzer Army gathered its strength and attacked south. The SS-Wiking was shifted to the east to assist the offensive, and along with the 23rd Panzer Division and the 111th Infantry Division, the SS grenadiers advanced on the Georgian Military Highway. Von Scholz's Nordland actually reached the road itself and cut it north of Grozny, but were overlooked by a feature denoted on German maps as Hill 711, near the village of Malgobek.

As long as the Russians held the high ground they could pour fire down on the hapless SS men. There was nothing for it, Hill 711 had to be captured. The Norwegians, Danes, Swedes and Germans of the Nordland attacked again and again, leaving piles of their dead on the hillside, but were unable to take it. Finally, on 16 October it was the turn of the Nordland's 3rd Battalion to go into the assault – it was time for Hans Collani's Finns. When the rest of SS-Wiking went into action at Rostov back in July, the Finns had been rested at Mokryj Jelantschick until the first week of August. Only then had they rejoined their comrades in the Nordland and fought in the western Caucasus. Now they took up positions in their line of departure (usually in dead ground away from direct fire where troops could get themselves ready for an assault), and at H-Hour leapt forward into the teeth of the Soviet fire. In small knots, the three Finnish infantry companies leapfrogged upwards, covered by the heavy weapons of their 4th Company. In desperate fighting the Finns took the summit and sent the Russians tumbling backwards. There was no time for congratulations, as the Soviets counter-attacked immediately. This time it was the turn of the Waffen-SS to hold the high ground against an advancing enemy. Assault after assault was broken up by concentrated Finnish fire. Come nightfall, Hill 711 was still in the hands of Collani's Finnish SS men, and Soviet resistance was broken. The toll was heavy. Hill 711 was rechristened 'Killing Hill' by its Finnish conquerors, with the battalion losing 88 killed and 346 wounded on its rocky slopes. With a further 80 men already in hospital, the battalion was almost wiped out. The arrival a month later of some 200 new volunteers, all combat veterans from the Winter War, was a great shot in the arm for the Nordland's Finnish contingent. These new men would go straight into action, as the battalion fought alongside its Nordic cousins to hold off growing Red Army attacks across the entire divisional front. Indeed, on 4 December two of them, Kalevi Könönen and Yrjö Pyyhtiä, held their machine-gun position unsupported for eight hours against furious Soviet assault. They were both awarded the Iron Cross 1st Class and the prestigious Honour Roll Clasp for their bravery.

The end of the line

With Killing Hill in Finnish hands, the rest of III Panzer Corps broke across the Terek River, smashed four Red Army divisions, took 7,000 prisoners, captured Alagir and by 5 November had cut the Ossetian Military Highway. Victory was so very close. The advancing Germans were feted by the local Muslim peoples as liberators from the atheist communist yoke. Nalchik, the capital of the mainly Muslim Kabardo-Balkiar region, fell in early November and there were public celebrations in the streets. But this was where the advance stopped. The armoured divisions had barely a handful of panzers still operational, and those they had were running on fumes. Even worse, ammunition was desperately short. The men were exhausted, their boots were worn out, and as the temperature began to drop they had little warm clothing, it was just like the last winter.

Ornulf Bjornstadt, a Norwegian volunteer in the Germania, was in the line on a stretch of high ground near Grozny:

> When I settled down for the night in my foxhole which was on a hillock, it was raining hard. The temperature dropped and the water trapped in the foxhole iced over while I slept. When I awoke it was iron hard and I was literally frozen to one wall. I couldn't move at all and my left side was totally paralysed. There was a bunker not far away where earlier there had been an attack by mortars which did plenty of damage, killing our company commander and wounding a lot of our men. Because of that there were doctors around and one managed to get to me after he heard me yelling. The only way to get me down the hillock was astride a motorcycle combination and I was bumped along until we reached a small town which had a hospital and spa baths originally used by senior Communist officials and now occupied by us.
>
> It was luxury to be between clean white sheets and the treatment was marvellous. There was even Norwegian staff, including nurses! I was in high fever when I arrived and then I became crippled with rheumatism, and it was a full month before I was able to be sent back to my unit, which was now in sight of a small Georgian village near the town of Osnokitsa. This was wooded country. The Elbrus, the highest mountain in the region and also all of Europe, towered above us. We set up a bunker in an abandoned house, establishing our mortar positions with infantry support, mine was near a creek – ideal because beyond was flat land leading to the village and it was good for observation.
>
> I was not on night duty at that time, which was lucky. One night there was a Russian scout patrol right in the path of my mortar position. Our men opened up. Next morning I discovered the body of a Russian officer slumped across my bunker. He had been caught in a burst of machine-gun fire.

The enemy was very active, striking out from the village again and again, mostly by day. The latest mortar grenades we were issued were very effective against them. They would land on the flat ground and then bounce up into the air before exploding with a deadly cascade of shrapnel splinters.

When we took Red Army prisoners we put them to good use, mostly digging trenches. I remember one wretched lad who was quivering with fear when we took him. He looked desperate and told me he wanted to be my friend. I took pity on him and put him to work as the company's cook. He had that job for about three months before I turned him loose to go back to his own lines. What happened to him after that I don't know.

What Bjornstadt didn't know at the time was that if the local Red Army commander had followed STAVKA's express orders the young cook would have been tried for cowardice, found guilty and shot. In Stalin's eyes there was no excuse for being captured.

Bjornstadt was not the only volunteer to be struck down by the terrible conditions in the Caucasus. Over in the Nordland's 7th Company the young Dane, Paul Hveger, was also suffering: 'I'd served in all the fighting in 1941 and 1942 right up to the Caucasus and never been wounded; but then I contracted jaundice and was sent home. That was the end of my service with the Nordland.'

With the Wehrmacht at the very end of its thousands of miles of supply lines, the increasingly bold Soviet forces launched attack after attack against their worn-out enemy. Bjornstadt and the rest of the Wiking's grenadiers had to cut their way through to the suddenly trapped 13th Panzer Division and pull them out to safety. All along the Front, the Wehrmacht began to pull back, and the withdrawal became official on 11 December. Army Group A was heading back north.

Stalingrad

The reason for the retreat was simple. Up north on the Volga River, the entire German Sixth Army was dying in Stalingard's choking ruins. The majority of Nazi Germany's allied armies – two Rumanian, and one each of Hungarians and Italians – had also been shattered in the encirclement battle that trapped von Paulus's men. In desperation, Hermann Hoth was leading his Fourth Panzer Army in Operation Winter Storm to try and cut a way through to their starving brethren. His panzers formed a wedge in front of a massive fleet of 800 trucks piled high with over 3,000 tons of supplies intended to revitalise the Sixth Army. All effort was thus focused on Stalingrad, and the cupboard for the Caucasus was literally bare. Now the threat was of destruction. If the Red Army could strike southwest from Stalingrad and take Rostov, then the whole of Army Group A would be cut-off in the Caucasus. One million men could be lost. For the Ostheer, the German Army in the East, it would be the end. There was no option, the Wiking's Scandinavians would have to retrace their steps all the way back to the Don. Case Blue had failed.

The cold reality of that summer's defeat demonstrated that Nazi Germany simply did not possess the resources or strategic focus to deliver a killing blow to the Soviet Union. They lacked what the great post-war German historian Paul Carrell christened 'the last battalion' that could make all the difference and bring final victory.

Away from the far south, 1942 was also the 'year of the legions'; the Norwegians at Leningrad, and the Danes at Demyansk and Velikiye Luki.

Leningrad – the DNL in the 2nd SS Motorised Infantry Brigade

Built on reclaimed swamp land at the cost of thousands of labourers' lives, Leningrad (the renamed St Petersburg), was an architectural jewel. The Neva River and its tributaries, then as now, flowed gently through picturesque canals and waterways, while the banks were lined with the imposing residences of Russia's pre-Revolutionary Tsarist élite. Romanov palaces jostled with gothic-style opera houses and world-class museums, while Leningraders strolled through beautifully laid out parks and squares. Like every Russian city, Leningrad also had its enormous factory complexes belching out smoke, but unlike Moscow, there was very little that was grim or grey about the place proud to call itself the 'Venice of the north'. When Barbarossa was launched, the citizens of the city felt they had little to fear given that the frontline was initially hundreds of miles to the west, but the huge German victories in the border battles and the loss of Lithuania, Latvia and Estonia had come as a great shock to the city, as the might of the Wehrmacht drew ever closer. A vengeful Finland had then launched its own offensive to the north of the city, recapturing all the ground it had been forced to cede to Russia after the Winter War. The Finns, though, did not press home their advantage, and were content to sit on the Svir River line and portray their advance as little more than the righting of a terrible wrong. The breathing space gave the Soviets the time and opportunity to turn their full attention on von Leeb's Army Group North and its three armies: the Sixteenth, Eighteenth and Panzer Group 4.

DNL legionnaires relax in the sun outside their bunker near Leningrad, 1942. (Erik Wiborg)

Dominated by foot-marching infantry, and having an area of operations unsuited for fast, mobile troops, the northern prong of the German invasion force was the weakest and least important in the Barbarossa plans. Priority for men and equipment went to the far more glamorous sectors to the south, as the likes of Guderian, Hoth and von Manstein raced through Belarus, the Ukraine and across the Dnieper. The commanders of von Leeb's infantry Armies, Ernst Busch and Georg von Küchler, were steady, professional soldiers, but not men to set the world alight. Erich Höppner, Panzer Group 4's tall, aggressive commander, was a different proposition entirely, driving his men relentlessly onwards and even being somewhat reckless on occasions. With the Baltic States captured, and the Germans at the very gates of Leningrad, von Leeb did not have the strength to capture the city outright, and so settled into an uninspired siege of the city hoping to bring about its surrender by bombardment and starvation. Tens of miles of trenches were dug, as the German infantry began a front life their forefathers in the last war on the Western Front would have recognised. Legion Hauptscharführer Bjørn Østring said of the conditions:

With temperatures below -30C it was terrible. The positions that we inherited from the attack units [elements of the 58th Infantry Division and the Leibstandarte] were established in a rush just after the cold weather started and after the Army were ordered out of the conquered parts of the city. An order from Hitler said that we would not take responsibility for the civilians of the city throughout the winter. The bunkers were virtually snow caves since the ground was frozen solid and was impossible to dig into. One of my units had it so low under the 'ceiling' of their bunker that our biggest

Bjørn Østring surveys the enemy in front of his trench near to Leningrad. (Erik Wiborg)

Norwegian DNL legionnaires dig in around Leningrad, winter 1942. (Erik Wiborg)

soldier could not turn around at night as his hip was too wide! The soot from our improvised cod oil lamps made us look like Africans, but with white skin around the eyes where the back of our hand sometimes would wipe the moisture away.

Making things worse was the fact that the already depleted formations of Army Group North had to besiege not one place but three. To the west of the city the Germans had been unable to take the huge naval base of Kronstadt and its environs on the Gulf of Finland, this was the so-called 'Oranienbaum Pocket' and was defended by the Soviet Coastal Army. To the east of the city the town of Schlüsselburg, on the shores of Lake Ladoga, held out. Both had to be invested, as well as Leningrad itself, and with the Red Army determined to break the siege from their lines on the Volkhov River to the east, von Leeb's weary divisions were stretched very thin indeed. With the majority of OKW's Strategic Reserve committed, and the lion's share of reinforcements going to the southern and central fronts, a series of scratch formations were hastily put together to try and hold the lines in the north. One such unit was the 2nd SS Motorised Infantry Brigade (2. *SS-Infanterie-Brigade* (*mot.*) in German). Along with its sister formation, the 1st SS Motorised Infantry Brigade, this unit was to have one of the most controversial records in the history of the Waffen-SS.

Originally formed from 'spare' Totenkopf regiments not required for the frontline divisions, the two brigades began life as anti-partisan security formations. They quickly established a reputation for brutality and ruthlessness. The cadre unit for the 2nd Brigade was Totenkopf Regiment 4, and a taste of its record can be found in its After Action Report for 26 October 1941. The report stated that after the radio interception of Soviet communications, the Brigade was put on readiness for an anticipated assault through the Skajadub Novka Bridgehead on the night of 25/26 October. The Soviets duly attacked, but had lost all surprise and were repulsed, with no SS losses, but '15 suspected terrorists and saboteurs from Tossno were sentenced to death and shot.'

Over time, the Brigades were to become heavily manned by foreign volunteers with several thousand Latvians on the books, along with the Flemings of SS-Legion Flandern and the Norwegians of the DNL. In fact, the arrival of the DNL instituted a reorganisation of the 2nd Brigade with the splitting off of several units to form *Battlegroup Jeckeln* (*Kampfgruppe Jeckeln*) on 17 February 1942. Alongside the Norwegians were a mixture of SS and Army units including elements from the departing 58th Infantry Division (Reconnaissance Battalion 158, Anti-tank Battalion 158, two batteries of Artillery Regiment 158 and seven infantry gun platoons), the

212th Infantry Division's 320th Infantry Regiment, four infantry gun platoons and the Artillery Regiment from the SS-Polizei Division, and last but not least, no fewer than five battalions of Order Police (*Ordnungspolizei* 56, 121, 305, 306 and 310). This curious mix of frontline and rear area units was commanded by a man who had already steeped himself in blood in southern Russia – SS-Obergruppenführer Friedrich Jeckeln. Jeckeln was a vicious anti-Semite who, following behind Army Group South the previous year as Higher SS and Police Leader for South Russia, had ordered and led mass executions of Jews and Communists across the Ukraine. He butchered 23,600 Jews at Kamenets-Podolsk in August 1941. Less than a month after the SS-Wiking took the town of Dnepropetrovsk and its massive dam, Jeckeln was there, slaughtering 15,000 of its inhabitants (almost all Jews) in October the same year.

Fortunately for the Norwegians, their contact with Jeckeln was strictly limited, and they were used in the frontline rather than in the infamous 'mopping up operations' behind the lines. Their first stop was the outer Leningrad suburb of Pushkin, right at the very end of the southern tramline out of the city. They were there only for a few days before being moved 13 kilometres to the west to Krasnoye Selo, the home of the old Tsarist summer palace. Here they dug in close by to the German artillery lines.

The DNL itself was organised in five companies; three of line infantry, and one each of heavy weapons and anti-tank guns, all commanded by Norwegians with minimal German liaison staff. Olaf Lindvig commanded the 1st Company, Karsten Sveen the 2nd, Jørgen Braset the 3rd, and Ragnar Berg the heavy weapons company. Finn Finson commanded the vital anti-tank gun company, curiously numbered as the 14th.

Each infantry section (and this was a battle for infantry and gunners, not dashing tankers) lived in a bunker deep underground, which they tried in every way possible to make liveable. Photos of sweethearts, family and friends were hung on the walls and the earthen floor was covered with boards or sacking. A stove, usually in the centre of the bunker, was kept going throughout the winter months in a desperate attempt to stay warm. Everybody then had their own bunk, hung with their kit and a few meagre personal possessions, woe betide any man who disturbed that. On a rota basis, the men would climb the stairs out of the bunker into the communication trench that connected all the bunkers together. There they would take turns to stand guard, the infamous 'stagging on', watching for any movement from the Soviet lines often built no more than a few hundred metres away across no-man's land. On occasions, each section would also go forward and take up position in a forward trench or outpost. Here they would be constantly ready to repel a Soviet attack or report back on any

Jonas Lie presents a medal to Olaf Lindvig. Lie was a part-time detective novelist before the war. He would go on to serve for several spells at the Front before dying in mysterious circumstances at Skallum at the end of the war. (James Macleod)

enemy movements. The exposed nature of these assignments meant they were very unpopular and the troops looked forward to their relief and a few hours rest back in the darkness of their underground home.

Trench life is a claustrophobic existence, where life is dominated by the most basic human needs and above all else, the weather. When it's cold, you freeze, when it's hot you swelter and no matter what, you are always wet and filthy. Everything stinks and everything rots, as the world shrinks around you to your own small piece of dirt. For the Norwegian volunteers of the DNL, the dirt around Leningrad was to be the backdrop to their war.

The Norwegians and the Siege of Leningrad

The siege of Leningrad, the longest in history, was an odyssey of human misery and endurance. The Germans lacked the strength to take the city and the Soviets the strength to free it. The result was a messy, vicious campaign, dominated by high explosive and hunger. German artillery and aircraft routinely bombarded the city, flattening buildings and killing civilians. With no food coming in and limited stocks, rationing soon became incredibly harsh. By late December 1941 Red Army soldiers in the line were receiving just 500 grammes (17.6 ounces) of bread per day, essential workers got 350 grammes (12.2 ounces) and everyone else a tiny 200 grammes, that's just four slices of a modern loaf of bread to hold together body and soul during a Russian winter. It just wasn't enough, and by January 1942 some 3,500–4,000 people were dying of disease and starvation every single day. The Leningrader, Valentina Fedorovna Kozlova, just 18 years old at the start of the blockade, said:

Opposite page: The DNL at the Siege of Leningrad. Top left: Bjørn Østring's bunker at Urizk in 1942. On the left is Bjørn himself, then his Company's German liaison officer Dieter Radbruch with the glasses, and on the right is Bjørn's second-in-command Henrik-Skaar Pedersen. Leningrad harbour is just visible through the window – Quisling's photo is on the wall above Radbruch. (Bjørn Østring)

Top right: The DNL gunner is manning an ex-French Army Hotchkiss machine-gun, indicating that the Legion was often armed with inferior weapons from captured stocks rather than the very latest modern German weapons.

Middle left: A friend tends the grave of the DNL officer Charles Westberg. Westberg served in the Norwegian Army and was a member of Quisling's Nasjonal Samling before joining the Norwegian SS. An experienced and well-liked officer he was killed by a direct artillery hit to his command bunker on the Leningrad front on 19 March 1942.

Middle right: Conditions in the Leningrad siege lines were primitive but there was always time for a smile with your comrades when the sun came out.

Bottom left: The low-lying land of the Urizk plain was prone to flooding so every trench was always half-filled with water.

Below right: Three volunteers come out of their subterranean bunker to take in some much-welcome fresh air (above) and Bjørn Østring and his section commanders from the DNL's 1st Platoon of the 1st Company, (below) in the moonscape terrain around Urizk; from left; the platoon second-in-command Henrik-Skaar Pedersen, Bjørn Østring himself, Einar Gill Fasting Jr and finally Per Bradley. (All Eric Wiborg)

Above left: A Norwegian DNL gunner with his MG34 in the lines around Leningrad. Conditions resemble the very worst of World War One trench fighting.

Above right: A Norwegian DNL volunteer uses a net to try and keep the swarming mosquitoes off his head, Leningrad 1942. (Erik Wiborg)

First and foremost the blockade meant hunger. I suffered from a state of extreme malnutrition. My pre-war weight of 60 kilos (132 pounds) fell to 39 kilos (86 pounds) by July 1942. There was no running water or sewer system. Hunger dominated, and the winter of 1941–1942 was intensely cold. German bombers raided frequently. Buildings burned and collapsed and people perished.

One constantly wanted to eat. I often dreamed on the way to work of suddenly finding a box of fat or an entire horse lying around.

It wasn't just Leningrad's desperate inhabitants who were obsessed by food in early 1942. Outside the city in the mud and squalor of the trenches, the besiegers felt hunger too, though nothing like what was happening on the Soviet side. The very drudgery of static warfare also increases the importance of food to alleviate boredom and break up the monotony. A good day in the trench was one where you had plenty to eat and it tasted of something more than the usual 'giddy-up-soup' (horsemeat goulash made from the supply of dead draught animals). This, at least, was an aspect of front life that the Scandinavians excelled at. Their homelands were not subject to extensive rationing or Allied bombing raids and food was still relatively plentiful. The result was a steady flow of parcels from friends and relatives packed with delicious goodies. Cheese, butter, pickled fish and jams were all sent to the ever-hungry volunteers, but this situation did not suit everyone. Jan Munk only half-jokingly said:

I liked the Norwegians a lot, good soldiers and nice to know as were the few Swedes I knew [there was one Swede, one Norwegian and two Danes in Munk's nine-man recruit squad in Sennheim training camp]. The Finns had a great reputation as fighters, the Danes were good soldiers too, but I didn't like them much personally as they used to get wonderful food parcels from home but didn't share them with us!

The DNL and the Battle of Urizk

Away from the food, there was no glory to be had in the trenches at Krasnoye Selo. No sweeping charges with massed tanks and aircraft, no grand pincer movements leading to prisoner bags in the tens of thousands. Combat was through shadowy night patrols, or the sudden launch of a brutal trench raid. Snipers abounded, as did artillery observers, ever waiting to unleash a salvo of rounds onto the unsuspecting. Bjarne Dramstad recalled his first experiences at the Front:

Above left: The Norwegian volunteer Bjarne Dramstad's identification picture from his official Wehrmacht papers, his *Soldbuch*. (Knut Thoresen)

Above right: The DNL's Olaf Lindvig in Russia posing with his MP40 sub-machine gun. (James Macleod)

First I did guard duty at an ammunition storage dump for a few weeks and then I was 'loaned out' as an infantryman to 2nd Company. My new platoon commander showed me my post in the trench and then I started my front-line service. This was around mid-March. I can remember a good friend of mine, Olav, was shot in the head – in the middle of his nose. The bullet came right out of his neck and there was a lot of blood.

It all started with the Russian sniper that killed Ola Strand [a volunteer and friend of Dramstad's]. Olav, who was one of the best snipers in the Legion, tried to spot the sniper but the Russian was expecting him, and shot him. Olav survived the war, and we actually served together later in Finland, but the Russian bullet gave him brain damage. He ended up living alone in a cabin on the Swedish border until he died in 1980.

But what I remember most from my first time at the Front was the grotesque sight of the dead Russians in front of our trenches. Their rotting bodies showed up as the snow melted, and blackbirds crawled into their chests to eat, it was horrible.

As always, infantrymen like Bjarne lived by the motto of 'keep your head down, dig fast and dig deep.' But being careful in war just isn't enough, and it was not long before the DNL started to suffer. In just over a week in the line, five Norwegians (including Ola Strand of course) were dead, and then on 19 March a well-directed artillery strike hit the command bunker of the 4th Company's 3rd Platoon. The ex-Norwegian Army officer, GSSN and NS luminary Charles Westberg was killed along with three of his men. It was a nasty shock to the still-acclimatising Norwegians, and the event bore a striking resemblance to the death of the Flemish volunteer leader, Reimond Tollenaere, killed just two months earlier less than eighty miles away on the Volkhov.

After Westberg's loss, the Front was relatively quiet for the next fortnight, with only sporadic shelling and the odd patrol. 1st Company's Commander, Olaf Lindvig said of these patrols:

> The orders were not to attack from the front, but to send out recce and fighting patrols which would be backed by infantry support as necessary. The strength of the patrols, which were organised by the company commanders, could range from eight to ten men, or in some cases be of platoon strength. Many of those who volunteered for the patrols used to be hunting enthusiasts back home, and they were undoubtedly among the best we had.

There were occasional full-on attacks as well, the first of which Bjarne Dramstad remembers vividly:

> Our closest point to the Russian lines was only about 75 metres away and that's where they attacked from. First we were hit by mortars, and after that came the infantry. We managed to stop them and lost no-one killed or wounded in that attack. It is possible someone was wounded behind us but I can't remember. The Russians lost several men. They were left behind lying in front of us. I was scared of course, but managed to do my job. Sometimes when the Russians started their bombardments of our positions, to soften us up, I sank down in the mud onto my knees praying to God. It was hell, sometimes I just thought of my mother, but when the attack came I always reacted like a machine, I acted without thinking.

The beginning of April wrought a change in position and in fortune for the DNL. The town of Urizk (also called *Uritsk*) was a small place, built at the junction where the main tramline going east from Leningrad to Oranienbaum splits and branches off south to Krasnoye Selo. It does not exist today. Utterly destroyed in the siege it was not rebuilt after the war. Its remnants were absorbed into the still-existent town of Staro Panovo, which stands looking out across the flat, reclaimed land of the area. The Urizk plain is relatively featureless, and criss-crossed with small waterways and drainage ditches. There is little cover and its very nature means a defender has excellent fields of fire. In the late summer of 1941 it was the western anchor of the main Russian defensive line built to protect Leningrad. An average daily total of 125,000 Leningraders expended a staggering 8,757,600 man-days building that line of fortifications, the majority of which fell to the advancing Germans in the autumn. So Urizk was in German hands, or more specifically from the beginning of April 1942, in the hands of 1,200 Norwegian Waffen-SS men. Bjørn Østring was now a Hauptsharführer commanding the 1st Platoon of the DNL's 1st Company under Olaf Lindvig. He said of the move:

It was heavenly to get to our new positions at Urizk, with a bunker we could actually stand up in and feel safe at the same time as it had an apparently thick roof. But as the spring progressed and the snow melted, we quickly realized that it was only some boards with snow on top, and that the walls rapidly crumbled because they were made with dirt mixed with ice and snow. What's more, everything that melted filled the trenches with genuine, wet, Russian mud. Our positions were at the top of a small hill, and so had some drainage. But for more than a kilometre around were wet trenches, from which flowed a continuous stream of muddy water. The result was that we were wet all the time. Often when going out to our positions, we had to wade through water up to our waists, and then stand guard for three to five hours while soaking wet. We then had to walk back to our bunker through the same water, which had then developed a thin layer of ice that we had to break. To rest, we had to climb a tall bank made to keep the water out. But after a while we couldn't keep all the water out, and sleeping during the day could only be done on the topmost bunk or on boards fastened to the ceiling. We never took our boots off, because our feet were blistered and swollen and we would never have been able to put them back on.

Under these 'drowned cat' conditions we wanted the winter back just to 'bind the water together'. Interestingly enough nobody became sick during these weeks. But we still had many men wounded or killed. It was very tempting to run along the top of the trench and stay dry, but with the closest snipers only 30 metres away this was the end for many of our men.

Østvig's company commander, Olaf Lindvig, agreed with him:

The Russians had set up a network of outposts and listening posts and seemed to have limitless numbers of troopers. They also seemed to have plenty of snipers whose aim was spot on. They would lie still for hours, observing through their binoculars. They were so sharp that they could knock a man's head off the moment he put it above the trench. The easiest targets were young Norwegian reservists, green and wet behind the ears. Some of whom were so trigger happy that they would sit on the edge of a trench and blast off their weapons. They didn't last long. The Russians would also send half-a-dozen or so bombers over at any time to attack our rear areas. The best occasion was when two Luftwaffe fighters shot down these nuisances and we were able to capture the crews after they baled out.

Such conditions have been the bane of soldiers through the ages. Both men would have recognised a description written 230 years earlier by the great British general the Duke of Marlborough, talking about his own men's experiences in Flanders during the War of the Spanish Succession: '… the continual rains, our poor men are up to their knees in mud and water, which is a most grievous sight, and will definitely occasion great sickness.'

Some things in the army never change. Another one of which is the necessity for any incoming unit, in this case the DNL, to familiarise itself with the lie of the land, and the enemy facing them. Patrolling is the standard method of accomplishing this, as well as beginning the process of dominating no-man's land and winning the initiative. It was no different for the DNL, so on the night of 15 April, Ragnar Berg led 18 men of his 4th Heavy Weapons Company on a trench raid against their opposite numbers in the Red Army's 56th Rifle Division. Berg was an experienced officer and the raid was well-planned, but it ended in disaster. In the nightmare ground conditions Østring described above, the assault troop inadvertently wandered into an uncharted Soviet minefield. A volunteer trod on a mine, and the blast alerted the Russians who plastered them with artillery firing on pre-set lines, so-called DFs (Defensive Fires). The Norwegians didn't have a chance, almost every man was hit and eight were killed outright including Berg himself, although the real miracle was that any survived at all. Under fire, the surviving wounded were brought out of the minefield by volunteers and sent to the rear for treatment. The survivors of Berg's Company were taken over by another Norwegian officer, Njaal Reppen. The DNL had now lost a company commander, a platoon commander and two dozen men in less than two months; and it would not be long before the entire Legion faced its stiffest test of the war so far.

To the southeast the Red Army spring offensive on the Volkhov had seen Andrei Vlasov's 2nd Shock Army crash through the German lines and flood west. In a scrambling defence, Army Group North had halted the advance and pinched off the assault. Every available unit was rushed east including the bulk of the 2nd SS Motorised Infantry Brigade (including by this time the SS-Legion Flandern – *see Hitler's Flemish Lions*). This left the siege lines around Leningrad badly stretched. The Russians took their chance to strike.

With all eyes on the Volkhov, the Leningrad Command thought a swift thrust along the coast through Urizk would enable a link up with the Oranienbaum Pocket. Plans were laid for an assault beginning on 21 April. By then the Norwegians had made some improvements to their positions. According to Bjørn Østring

> … the conditions got somewhat better, which enabled us to improve many of our positions while the sun started to dry everything up. The guard duties were changed and everyone – even the commanders – was able to get some sleep almost every night. But as soon as an attack was imminent we all worked every minute. We worked between flares at night, where we were like ants that took cover and froze once another flare erupted above us in the sky.
>
> For machine-gun and single soldier positions, new spring enforcements were built into the existing trenches, while 'Spanish riders' were moved forward to strengthen the sparse barbed wire fences. This job was extremely dangerous, as the Bolsheviks and us were working on our various projects almost shoulder to shoulder and just metres apart.
>
> A company of Latvian volunteers helped us out during this time. Their eagerness to work was great, but their hate towards the Russians was so enormous it scared us. They were not like us Norwegians, individuals with independent responsibilities, they did everything as a group. They always needed to have a leader in charge. From this point onwards this was the way we pictured our enemy as well, and we learned who we should go after first when the attack eventually came.

Bjarne Dramstad agreed with his fellow legionnaire on the quality of these Baltic soldiers; 'The Baltic nationals were very well regarded as soldiers, good fighters and highly motivated.' Bjørn Østring fought in the Urizk battle in late April 1942, and while it did not grab the headlines like the bloody mass slaughter going on in the primeval Volkhov swamps at the same time, it was typical of the vicious, intense, small-unit combats that characterised the DNL's record in Russia. As such it is worth recounting Bjørn's extraordinarily vivid story of the fight in full:

> Already in the week before the attack we started seeing the first defectors coming across the frontline. We also noticed that the enemy aimed their artillery very differently than they previously had done. Very seldom more than

two or three rounds against a given target, and the rounds were fired more often and with much more precision than before.

During the daytime we also noticed significantly more activity in the open area between us and the city of Leningrad, and during the night new sounds we hadn't heard before came out of the darkness. Of course the sun and warmer weather could be the reason for some of this. But the number of defectors increased, they seemed much better fed and were obviously new at the front. Their main reason to defect was obvious – the ever-present desire to survive! This was evident. An attack was clearly imminent and their thoughts must have been – 'If I cross over the mines will still be there and I will also be shot at. If we don't succeed with the attack, I will also have to withdraw over the same field. Then the NKVD will be in place to fire at the withdrawing troops and I will be shot regardless!'

And so they came, one or two at a time. They especially used the low ditches, which gave their own people a poor view of their escape across to our side. We started to call these ditches, the 'Defectors Ditches'. It appeared the Russian soldiers were thinking the same way we did, believing that only the Germans would win in the end.

The Company was organised with Ole Hjalmar Jacobsen's platoon on the right as seen from the enemy (Jacobsen was from Vestfold). In the middle was the platoon of Per Wang from Oslo, he had a theology education. My platoon was on the left, and then there was a small open area to the 2nd Company commanded by Karsten Sveen from Biri. The closest platoon to me on that side was led by Sophus Kars from Bergen.

The positions of our Company had an angular shape, with the right leg defended by the other two platoons. The terrain between them and the Russian trenches about 200 metres in front was relatively flat. The point of the triangle was at the 'Red Ruin', and my leg was on the hill with the road between Oranienbaum and Leningrad about 250 metres to our front. The road ran parallel to our frontline and went through the swampy lowlands stretching into town. Ivan's [Wehrmacht slang for the Red Army] trenches followed Ufer Street's other side. From my vantage point, at the point of the triangle, I had one trench stretching straight forward towards the enemy positions. From this position we had a backward view straight into the area of Red Ruin. In this area Henrik-Skaar Pedersen and his section had their bunker, which was one of many that we maintained. He was so exposed to the enemy in this position that we twice noticed enemy footprints on the roof of the bunker. At the end of the trench we had a machine-gun position manned by Arnold Schee from Oslo. Just before this machine-gun nest, a separate trench was dug northward on our side parallel to Ufer Street. Every night we placed a listening post here. There was also a period when Ivan controlled this trench during daytime. Because the trench going to Schee's machine-gun nest was pointing straight towards the enemy, we had it covered with snow throughout the winter. But now during spring and summer it was just covered with boards and twigs etc, which gave us some sort of secure feeling.

The second-in-command of my platoon, Naval Cadet Arne-Wilhelm Nilsen from Østfold, was a very capable leader and soldier. He had a good sense of humour and was always calm. The three section leaders were: engineering student Einar-Gill Fasting Jr of Hamar, world traveller Per Bradley from Bergen who had an exceptionally beautiful voice and had held church concerts throughout Norway, and Henrik Skaar-Pedersen from Egersund who used to study at Kotpus. The mortar section was headed by Olaf Hilde, a farmer from Stokke in Vestfold. All of them were top notch soldiers and all very proud to be a part of our platoon as well as being Norwegian soldiers. We were the very first recruits to show up at Bjølsen School, and subsequently formed the 1st platoon in the 1st Company in the first battalion to be set up! This became Viken Battalion of Den Norske Legion. We all knew each other's strengths and weaknesses, but seen from the Germans' point of view we were probably no parade-ground soldiers. We had all volunteered and were of the opinion that everyone in the Battalion was making an effort to stop the communists taking over Europe. We were also past the stage where we were afraid of becoming casualties of the war, for us this wasn't about 'fields of honour' but only bitter reality. Everyone was either going to be lucky, or unlucky. What we feared most was losing an arm or a leg, or becoming blind. But when the battle rolled on at its worst, we were all thinking 'and you volunteered for this?'

The night before the 21st of April we heard the Russian tanks crawling around. During the briefing I had with the Company Commander that morning, I received orders to gather a group of soldiers with Pioneer [assault engineer training that included destroying tanks] training and go out on a hunt over Ufer Street to damage any tanks getting ready to attack us from the road. Straight behind us was a building we called 'The Dairy', and our 14th Company (Finn Finnson's anti-tank company) had an anti-tank cannon nearby which now had to change position. Earlier I had gotten hold of explosives and fuses, which were now put to good use. We also agreed that as soon as the attack started we would get the men as close as possible to the enemy. This was thought to be the best option under the circumstances [to help nullify the effect of the Russian artillery]. I crawled over to 2nd Company's positions and agreed with Sophus Kars how his men and machine-gun could cover the area in front of us as we were going to move forward. During our conversation an intense bombardment began, which lasted several hours. I had to get back at some point, but this was incredibly difficult as shells were landing all around us. I thought at that time that no matter what I did it would be very dangerous. I was forced to take chances that morning that normally I wouldn't let any of my men take.

It went quiet just before dark fell, and Radbruch gave orders to move forward as planned. While we moved forward towards the enemy, Arne Nilsen was to take responsibility for our vacated position. It took us a long time to carry all the explosives forward without the enemy noticing, but we did put some charges and Teller mines [anti-tank mines] in place. We were so close we could hear the enemy talk, it was a pity none of us spoke Russian. The enemy trenches were heavily manned, but they seemed nervous and it was clear that the soldiers were conscripts fresh out of training.

Just before we reached our own positions I heard someone calling quietly for me, it was my assistant Erik Bratlien from Nannestad, who had been asked by the Company Commander to get hold of me and call him up on the field telephone. This I did and told him that everyone was in position as agreed. Just as I climbed back into the trench a bombardment started that was so intense I have a hard time describing it. It was estimated later that about 10,000 shells landed on the small area covered by the 1st and 2nd Companies. This must be true, it was so strong that our bunker actually sank lower into the ground because of the force of the explosions. All this while I was lying down at the bunker entrance with the phone held to my ear. We'd established the password 'Kochloffel' ['cooking spoon', or 'ladle'] that night for the three of us on the same phone line. Per Wang came on the line and told us that the first enemy soldiers were already crawling towards Red Ruin, and that his comrade Per Olav Fredriksen from Fredrikstad was taking over the phone in his place. He then disappeared outside and just a couple of minutes later Fredriksen yelled on the phone: 'Wang has gone down!' Soon after that the phone line took a direct hit and the connection was broken. My second-in-command, Nilsen, had responsibility for Ufer Street and held it against the enemy, with fire support from 2nd Company. This all happened while I was crawling towards Red Ruin to take over command. At this point I wasn't even sure if it had already been taken by the enemy. But I had the feeling that everything was moving around me. The noise was intense, and the shockwaves from the explosions constantly threw me off balance. Taking cover had no effect and there was no safe place to hide.

All of a sudden everything went completely quiet, and I thought I could be the only survivor as surely no-one else could have lived through a bombardment like that. Our trenches and positions were all completely gone. Where the platoon's sole machine-gun should have been was just a patch of splintered wood. Then, like a miracle, from a pile of rubble I suddenly heard Fasting's voice 'All OK!' I then had to take charge of the trench leading to Ufer Street because of how important that lone machine-gun was. The enemy now had a perfect view into the trench and fired shots directly into it from below. The trench was completely exposed with no cover at all, and I suddenly became aware of shots being fired along it towards me, so I took cover in a spare firing hole we had dug earlier. Here I was completely covered in dirt from the next two shell bursts which luckily didn't hit me. With me were two German 'office soldiers', Bauer and Wieland, who had requested frontline experience. I had put them down here with cases of hand grenades and with a view directly down into Red Ruin from the rear. Red Ruin was now infested with Russians who had orders to keep on going forward. From our position all we could see was a forest of bayonets, which the two Germans were busy throwing grenades into. Throughout this, Schee somehow kept on firing his machine-gun.

The other side of the barbed wire, as well as the open ground between me and Red Ruin, seemed like some sort of 'moving carpet' consisting of dead and wounded Russian soldiers. The air was filled with screams, and it was impossible to hear any orders or commands from anyone. Throughout this our closest machine-gun was continuously firing accurate bursts into the advancing enemy. This machine-gun was the most important in our whole line, but then I suddenly noticed a change in its rate of fire – it was a jam! I sent a soldier to go and fetch Saxlund's machine-gun, while I ran to the position of the jammed gun. When I got there the gunner had already taken it apart and was cleaning it as if at a relaxing day at the ranges! I blessed the hard SS training we'd received, which caused us to behave automatically in situations like this. Jacob Kynningsrund from Østfold had crawled up onto the bunker roof where he was being passed grenades by Stener Ulven from Valdres. Stener took the pins out before handing them to Jacob, who in turn would coolly throw them directly into the enemy at the points of greatest danger. The third member of the machine-gun team was using his K98 rifle and firing without stopping. In no time at all the machine-gun was operational again, and we had to order Kynningsund down to man it, even though he felt he was doing more damage to the enemy by throwing hand-grenades at them, and that Ulven could replace him in case he was hit.

I made a quick visit to Per Wang's bunker while he was still alive. He seemed very proud when I told him that his men were fighting bravely and holding their positions. Two days before he had managed to get hold of a couple of fresh eggs from behind the frontlines. Our bunker had got one of them on condition I promised to read him his last rites if he fell in battle. Somehow he 'knew' he wasn't going to survive so I granted him his wish.

Immediately afterwards, while making an inspection of Per's platoon, I passed another Norwegian soldier sitting across one of his fallen comrades filling machine-gun belts – his friend's back was the only dry spot he could find. He carried on with tears flowing down his cheeks.

Per's second-in-command, William Andersen from Moss, who previously had responsibility for the right flank, now took over full command. Radbruch moved forward but four members of his staff stayed behind to help us cover the area. Per Wang's body was carried past us to the rear.

There were no more Russian cheers to hear when I went forward again through the trenches, only horrible screams. Hilde was constantly firing mortar rounds over my head, which flew in a low trajectory before exploding alongside rounds from 14th Company's anti-tank gun positioned at The Dairy. Now even heavier firing was coming down as Arnfinn Vik's infantry guns also hit the enemy. With surgical accuracy, and only yards away from us, they protected Red Ruin as well as the area immediately behind where our men were taking cover. The effect of the bombardment must have been enormous, and we could clearly see the endless streams of Russian soldiers withdrawing before coming up against the machine-guns of their own 'political officers'. These politicals, greatly feared by all, had the power to slaughter their own troops in case of retreat. The poor enemy soldiers were utterly massacred.

When I reached Schee's machine-gun nest, I met my assistant Erik Bratlien, who was wading through waist-deep water in a trench we no longer used as spring flood water had submerged it. With several packs of cigarettes in one hand and half a bottle of cognac in the other, he blurted out; 'Sir, shouldn't our reserves be used before they get a direct hit?' I decided to hand out shots of alcohol to everyone, including those who were banned from drinking. Schee, still manning his machine-gun, put a cigarette in his mouth just as two Russians popped up in front of him. He knew they would throw hand-grenades at him unless he could get them first. As he burned off a series of rounds at them he yelled; 'Sir, can you give me a light please?' It wasn't just the training that made good soldiers, being Norwegian was equally important.

Looking forward over the front it looked extremely dangerous. There were so many Russian soldiers hanging over the barbed wire that you could have literally walked over it. But there were no further enemy attacks, only the medics who we tried to help as best we could. The Russian artillery eventually started firing again, but the shells landed way behind us. We were sure they believed they had wiped us out and that any survivors were running away. Even though exhausted, we grabbed our shovels and set to, to improve our positions again.

A heavy-set Russian officer was hanging dead over the barbed wire with a map or document case around his neck. We needed the case for our intelligence and agreed to drag him in once darkness fell. But after a short while Per Wang's man, Per-Olav Fredriksen, handed it to me. He had crawled out there himself and cut it loose from the body. The documents were sent to the rear immediately.

So what had happened? There were perhaps 50 of us altogether from Per's platoon and my own plus some panzer-grenadiers, defending against the main attack launched at the Red Ruin. But we only had three dead including Per. The Russians must have sent more than a thousand soldiers against us, but since the assaulting troops weren't the men we normally faced in the line they seemed totally unaware of our positions and any weaknesses we may have had. To throw your own soldiers across the frontline in this fashion should be considered a criminal act. The fact that we had stockpiled ammo, especially hand-grenades and mortar rounds, during the week before the attack, helped us tremendously.

It was relatively quiet for about three weeks after that before a smaller attack came in along Ufer Street, at the point where our 2nd Company's positions crossed the road. The attack was thrown back. During the ensuing counter-attack we even destroyed several of their bunkers. Afterwards when we searched these bunkers we discovered a large quantity of American canned foods. This came as a real shock to me at the time, the United States was actually helping communism! After the counter-attack I was given a radio receiver, which later on saved my life when it shielded my head from grenade shrapnel.

A few days later I was promoted to become an officer. The promotion was solely given me for my accomplishments on the battlefield. I was at that time, and still am today, very proud of what happened during those days on the Leningrad front.

For me personally, Urizk was the battle that stood out as the fiercest and most violent that I fought during World War II. For some of my closest friends, as well as many enemy Russian soldiers, the battle of Urizk would be their last. They paid the ultimate price.

In the aftermath of Urizk some 12 Norwegians were awarded the Iron Cross 2nd Class, including Østring, his second-in-command Arne Nilsen and the grenade thrower Stener Ulven. Quisling also made a visit to the DNL at the time, and met both Qvist and Østring (whom he knew well personally anyway of course) along with some of the other volunteers.

The DNL then mounted an attack of their own with Østring's company commander, 25-year-old Olaf Lindvig, taking a leading role. Lindvig had been a platoon commander in the Royal Norwegian Infantry Regiment No.5 before the war, he had then fought the Germans during their invasion in 1940 and was a hugely experienced officer:

Following the Urizk battle, Quisling himself (centre in the black uniform with cap and no helmet) came to see the DNL and present awards. Bjørn Østring (talking to Quisling) organised an honour guard, much to Qvist's annoyance, who is helmeted just to the left of Quisling. (Erik Wiborg)

Quisling uses the opportunity of his post-Urizk visit to the DNL to catch up with his friend and devoted follower, Bjørn Østring. (Erik Wiborg)

Co-ordination for the attack was textbook. The leader of our assault troops fired a flare pistol which was the signal for the grenade launchers to start. The time was 1300hrs on 2 May. Our troops on the ground then opened up with MG34s (machine-guns type 34), submachine-guns, rifles and hand grenades. For these we had previously concocted a crude device in which we attached five hand grenades in a single bundle. This was tossed into the enemy's bunkers and trenches. One of our volunteers was half Russian and half Norwegian, and soon he was shouting to the Russians in their own language to put their hands up and come out. The heavy machine-guns were emptied into those that didn't surrender as they broke out of their trenches and ran back towards the city. It was sheer slaughter, a horrific massacre.

I remember five of them who surrendered. They were miserable specimens. One was a commissar who had the Communist hammer and sickle on his helmet. I remember that he ripped these off and stamped on them in a blind rage. There were two others with a single Norwegian guard in charge. At one point our man took out some tobacco to roll himself a cigarette. The Russians stared at the tobacco hungrily since they didn't have any. But in their pouches they had some butter so a gentlemanly swap was agreed. The prisoners were also persuaded to part with their waterproof rubber boots.

I was anxious to have a look at the captured trenches, but as I made my way towards them, an explosion sent me flying. I had stumbled either on a small mine or bomb which could have been dropped from an aircraft.

With Lindvig out of action and sent to the rear, Østring continued: 'All the commanders in the Company requested that our German advisor, SS-Hauptscharführer Dieter Radbruch, take over from Lindvig. Radbruch was educated in England and was eventually recognised by us as "Norwegian".'

Post-Urizk: Arnfinn Vik and his anti-tank gunners

After the Urizk battles, the DNL was detached from the 2nd SS Motorised Infantry Brigade, and transferred to its sister formation almost next door, the 1st SS Motorised Infantry Brigade, before being pulled out of the line to rest near the town of Konstantinovka (modern-day Golorowo) just north of Krasnoye Selo. After several weeks of well-earned rest the DNL went back into the line in June. The usual state of play with patrols and random artillery salvoes resumed until 20 July, when the neighbouring Latvian SS battalion was hit by a major Soviet assault. One of Finn Finson's teams, a two-gun troop led by SS-Oberscharführer Arnfinn Vik, was close by, and when Vik saw the danger he and his men dragged their obsolete 37mm guns almost a kilometre to a blocking position near Novo Panovo. From their new position the Norwegian gunners poured fire into the advancing Soviet infantry, and continued to do so even after one gun was knocked out. Eventually a German police battalion counter-attacked, along with the remaining Latvians, and restored the line.

As the line stabilised, the Germans were finalising plans for Operation Northern Lights (*Unternehmen Nordlicht*), the capture of Leningrad. Having successfully assaulted the Black Sea fortress of Sevastopol, Manstein and his entire Eleventh Army were slated to travel north and repeat their feat against Russia's second city. September 14 was chosen as the start date for the offensive, but the operation was thrown into disarray when the Red Army beat the Germans to the punch and launched their own attack to relieve Leningrad on 24 August. Army Group North struggled to repulse the Soviet assault, and the resources carefully husbanded for Northern Lights were expended in bitter defensive fighting. The DNL's neighbouring Corps, the Army's XXVI Corps, was the Soviet point of main effort and suffered badly. The Norwegians were caught up in the fighting and took heavy losses as well. Although Manstein managed to pinch off the Soviet breakthrough, just as with Vlasov's earlier Volkhov offensive, and destroy seven Red Army divisions and six brigades into the bargain, the attack fatally delayed Northern Lights. As Case Blue began to stall and the nightmare of Stalingrad unfold, the capture of Leningrad fell down the Wehrmacht priority list. Troops began to be pulled out of the region to shore up other fronts and soon the siege lines were stretched thin indeed. Although Leningrad was still surrounded, the Ostheer would never seriously threaten to take the city again.

Jonas Lie and the 1st SS Police Company

As the September fighting died down, the DNL received some welcome reinforcements from a rather unexpected source. Back in Norway, members of the police were encouraged to volunteer for service with the DNL in a company all their own, to be led by the Minister for Police himself – ex-Leibstandarte war correspondent and Iron Cross 2nd Class holder, SS-Sturmbannführer Jonas Lie. Some 160 came forward, were formed into the 1st SS Police Company (*1. SS- und Polizei-Kompanie*, also called the *1. SS-og-Polit Kompanie*), and were dispatched east to join their comrades in the trenches. They ended up fighting through the whole autumn and winter. Lie received the Iron Cross 1st Class for their endeavours, as did Artur Qvist for the DNL as a whole.

Two months after the Norwegian policemen arrived in the line, a worn-down DNL was thrown into the fighting near Krasny Bor on 4 December, where the Dutch volunteers of the *SS-Legion Niederland* were receiving a pounding. The Norwegians' 3rd and 4th Companies counter-attacked in support of the Dutch, and once again the Front was restored. As usual it was to be only a temporary respite, and by now the DNL was down to 20 officers and 678 other ranks from the original roster of over 1,200 volunteers.

A quiet Christmas was followed by a vicious new year, as the Red Army once again tried to reach Mga near the Volkhov and lift the siege of Leningrad. Army Group North was equally determined to stop them doing just that. In what became known as the Second battle of Lake Ladoga, Finson's men went to the aid of the Spaniards of the 250th Infantry Division (the *Blue Division*) who were struggling to stop wave after wave of Soviet tanks. The Norwegians old 37mm peashooters had been replaced by far more powerful 75mm guns (38/97 models based on First World War French Army gun barrels) which were big enough to blow the Russian T-34 tanks to pieces. As the Soviets came on, tank after tank fell to the Norwegian gunners, but the odds were hugely against and an entire battery had to be spiked and abandoned when it was encircled. The men only just got out alive. By this time Bjarne Dramstad had left 2nd Company and was back as an anti-tank gunner in the 14th Company:

I was wounded in January 1943 at the battle for Mga, this was hard fight-ing, my 75mm PAK [*PanzerAbwherKanone* – anti-tank gun] destroyed the first T-34 in the battle. I was wounded when a Katyusha rocket hit a load of Tellermines that exploded. I was flung several metres up in the air and my friends had to dig me out. I came to, lying wounded, and was transferred to a first aid post behind the lines. At the end of this battle there were so few survivors from the Company that the PAK cannons were given to the Dutch. I later found out that my cannon was given to Gerardus Mooyman, who destroyed so many tanks at Mga with this cannon that he became the first foreigner to be awarded the Knight's Cross.

Mooyman was only 19 years old at the time but that didn't stop him from knocking out 13 Soviet tanks on 13 February alone.

Somehow though, the defenders hung on, and the Norwegians of 14th Anti-tank Company in particular were singled out for praise by grateful German commanders. Three members of the DNL – SS-Hauptscharführer Arne W. Nilsen and SS-Unterscharführers Per Meidell and Nils Lande – received the Iron Cross 1st Class for bravery during the fighting.

The DNL's swansong

The Ladoga fighting turned out to the last for the DNL. Even with fresh drafts of men coming in over the winter, the Legion was still only some 700 men strong, and was withdrawn back to Krasnoye Selo in late February as the two-year terms of its original enlisters came to an end. The grind of trench warfare had slowly eaten away at the fabric of the unit, and although it suffered the fewest casualties of all the legions (some 158 Norwegian legionnaires were killed in action during its lifetime), the DNL 'felt' battered and bruised. Thus the decision was taken in Berlin to withdraw the unit back to Norway and decide from there what to do next. The ex-policemen of Lie's Company led the way and left for home on 1 March, to be followed a few days later by the rest of their comrades. Given two weeks welcome home leave, the DNL then reformed in Oslo and held one last parade through the city to the Slotts Palace. There, at an official ceremony, the Den Norske Legion was disbanded and its members released from service in the Waffen-SS. Most would never wear the uniform again, and one of those was Bjørn Østring:

> After my leave in Norway I was retained there at home by Quisling for Party service, i.e. as head of his 150-strong Førergarden personal bodyguard at his residence 'Gimle', and that was where I was when the war ended. I had an awkward feeling of 'letting down' my comrades out East, but orders are orders. That then was the end of my front service. I had been wounded, but so slightly that I made no fuss about it. It wasn't until many years later that I began to feel 'uneasy' in my neck, a doctor gave me a local and removed a 'wandering' shell fragment.

Many other volunteers felt they had 'done their bit' out East, and either went back to civilian life or, like Bjørn, served instead within NS party functions or paramilitary bodies. But not all followed this path. Some would sign on again, and they would join their Danish, Swedish and Finnish brethren in a whole new venture.

The Demyansk Pocket

The siege of Leningrad was not the only battle Army Group North was fighting in 1942. In the swamps and forests around the Lovat River to the south, some 95,000 of its men were cut off and fighting for their very lives in the Demyansk Pocket.

As elsewhere along the Russian Front that winter, the Red Army had launched itself at the invaders on the Lovat, determined to deal them a shattering blow. South of Lake Ilmen, Marshal Georgi Zhukov, arguably the Red Army's finest commander of the war, had sent three entire armies crashing into just two German infantry divisions on the night of 7 January 1942. The poor German *landsers* (German equivalent to 'Tommy') were all but wiped out. The resulting crisis cost von Leeb his job as he was replaced by Eighteenth Army's commander, Georg von Küchler. But sacking von Leeb did not stop the Soviet tanks rolling and linking up west of Demyansk a few days later. In the pocket were no less than five German infantry divisions and Theodor Eicke's 3rd SS-Totenkopf Division. In temperatures that often plunged to minus 30 degrees C, and in snow three feet deep, the encircled Germans fought like demons to avoid disaster. Thousands died, despite the Luftwaffe successfully delivering the required 200 tonnes of supplies a day the troops needed, and evacuating some 35,000 wounded men.

Eicke especially was incandescent with rage that his treasured division was being bled to death in the wastes of Demyansk, and demanded reinforcements to keep it alive. Few were forthcoming, but OKW was on the lookout.

The Danish Waffen-SS arrives

Meanwhile back in Posen-Treskau, the charismatic Christian von Schalburg had transformed the Danish Frikorps from a fledgling organisation riven by internal dissention, into a solid, well-drilled, reinforced infantry battalion. He had integrated 10 experienced German officer instructors into key posts to help stiffen the unit, and had led it through a tough training régime. The Danmark now had three infantry companies, and one heavy weapons company with two platoons of 75mm infantry cannons, one platoon of 50mm anti-tank guns, and a combat engineer platoon, all at full-strength. That were still only a paltry *seven* heavy calibre weapons, but at least it was something. Many of its men were untried and untested, but at its core was a strong cadre of professional officers, NCOs and men, most of whom had some sort of battle experience, either in the Winter War, with the SS-Wiking, or indeed against the Germans themselves.

When the Frikorps was finally declared combat-ready in May 1942, the German High Command made a momentous decision regarding its future. Up until then the volunteer legions had almost uniformly been viewed as second-rate in comparison to German formations, and unsuited to anything more than static warfare, hence their concentration around

Left: Per Sörensen – a well-regarded pre-war Danish Army officer, Per Sörensen led the Frikorps Danmark's 1st Company at Demyansk before transferring to the Nordland Division. He would eventually command the whole Danmark Regiment before being killed in action in Berlin in April 1945.

Below: From left, Per Sörensen, the only ever Danish commander of the Danmark Regiment, Rudolf Ternedde, the highly decorated German officer who ended up commanding the remnants of both the Norge and Danmark Regiments in the ashes of Berlin, and finally the Danish volunteer Alfred Jonstrup. Jonstrup recovered von Schalburg's body after his death in the Demyansk Pocket and was awarded the Honour Roll Clasp for bravery during the Courland battles of 1944.

Leningrad and in anti-partisan fighting (the French of the LVF were an example of the latter). Now, this situation was to change dramatically as the order went out to send the Danes into Demyansk. A land corridor to the beleaguered defenders had finally been established on 22 April after 73 days of brutal combat, but the fighting was far from over, and the Frikorps was actually flown into the Pocket, from Heiligenbeil near Köngisberg, to fight alongside the battling Totenkopf veterans.

Even in the spring sunshine, Demyansk, as already described, was definitely not for the faint-hearted. This was not a period of brief skirmishes and light patrolling, but a vicious and brutal battle for survival. The Soviets were still determined to crush the defenders and register a historic Red Army victory, and were throwing all they could muster into it. They had already devastated the area, dropping incendiary bombs on every building in the winter to deny shelter to the Germans and their own civilians. Massed artillery regularly worked the ground over and waves of tanks and infantry were constantly trying to stave in the sides of the Pocket and stir up panic among the defenders.

Left: Von Schalburg confers with men from his Frikorps Danmark in the Demyansk Pocket, 1942

Below: The German Frikorps Danmark officer, Obersturmführer Hennecke, talks to his men during the Demyansk fighting. As with its sister formation the Norwegian DNL, the majority of the Frikorps commanders were actually Scandinavians and not Germans.

Death of the commanders

From day one the Danes were thrown into the fighting. Taking up positions on the River Robja, the Frikorps was given the task of stopping the Red Army from expanding their bridgehead in the area of Ssutoki. The Soviets were on the far bank and had managed to get some troops over to the German-held side. If they could get across in any numbers, and bring tanks, they could expand it out until they had a solid base from which to launch a full-scale attack. This would spell real trouble for the hard-pressed defenders. Von Schalburg knew the Soviet toehold had to be destroyed and ordered the Winter War veteran Johannes-Just Nielsen to carry out an the assault on the night of 27/28 May. Nielsen was one of the Frikorps's real characters. Young, engaging, and immensely popular with his soldiers, he was also one of the Frikorps's best platoon commanders. After planning the attack, Nielsen divided his men into two groups and led them silently through the darkness towards the bridgehead. Sneaking up unnoticed on the Soviets, Nielsen threw a hand-grenade into the enemy to signal the attack. From both sides his men rushed forward and machine-gunned the Russians. Those that survived jumped into the river and swam to safety. The operation was a complete success. Then disaster struck. Dawn arrived and Nielsen ordered his men to withdraw back to the defence line, but they were hit by an artillery barrage and Nielsen was killed. Caught full on by a shell blast his body was blown into the river and disappeared. His men took cover in the abandoned Red Army trenches and waited out the barrage. When it finally stopped they withdrew under the leadership of Oberscharführers Kern and Jens 'Lightning' Nielsen.

Nielsen's death at Ssutoki presaged an even bigger blow for the Frikorps, when just a few days later the Red Army lunged across the river yet again to re-establish a bridgehead at exactly the same place. Another attack was needed to repeat Nielsen's success, so on 2 June the Danish SS once again were assaulted at Ssutoki. The Soviets knew what was coming and showered the Danes with artillery, trying to blow the attack away before it really got going. Von Schalburg went forward himself to encourage his men, but was badly wounded when he stepped on a mine. With one of his legs shattered in the explosion, he needed to be carried to safety, but as his men grabbed him they were hit by a salvo of Russian mortar shells. Von Schalburg and two others were killed instantly. Another Winter War veteran, Alfred Jonstrup, managed to retrieve von Schalburg's body for burial, but the shock of his death caused the attack on the bridgehead to fizzle out. The Frikorps lost 21 men killed and 58 wounded on that day, and the Soviets still had their bridgehead.

A portrait of the Danish Frikorps commander Knud Börge Martinsen while undergoing officer training at Bad Tölz. After service on the Russian Front he would go on to found the paramilitary Schalburg Corps back home in Denmark in homage to his dead friend, before himself being executed after the war for the murder of a fellow Danish SS officer whom he accused of having an affair with his wife.

Danish SS officer Count Christian von Schalburg with his son Alex.

A close friend of von Schalburg's from Finnish War days, SS-Obersturmbannführer Knud Börge Martinsen, immediately took command and stabilised the situation over the next few days, while the Frikorps waited for a new leader to be appointed. Within a week this new man had arrived, the SS-Wiking veteran, middle-aged aristocrat Hans Albert von Lettow-Vorbeck. Von Lettow-Vorbeck was a nephew of the famous World War One East African hero, and had been appointed to command the *SS-Legion Flandern*, after Michael Lippert's loss through injury. However, with von Schalburg's death, the Danmark was deemed a higher priority and he was re-routed to Demyansk. At the same time, parts of the SS-Totenkopf were preparing to launch Operation Danebrog to recapture the area up to the Pola River and re-establish a defensible line. The Frikorps was slated to play its part in the attack by taking the important local town of Bolschoje Dubowizy. Von Lettow-Vorbeck arrived on 10 June, was briefed by his officers on the situation, and as dawn lit the sky the Danes made a frontal assault on the town. German artillery fired on the Russians to the city's north, as the Danes struggled through swamps and flooded meadows before bursting into Dubowizy and starting to clear it house by house. In the face of bitter resistance the advance stalled, and the Red Army counter-attacked, killing two of the Frikorps' company commanders – Untersturmführers Boy Hansen and Alfred Nielsen. By 11 o'clock the Russians were on the verge of surrounding 27-year-old Per Sörensen's 1st Company and cutting it off. Von Lettow-Vorbeck was on his way forward to personally order Sörensen to withdraw, when a Soviet machine-gun cut him down. His death took the steam out of the Danish attack and by the end of the day Dubowizy was still in Russian hands. The Frikorps lost 25 men that day. All were buried in the cemetery at Biakowo. Yet again, Martinsen had to take over. The Danmark had now lost two commanders in just over a week, as well as over a hundred men killed and wounded in the Ssutoki and Pola River fighting. With von Lettow-Vorbeck dead, Berlin made no more attempts to 'import' officers, and Martinsen was confirmed as the Frikorps' leader for the rest of its existence.

Back in Denmark, von Schalburg was given a hero's send-off and buried with full military honours. He became a martyr for the Danish Nazis, and his example encouraged a fresh wave of volunteers to come forward. The Frikorps would come to need this new draft, as the Demyansk battles ground on over the summer.

A month after von Schalburg's death, the Danes were defending an overly-long line between Biakowo and Vassilievschtshina. Everything was quiet and the men were waiting for hot food to be brought up from the field-kitchens about a kilometre behind them, when all hell broke loose. For more than an hour the volunteers were lashed by artillery fire, after which the Red infantry flooded forward. The dazed Danes fought back, but it was not long before they had lost contact with the German unit on their right flank and were in danger of being overrun.

Every man who could hold a rifle – cooks, clerks, signallers – was sent forward to try and hold off the attack. The Luftwaffe was called in to provide support with its 'flying artillery', the Junkers Ju-87 Stuka dive-bombers. Just as at Dubowizy, Per Sörensen's 1st Company was involved in the fiercest fighting and was soon down to just 40 men from its earlier complement of 200. Sörensen himself was another pre-war professional Danish Army officer, having been Adjutant of the Viborg Battalion, when handpicked by Kryssing to come over to the Frikorps as one of the original officer cadre. Selected for training at Bad Tölz, the SS recruiting office in Copenhagen described the tall and slender Dane as 'a competent and reliable officer. Lieutenant-Colonel Kryssing is very interested in his accession and posting as an SS-Obersturmführer. Sörensen is an officer of exceptionally good appearance. He disposes of a sure and deliberate bearing.'

After graduation, he took command of the 1st Company at Demyansk and would eventually rise to lead the whole Danish Waffen-SS, before dying in the ruins of Berlin in 1945. But back on the afternoon of 16 July 1942 that fate was a world away, as he and his men desperately tried to hold out against the Russian attack. He telephoned Martinsen and told him he might not be able to beat off another Soviet assault, but no matter what, his men would not abandon their positions. The fighting went on through the night, right in the heart of the Frikorps defensive position. An entire Red Army infantry battalion, with tank support, crashed into Sörensen and his remaining men. They were in the Danish trenches in a moment; and so began several hours of hand-to-hand fighting as Danes and Russians killed each other with knives, grenades and entrenching tools. Just after midnight the Soviets had had enough, suddenly they were breaking and running. Miraculously, 1st Company had held. The battle was not over though, as the Soviets threw in reinforcements, as did the Germans with the arrival in the early hours of Silesian 28th Jäger Battalion, along with a battalion from the 38th Jäger Regiment. These fresh German units attacked along the road to try and link up with their comrades to the east of Vassilievschtshina but were repulsed with heavy losses. The next day waves of Red Army infantrymen charged forward yet again, supported by clusters of T-34 tanks and with fighter-bombers roaring in overhead. As with their Norwegian comrades, the Danes had no armour or anti-aircraft guns of their own, and could only reply with their three anti-tank guns and four infantry cannon. They just had to crouch and bear it as casualties mounted. Nevertheless, the Danes and the Jägers managed to see the Russians off and stabilise the line over the next few days. By the 21st the crisis was over. That fight was typical of combat in the Pocket. Unsurprisingly, casualties under these circumstances were high – over 300 Danes were dead by early August and only 150 or so of the original Frikorps remained in the line. In effect, the unit was no more. Down to a couple of weak companies, the decision was taken to withdraw the Frikorps for a rest and a refit.

Their sacrifice had not gone unnoticed though, and the Pocket Commander, General of Infantry Graf Walter von Brockdorff-Ahlefeldt, wrote to them thanking them for their bravery:

> Since the 8th of May the Danmark Legion has been positioned in the fortress. True to your oath, and mindful of the heroic death of your first commander, SS-Sturmbannführer Christian von Schalburg, you, the officers and men of the Legion, have always shown the greatest bravery and readiness to make sacrifices, as well as exhibiting exemplary toughness and endurance.
>
> Your comrades of the Army and Waffen-SS are proud of being able to fight shoulder to shoulder with you in the truest armed brotherhood. I thank you for your loyalty and bravery.

With this endorsement ringing in their ears, the Danes were withdrawn to Latvia at the beginning of August, before heading home to Denmark for a homecoming parade through Copenhagen and three weeks well earned leave. The Frikorps had been in combat for three months straight, and in that time had lost two commanders, a host of junior officers and NCOs, and hundreds of men. Having flown into Demyansk with a fighting strength of 24 officers, 80 NCOs and 598 men back in May, only 10 officers, 28 NCOs and 171 men took part in the Copenhagen parade. Many were wounded rather than dead of course, so some would return to the unit in time, but there was no getting away from the fact that Demyansk had decimated the Frikorps. They'd given as good as they got, for sure. The SS-Totenkopf's Order of the Day on 3 August credited them with killing 1,376 Soviets and capturing 103 others, along with over 600 heavy weapons. Gratifying though this recognition was, the fact that some of the crowd watching them parade in Copenhagen jeered them did little to lift the spirits of the surviving volunteers.

One Dane who did not take part in the parade, indeed he had not served with the Frikorps since before Demyansk, was Erik Brörup. The ex-cavalry officer had initially worked with Kryssing and his team during the training in Hamburg Langenhorn, and had then had his place confirmed at Bad Tölz. Along with Per Sörensen and several other European volunteers, Brörup spent the first half of 1942 at the academy, before graduating on 8 May. Given his love of his old arm, he had applied not to return to the Frikorps but instead to be sent to the Waffen-SS's own cavalry formation, the 8th SS Cavalry Division Florian Geyer. This new division was being built around the existing SS Cavalry Brigade, augmented by the addition of more than 9,000 volksdeutsche from Hungary. On formation it was allocated to Army Group Centre, as part of the Ninth Army. Brörup joined the 4th Squadron of SS Cavalry Regiment Nr. 3 as a troop commander, before being transferred to a new posting during the fighting at Orele:

With the onset of winter in November 1942 I was transferred to Reconnaissance Battalion 8 [*Aufklärungs Abteilung 8*] as a platoon commander. The recce battalion was now a ski-troop outfit and an interesting form of warfare began for us. It was similar in content to the way the Finnish ski-troops operated. Fighting in trees is a little different from a traditional battle, where you usually have all kinds of fireworks – artillery, mortars, rockets, machine-guns – and all kinds of other hardware to back you up. In the trees you are on your own. The weapons we used for forest fighting were just rifles, machine pistols and grenades. It is also very sneaky. You work in circles around each other in a kind of deadly 'hide and seek'.

I got the Iron Cross 2nd Class on 1 December 1942 for a raid into a forest when we ran into a Russian battalion. My job was to establish how far the Russians had penetrated into the forest. We killed some of them, lost one man, and brought back six prisoners, two of them NCOs.

Return to Russia

While Erik Brörup was fighting in the vast forests of central Russia, his old Frikorps comrades finished their post-Demyansk leave and reassembled at the Citadel garrison in Copenhagen. From there, they were sent to the Mitau (now Jelgava) training area in Latvia to reform and prepare for another stint at the Front. The Danes spent two months absorbing new volunteers and welcoming back many men returning from convalescence. Unbelievably, owing to the efficiency of the Wehrmacht's medical services as well as the SS recruiters, the Frikorps was back up to a strength of over 1,000 men by the beginning of December and the first serious snows of the winter. Whilst there, they were visited by the 'grocer from Slagelse' – a nickname for the popular pre-war DNSAP politician, Einar Jörgensen. When Denmark was invaded in spring 1940, Jörgensen and a handful of fellow Danish Nazis had attempted to take over the Danish parliament building. In a somewhat comical scene they were quickly arrested, given a telling-off – and then sent home. Now a cheerleader for the Frikorps, he addressed the men on the Potential NCO's Course and their Danish commander, SS-Untersturmführer Egil Poulsen:

> When I first arrived in Berlin at the SS-Main Office to get permission to follow you up here, we all forgot one thing. What uniform should I wear and what rank should I have? It was clear I couldn't go to Russia in my brown DNSAP uniform or as a civilian either. They had to give me some kind of a uniform, but what rank do you give to an older member of the Danish parliament? [By this time he had been elected to the same parliament he had tried to overthrow two years earlier.] Surely not the rank of private. Someone suggested a senior NCO rank, an Oberscharführer or Hauptscharführer, but then someone reminded us that people would expect some sort of military experience from those ranks. Then I was appointed an officer as an Untersturmführer.
>
> I guess they don't expect any military knowledge from that rank!

As a standard junior officer wisecrack, the men loved it. A few short weeks later the Frikorps was deemed fit for action again, and Martinsen led his men to the River Lovat, at the junction of Army Groups' North and Centre. In the nearby city of Velikiye Luki some 5,000 men from the German LIX Corps had been cut off since late November, and were still holding out for relief. Even as fighting for the city raged, all eyes were on the unfolding cataclysm of Stalingrad far to the south.

Unlike the experience of Sixth Army and the men of the LIX Corps, frontline life for the Danish SS was relatively quiet with only a few sporadic firefights and normal patrolling activity. The situation altered dramatically on Christmas Day when an élite NKVD division, fresh to the line, launched a full-scale assault that drove the Frikorps out of most of its trenches. Taken by surprise, the Danes rallied and counter-attacked the next day. They retook their old positions in close combat, and were then used to restore the line further north at Taidy. Casualties among the volunteers were heavy. But by now the Frikorps's sector was, officially at least, a backwater on the Eastern Front.

To the south von Kleist was abandoning the Caucasus and the Wiking was retreating north, whilst von Manstein and Hoth were desperately trying to rescue the beleaguered Sixth Army on the Volga. To the north the increasingly powerful Red Army was carrying out yet another offensive on the Volkhov, with the intent, as ever, to break the siege of Leningrad and destroy Army Group North – and the DNL of course. Everywhere resources were stretched to breaking point. The Volkhov attack alone was launched by 296,000 Soviet soldiers, with more than four times that number involved in the southern fighting. The result in the Danish sector was that there was no relief for Velikiye Luki and the city finally fell on 15 January after a last relief attempt failed. Only 180 men of the trapped 5,000 made it back to their own lines.

In a savage postscript to the battle, the stubbornness of the defenders had so enraged the Soviets that when the war finally ended they rounded up the survivors from the POW camps and sent them back to the ruined city. Once there, one man of each rank who had fought there – so one general, one colonel, one lieutenant-colonel, one major, one captain, one lieutenant, one warrant officer (senior sergeant), one sergeant, one senior corporal, one junior corporal and one private soldier – were selected at random, 'tried' and sentenced to death. They were publicly hanged in Velikiye Luki's Lenin Square in front of their comrades on 29 January 1946. Victors' justice indeed.

It all made the fate of a few hundred Danes on the Lovat River seem insignificant in the grand scheme of things. Needless to say it was not insignificant for the men themselves, who continued to man their bunkers and trenches and watch out for snipers and mortar salvoes. As dangerous as ever, life at the Front was also relatively quiet during this period, so Martinsen took the opportunity to go back to Denmark to form a Danish branch of the Germanic SS (as the Norwegians had done with the GSSN).

He named the new formation the 'Schalburg Corps' in honour of his old friend and fallen leader. The Corps would become the most important paramilitary organisation in the country, very much along the lines of the Norwegian Hird, and would provide a steady stream of volunteers to the Waffen-SS throughout its brief life. In Martinsen's place, another ex-Danish Army officer took charge of the Frikorps, SS-Hauptsturmführer Per Neergard-Jacobsen.

After a few more weeks of rather desultory activity on the Lovat, Berlin made the decision to wind the Frikorps down. As with their Norwegian counterparts, the initial two-year enlistment period of the volunteers was coming to an end and there was widespread recognition in the Waffen-SS hierarchy that the Legions had had their day. Neergard-Jacobsen took his men out of the line and the unit went by train to the Grafenwöhr training area in Bavaria at the end of March 1943. There, in a final ceremony, the Frikorps Danmark was officially disbanded on 20 May 1943 after just under two years of life. The Danes had lost a total of nine officers, 17 NCOs and 133 men killed in action during that time, along with

The DNL fighting in Russia, from top left, left to right.

A Norwegian DNL rifleman in the winter 1941/42.

One of the DNL's 14th Anti-tank Company gun crews during the Volkhov fighting in 1942.

A Norwegian DNL mortar crew go into action.

The horrors of army dentistry – Russian Front-style!

Norwegian DNL volunteers sit on a destroyed Russian tank, winter 1941.

A Norwegian DNL volunteer leans against a destroyed Soviet light tank.

Norwegian SS machine-gun crew prepares to fire on fixed lines.

Norwegian DNL grenadier guards dazed Soviet prisoners taken in the fighting around Leningrad, 1942. (All Erik Wiborg) hundreds of wounded. Amongst their dead was their most inspirational leader; but they had gained invaluable experience in Demyansk, fighting in some of the hardest defensive battles of 1942. A good number had been decorated for bravery with the Iron Cross, including Martinsen himself, SS-Untersturmführer Hans-Olsen Muller (as a platoon and company commander), SS-Unterscharführer Adam Andersen, and SS troopers Erik-Herlöv Nielsen and Andreas Mortensen, the former as a Russian speaker dealing with prisoners and the latter as a foot messenger.

Back home in Copenhagen, Frits Clausen, as head of Denmark's Nazis, complained loudly to Himmler about the disbandment of the Frikorps and asked for the resurrection of a purely Danish SS unit. The Reichsführer made a rather tart response: 'It depends on him when the Grenadier Regiment Danmark becomes a Danmark Division!' Clausen was firmly put in his place, and proceeded to sink further into the alcoholism that was rapidly killing him.

Attrition and mobility

The Danes, Norwegians, Finns and Swedes of the Wiking had endured a bloody and ultimately unsuccessful 1942. Some places where their boots had trodden no other members of the Wehrmacht would ever reach again (except as POWs). They had proved conclusively that although their numbers were few, they could stand shoulder to shoulder with the very best the Germans had to offer. The green, inexperienced volunteers of 1941 had come of age. Thousands of miles away in Berlin the powers-that-be took note.

The time of the Legions, though, was at an end. They were too small and too lightly armed to remain effective for any length of time in the cauldron of the Russian Front. In the attritional warfare of the Eastern Front it was impossible to keep the Legions at full strength and relatively quickly, losses in key personnel especially eroded the combat effectiveness of the units. The Frikorps Danmark was a perfect example. It lost over 75% of its original strength in less than three months fighting at Demyansk. It wasn't then combat-ready again for another three months, and losing that amount of precious time was something the Wehrmacht could ill afford. The overall usefulness of static infantry like the Legions was decreasing too, as the Red Army became ever more mechanised. With resources stretched to the limit in the frontline, it was increasingly vital to be mobile to cover the ground and concentrate scarce forces quickly. Delivering that mobility was a production race, and it was a race being won by the Soviets. Stalin's factories, mostly situated far from possible German air attack, produced a staggering 24,446 tanks in 1942, as well as 30,400 other motor vehicles. That's eight times more than the Wehrmacht had when it invaded the country the previous year. In reply, Nazi Germany made just 6,180 panzers that same year. The Third Reich was beginning to be overwhelmed, and all the Wehrmacht's old advantages were fast disappearing.

The disbanding of the Legions made the volunteers reassess their options. Many decided enough was enough, hung up their weapons and headed home. Some did so only to join other paramilitary organisations such as Martinsen's Schalburg Corps. However, for most it was the end of their wartime career. Others wanted to stay in the conflict and felt that fighting alongside their Finnish cousins was the best thing to do, and so went north and put on yet another uniform. The majority of those that did stay on in the Waffen-SS would go on to form the core of the Scandinavian Waffen-SS for the remainder of the war.

IV

1943: The End of the Legions, the SS-Nordland is Born

War is cruelty and cannot be refined.

General Sherman to the Mayor of Atlanta on burning the city to the ground in 1864.

In 1942 the Scandinavians of the SS-Wiking had spearheaded the main offensive effort of the Wehrmacht in southern Russia. Months of fighting had whittled away at their numbers, but the division had kept its cohesion and it was still a formidable fighting force at the end of the year. It was not the same story for the national Legions. The Norwegians of the DNL had fought well in the trenches around Leningrad, as had the Danes of the Frikorps at Demyansk and Velikiye Luki. Now there would be a new chapter for the Scandinavian Waffen-SS.

1943 would turn out to be a watershed year for the Waffen-SS in general and its foreign members in particular. As a fighting force the black guards had come of age, and were now about to undergo a massive programme of expansion, along with a root and branch reorganisation. The élite divisions, the Das Reich, Leibstandarte and the Wiking, along with three new ones (the *SS-Hohenstaufen*, *SS-Frundsberg* and the *SS-Hitler Jugend*), would be converted to mighty panzer divisions boasting hundreds of tanks and assault guns. Just down the pecking order there would be a tier of new, partly-armoured, panzer grenadier divisions, and finally the floodgates would be opened for foreign volunteers to establish large numbers of new formations, both divisions and assault brigades – the so-called *SS-Sturmbrigaden*.

However, if the new divisions and brigades were to become a reality, something was going to have to be done to improve foreign recruitment and leadership. Not only were there not enough volunteers overall to fill

The Germanske SS Norge (Norwegian SS) parade through Oslo in 1943 on the official 'SS Day' – which was also Norway's National Day. (James Macleod)

Two Norwegian SS men (GSSN) put the finishing touches to their uniforms before joining the same parade through Oslo in the spring of 1943. (James Macleod)

the ranks, but even more acute was the lack of trained NCOs and officers. Even with the likes of native, ex-regular army officers like the Brörups, von Schalburgs, Sörensens, Østrings and so on, across the Wiking and the national Legions it was Germans who had too often commanded Germanic soldiers; (as an extreme example, when the Flemish Legion went into action it had only one Flemish NCO and 80 German ones). As for administration, Jüttner still had not sorted out issues such as retention of rank, liaison with home, and even mail. The gap between the recruiters' promises and the reality was then widened when the volunteer arrived in the SS training establishments, which were not exactly bending over backwards to accommodate the young foreign entrants. The result was dissatisfaction and resentment and the flow of recruits slowing to a trickle, just when the Reich needed them most.

Gottlob Berger understood exactly what the problem was and he knew how to solve it. He made a detailed report to Himmler recommending a sea-change in the way foreign volunteers were treated from the moment they were recruited and all the way through their training, with national differences being acknowledged and given due regard. The weight of evidence in the report was crushing and Himmler accepted all the recommendations in full. In a personal directive, the Reichsführer clearly set out how the fortunes of the foreign Waffen-SS were going to be revived. The 'Instruction and Care' orders (*Erziehung und Umsorgung*) set out a range of changes which were to be enacted immediately:

- All Germans officers and NCOs scheduled to serve with foreign volunteers would now be given two full weeks induction training on handling foreign volunteers

- All instruction on the superiority of Germany and the Germans was to be dropped immediately

- Legionary status, seen as second-best by volunteers, was abandoned and volunteers were to be treated as having full SS membership with all of its benefits for them and their families

- A major drive was to be launched to select, train and rapidly promote non-German junior leaders. So by February 1943 there were 47 officers and 172 cadets from Norway, Denmark, Sweden (some 20 Swedes passed through Bad Tölz during the war with two of them graduating top of their class), Finland, Flanders and Holland training at Bad Tölz on the standard six-month course, with special courses designed specifically for foreign volunteers ordered to begin in May of that year.

From then on officer promotion for foreigners was made strictly dependent on attending and passing Tölz, and while this made the Waffen-SS foreign officer corps extremely professional, it also meant that demand for leaders always outstripped supply by a huge margin. The new leaders were excellent but were killed at the Front far quicker than new ones were trained.

Himmler's instructions were all well and good, but the new crop of Scandinavian Waffen-SS leaders coming out of Tölz would need men to lead, and they were scarce. When the SS-Wiking had gone into the assault at Rostov back in the summer of 1942, it had counted 947 Norwegians, 630 Danes, 421 Finns and a handful of Swedes in its ranks. The DNL had taken 1,218 men to Leningrad, and the Frikorps Danmark 1,164 to Demyansk. Close on 4,400 Nordics all told. But half a year of pitched battles like the Ssutoki bridgehead, Killing Hill and Urizk, had haemorrhaged the Scandinavian Waffen-SS. So, despite fresh drafts of volunteers arriving throughout 1942, by 6 February 1943 there were just 612 Norwegians and 633 Danes in SS-Wiking, with around the same number of Finns and a couple of dozen Swedes. There were just over 600 DNL veterans in Oslo parading to be disbanded, and another 650 Frikorps Danmark men in Bavaria awaiting the same fate. The Scandinavian Waffen-SS could now just about muster 3,000 men – in Wehrmacht terms a single regiment. More men were desperately needed.

The end of the road for the Finns

Things then proceeded to get worse. Collani's battalion, universally recognised as being first rate, was coming to the end of its two-year enlistment period. Himmler wanted to use it as the cadre for a new unit, the SS-Motorcycle Regiment Kalevala (named for the Finnish saga). But Helsinki had other ideas. The Finnish government was watching the ominous Red Army build-up on its northern border with real trepidation, and it wanted every trained man back home to face it. They also had real doubts about Nazi Germany's ability to win the war, and wanted to plough their own furrow. Himmler argued his case, but in the end Hitler himself stepped in and agreed to send the Finns home. Pulled from the frontline in early May, the battalion first went to Grafenwöhr, then Ruhpolding in Bavaria, before entraining for Reval (modern-day Tallinn) in Estonia on 28 May. Shipped across the Gulf of Finland to Hanko (liberated from the Red Army in 1941 and the name of the all-Swedish battalion fighting with the Finns – in Swedish Hangø), the unit was officially disbanded at a parade on 11 July 1943. Hans Collani walked down each rank, personally shaking hands with every single man, and thanking them on Germany's behalf for their bravery and service. In a gesture loaded with symbolism, the volunteers then changed into Finnish Army uniforms. Their combat fatigues with the SS runes were thrown in a heap, and with that the official Finnish Waffen-SS was no more.

Their place in Wiking's Order of Battle, as the Nordland's third battalion, was taken by a new formation of Estonian volunteers; the SS-Volunteer Battalion Narva (Estnisches SS-Freiwilligen Bataillon Narwa), commanded by the veteran German officer, SS-Sturmbannführer Georg Eberhardt.

The Finnish SS Battalion arrive home in Helsinki, 1943, prior to disbandment.

The Wiking's Finnish Battalion parades for the very last time in Ruhpolding before being officially disbanded, 11 July 1943. (James Macleod)

Two hundred and twenty-two Finnish volunteers had been killed in action and 557 wounded during the unit's brief lifetime. Some 230 Iron Crosses (both classes) were awarded to the volunteers, and 42 Finns attended Bad Tölz (21 graduated, most of the rest were in training when the battalion was disbanded and so were sent home before the course finished). Several individual volunteers stayed on – notable among them SS-Obersturmführer Ulf-Ola Olin and Lars-Erik Ekroth – and continued to serve across the Waffen-SS in the Wiking, the Nordland and in the Kurt Eggers War Reporters Regiment. As for Collani, he went on to command the Dutch SS-Panzergrenadier Regiment 49 De Ruyter, and was post-humously awarded the Knight's Cross after being killed in action in the Narva fighting the following year.

As to the rank-and-file volunteers, when Finland later switched sides in 1944, at least six of the battalion's veterans were killed fighting against their former German allies.

The Germanic Corps

Back in Berlin, Himmler's grand vision for 1943 was nothing less than a massively-expanded Waffen-SS with a whole series of Corps-strength for-mations – each Corps totalling roughly 30–40,000 men split into two or three divisions. In the Balkans there would be two mountain corps made up of local Yugoslav volksdeutsche and Bosnian and Albanian Muslims (see *Hitler's Jihadis*). The wholly German (Reich and volksdeutsche) armoured might of the Waffen-SS would be concentrated in two panzer corps, with two further corps on the Russian Front comprising one made up of the SS cavalry divisions (Brörup's Florian Geyer plus another new volksdeutsche division, the Maria Theresia) and another of assorted SS grenadier divisions.

Additionally, Felix Steiner and Dr Franz Riedweg (Berger's influential Swiss-German Chief of the Germanic Directorate), also advocated concentrating all the Nordics into one single division and using it as the basis of a 'Germanic Corps' under Steiner's command. Himmler enthusiastically accepted the idea, and so was born the III SS-Germanic Armoured Corps (the III. (Germanische) SS-Panzerkorps). This Corps was to become famous, both for its fighting prowess and its multi-national composition. No other formation symbolised the foreign nature of the Waffen-SS quite like it, and although there was always a large number of Germans in it from the start, there were also contingents from almost every country in Europe – Danes, Swedes, Norwegians, Finns and Spaniards ('unofficial' ones anyway), Latvians, Estonians, Dutch, Flemish, Walloons, Swiss and even Britons. All would pass through the Corps and leave their mark on its unique history. The Corps was envisaged as two divisions; the tried and newly-upgraded 5th SS-Panzer Division Wiking, and a new division, the 11th SS-Volunteer Panzergrenadier Division Nordland (in German the 11th SS Freiwilligen-Panzergrenadier Division Nordland) formally established on 22 March 1943, and commanded initially by the experienced Austrian Waffen-SS officer, Franz Augsberger.

The Swiss-German Dr Franz Riedweg, who along with Felix Steiner convinced Himmler to establish a new division for the Scandinavian Waffen-SS – the SS-Nordland Division. He later became the Chief Medical Officer for Steiner's 3rd Germanic SS-Panzer Corps. (James Macleod)

The 11th SS-Panzergrenadier Division Nordland

Originally named the 'Waräger' by Himmler ('Varangian' in English – after the ancient Viking bodyguard of the Byzantine Emperors), the intention was to bring together all of the Scandinavian and Dutch Waffen-SS into one division. Hitler liked the idea, but disliked the name, thinking it far too obscure even for his taste. Casting around for something simpler, he settled on one already in use – Nordland. This made sense as the cadre unit (the *Stamm Einheit*) for the new formation was, understandably enough, to be the Wiking's veteran SS-Nordland Regiment. As was usual practice, the veterans would then be split amongst the division's sub-units, filling key command appointments and providing backbone to the ranks. New recruits would then be grouped around these experienced men to learn the ropes. The 'new' Nordland's order of battle would comprise three infantry regiments of three battalions each, a panzer regiment of three battalions, an armoured reconnaissance battalion, an artillery regiment, an assault gun battalion and the usual assortment of other battalion-sized divisional troops such as anti-tank and anti-aircraft guns and combat engineers. The main sub-units were given national rather than German names, as proof of 'Germanic' identity, and were designated as the following:

Above right: The DNL veteran Olaf Lindvig leads a company of volunteers from the Norwegian SS (the GSSN) on a parade through Oslo on 16 April 1943. This company was raised as a response to the establishment of the Nordland Division and would go on to form the Norge Regiment's 1st Company. Lindvig became an outspoken figure after the war before passing away in 2007. (James Macleod)

SS-Panzergrenadier Regiment 23 Norge
Comprising Norwegian volunteers, commanded initially by Wolfgang Joerchel, who then went to command the Dutch SS General Seyffardt Regiment, and was replaced by the highly experienced Regiment Nordland officer Arnold Stoffers. The three grenadier battalions, 1–3, were commanded respectively by the Norwegian Finn Finson (succeeded by Fritz Vogt) and the Germans Albrecht Krügel and Hans-Heinrich Lohmann.

SS-Panzergrenadier Regiment 24 Danmark
Comprising Danish volunteers, commanded by another German, the aristocratic *Graf* Hermenegild von Westphalen. The 1st and 3rd Battalions were led by the old Frikorps commanders Knud Börge Martinsen, lured back from the Schalburg Corps, and Per Neergard-Jacobsen respectively. The latter was succeeded in due course by Kryssing's former protégé Per Sörensen, another Frikorps veteran of course. Martinsen's tenure didn't last long. A political fanatic with a volatile temper, he felt snubbed at not being given command of the regiment as a whole, so headed home and left the Waffen-SS all together. Back in Copenhagen he devoted his considerable energies to combating the Danish resistance and converting his fellow-countrymen to the National Socialist cause he revered so much. His place as battalion commander was eventually taken by Siegfried Scheibe. The 2nd Battalion was led by Kurt Walther. Both of these latter officers were German.

SS-Panzergrenadier Regiment 25 Nederland
Comprising Dutch volunteers, see below.

SS-Panzer Regiment 11 Hermann von Salza
Named after the legendary thirteenth-century Grand Master of the crusading Order of Teutonic Knights, commanded by the German ex-Wiking artillery officer Paul-Albert Kausch. Having a three-battalion panzer regiment would, in effect, have made the Nordland a panzer division, but this turned out to be a pipe dream, and the division's armoured component was scaled down to a single battalion.

The Norge and Danmark

This all looked great on paper, however, from the start the new division struggled for manpower and equipment. The Dutch were the first hurdle, with Holland's collaborationist leader, Anton Mussert, protesting that they deserved an all-Dutch SS division. No other nation in western

Europe contributed more volunteers to the Waffen-SS than Holland, and so, given that fact, Himmler gave way. There would be no Nederland Regiment in the Nordland. Instead, the surviving 2,500 Dutch Legion veterans were combined with a fresh draft of 3,000 volunteers to form the 4th SS-Volunteer Panzergrenadier Brigade Nederland.

With no third grenadier regiment, it was doubly important that the Norge and Danmark were full-strength units, and that meant finding around 6,000 men ready and willing to fill them. But the entire Scandinavian Waffen-SS was only half that total, and they were spread across a number of formations, mainly the Wiking and the disbanding Legions.

Berlin's first step to address this issue was to appeal to the existing volunteers to sign on again. This policy was only partially successful. Of the 2,296 Norwegians and 1,896 Danes who had enlisted in the lifetime of the DNL and Frikorps, 824 Norwegians (36%) and 311 Danes (16%) asked to be discharged at the end of their enlistments. Of the rest, over 600 Danes re-enlisted, but only around 300 Norwegians did the same, with many joining the new Norwegian SS-Ski Battalion instead (see below for this unit's history). One Dane who did transfer over to the Nordland was the 16 year-old Vagner Kristensen:

> Having been born in 1927 I was too young to volunteer before 1943, but I became a member of the NSU and was eventually allowed to enlist in the Frikorps Danmark only to see it disbanded. We were told about the new Danmark Regiment and transferred over, we didn't even see it as a choice really, we just did as we were told.

Secondly, Berlin made it official policy to combine all the existing Scandinavian Waffen-SS volunteers into the new division. The Legions were already in the process of disappearing of course, but the biggest effect of this decision would be to bring to an end the Scandinavian presence in the division that bore their ancient name – the Wiking. Most of them were in the Nordland Regiment anyway and came over as cadre, but others were combed out of the divisional sub-units to transfer across. This resulted in several hundred Danes, and over 250 Norwegians, joining their fellow-countrymen in the Norge and Danmark. In truth, not all Scandinavians transferred over, some stayed due to the vagaries of the system and individual choice. So by the summer of 1944 the Wiking officer Peter Strassner noted that there were still 177 Danes, 47 Norwegians, 5 Swedes and 2 Finns serving in the Wiking; but by and large the vast majority of Nordics would, from now on, fight in the Nordland. The symbolism was potent , with the 'baton' of the Scandinavian Waffen-SS being passed on from the old to the new. Scandinavians in the Wiking, always a relative minority, would now become a pretty rare species.

The transfers from the Wiking and the Legions were a start, but the Norge and Danmark were still desperately short of manpower, which meant a new impetus was put into recruiting fresh volunteers. In Norway, Quisling called for no fewer than 3,000 NS men to step forward, but he was hardly knocked down in the stampede. In the end, only about 100 new recruits came forward from the Party. A greater number of recruits did come, unsurprisingly, from among the ranks of the GSSN. When Olaf Lindvig was wounded at Urizk, he was sent home to convalesce and took up the post of acting Chief-of-Staff of the Norwegian SS. A big man in every sense, Lindvig was incredibly keen to get back to the Front, and on 11 March called for other GSSN members to join him once more in the struggle out East. Some 160 put their hands up and were paraded through Oslo in front of Quisling on 16 August, prior to joining the new division. There they would become the mainstay of the Norge's 1st Company under Lindvig's command. The picture was much the same in Denmark, and welcome though all these men were, numbers were still in the low hundreds and not the thousands the Norge and Danmark needed. Nils Per Immerslund was clear as to the reasons for this poor response:

> Norwegians had volunteered to fight for Norway on a contract basis, not to fight for Germany throughout the war's duration. Norwegian volunteers had been spread too thinly in German units, and most would fight better if they could stand alone as Norwegians and just go where the Germans indicated.

Unrest and resistance back home

One factor that greatly affected recruitment was the growing domestic turmoil in Denmark and Norway. In Denmark, dissatisfaction and resentment of Nazi Germany was escalating with frequent strikes and increasingly overt protests. The Danish Waffen-SS veteran Paul Hveger, now serving back home after being invalided out after the Caucasus, was caught up in the troubles: 'After leaving hospital I went to Copenhagen and served under Standartenführer Boysen as a driver in the Germanic Liaison Office. Things were fine at first, but trouble really started in 1943, I myself was involved in violent rows in the street with civilians.'

Some 5,000 Danes had even crossed to neutral Sweden and, with an official blind eye turned, had formed the so-called Danske Brigade ready to intervene back home once the Germans had left. Alongside them were some 15,000 Norwegians training to do exactly the same thing in their own homeland, although as it turned out neither force ever actually saw any combat. For those who stayed, the level of resistance to German occupation started to step up. The Norwegian underground tried to avoid killing collaborators so as not to incite reprisals, but things were different in Denmark where an increasingly vicious campaign of tit-for-tat killings between the Resistance and pro-Nazi groups, such as Martinsen's Schalburg Corps, began to spiral. The Germans began to lose patience with their 'model occupation' and resorted to oppression. Firstly they disbanded the Danish armed forces in March 1943, partly because they hoped this would spark a rush of recruits into the Waffen-SS. That did not happen. Next, a State of Emergency was declared in August, and the decision was taken in Berlin to round up Denmark's 7,500 Jews and send them to the Theresienstadt Concentration Camp prior to their murder. A locally based German maritime attaché, Georg F. Duckwitz, warned the Danes just days before the deportations were due to start on 1 October. The Danish response was magnificent. With the direct collusion of the police, the civil service and the coastguard, Denmark's Jews were smuggled en masse to safety in Sweden. The German squads swept through the streets and found their quarry had escaped them. In all over 7,000 Jews were saved and only 472 were arrested, of whom 52 died in Theresienstadt. The Nazi reaction was to disband the elected government and rule through an unofficial board of civil servant technocrats headed by Niels Svenningsen.

Simultaneously over in Norway the German defeat at Stalingrad was having a marked impact on the population, as related by Ornulf Bjornstad:

At the start of the war we made it clear to everyone we were fighting with the Germans because they offered the best chance of defeating communism. I had a lot of encouragement from my family and friends, but when the war started going against Germany their attitude changed to hostility against the whole German cause. This change of attitude dated from the defeat at Stalingrad in 1943 and the subsequent retreat.

The resistance grew bolder and scored a massive success when it destroyed Nazi Germany's stocks of heavy water in Telemark (an act made famous by the film *The Heroes of Telemark*).

This action effectively prevented the nightmare of a Nazi atomic bomb. Unsurprisingly, any sign of defiance was treated extremely harshly after that, and some 40,000 Norwegians (including Norway's tiny Jewish population) were either imprisoned in the nation's jails or deported to concentration camps. Two thousand of these unfortunates would die in captivity, of whom 700 were Norwegian Jews murdered in the Holocaust. Another 500 Norwegians were either executed as resistance or died in direct clashes with the Germans during the occupation.

Speer and the labour pool

As Berger cast around for more men for the Nordland that spring, two further policy changes were made by the Berlin authorities, one which helped the recruitment effort, and one which hindered it. Firstly, there were vast pools of foreigners in the Reich at the time working in every conceivable industry from farming through to armaments production, often living in desperately harsh conditions. Those from the East tended to have been press-ganged and were virtually slave labour. But many from the West had been enticed with the promise of better wages and conditions. There were, for example, some 100,000 Danes working in Germany in the spring of 1943, and up until now their work had taken precedence and they were off-limits to recruiters. Indeed, Albert Speer (the architect turned Armaments Minister) guarded them jealously. However, with the disasters at Stalingrad and Tunisia wiping two entire field armies from the Wehrmacht's establishment, this position was no longer tenable. As a result, recruitment among Germany's foreign workers was allowed from April onwards, and Berger's men went at it with gusto.

By mid-August the SS had recruited 8,105 foreign labourers, of whom 3,154 passed Waffen-SS selection, but there were only 119 Danes and just two Norwegians among this draft. Part of the problem was that it was not just the Waffen-SS who were allowed to recruit, it was everyone else too, and service in other arms usually carried far less risk and the same level of reward. Thus many Scandinavians joined the Kriegsmarine or the Luftwaffe (there were even two Norwegian Luftwaffe pilots, one of whom was the decorated SS-Wiking veteran Alf Lie) and its anti-aircraft units. More than a few Norwegians opted for the SS-Ski Battalion Norge.

The volksdeutsche arrive

In the end, the Danmark could field 1,280 Danes, and the Norge just 810 Norwegians. Senior command down to regimental level was filled by Germans. Below that about half of all battalion and company level posts were filled by Scandinavians. For instance, the Danmark had 16 German officers and 16 Danish officers giving it a much-needed Nordic 'feel'. But there was no hiding the fact that the concept of wholly-national Scandinavian regiments had failed. The SS had no choice but to look elsewhere for thousands of men to fill the ranks. Their first port of call was German nationals, with 4,131 brought in to make up a full third of the division. However the biggest contingent by far were Rumanian volksdeutsche from the Siebenbürgen region, the so-called Transylvanian Saxons. Many of these men had previously served in the Rumanian Army, and were transferred over according to an agreement between the Bucharest and Berlin, while others had been recruited direct from their home towns and villages. In the end almost half the division, 5,895 men, would be volksdeutsche. The effect was felt across the Nordland – for example, alongside the Danes in the Danmark Regiment were 1,120 volksdeustche and 800 German nationals. The proportions in the Norge were even more heavily skewed towards the volksdeutsche. There were some Nordics in divisional posts, but overall the division contained just 2,491 Scandinavians out of an establishment of over 12,000.

The rest of the Corps had the same problem. The Nederland struggled to recruit and was majority non-Dutch, with 40 per cent volksdeustche and 20 per cent German nationals, and only 181 members of the 900-odd non-divisional Corps troops were Germanics. The reality of the situation was that it was ethnic Germans, and not Germanics, that were the mainstay of the Corps from the very start, and then, as now, controversy surrounds them and their role in the Waffen-SS. Many saw them as second-rate soldiers who couldn't even speak German properly. The language of command in the Nordland was German, as usual, and this gave the volksdeutsche as many problems as it did the Scandinavians. They only really started to appear in the Waffen-SS in large numbers from 1943 onwards, and unsurprisingly the first waves of recruits seemed to be of a higher quality than those that came after. From veterans' testimonies it would seem the Nordland and the Wiking received some of the best. The Wiking's Jan Munk fought with them:

It was July 1943 and we were near the Donets, at that time I had an MG34, a beautiful machine-gun, very reliable and accurate. My Number 2 was a Rumanian farmer's son. His German was not too good but his willingness to help was enormous, and so was his strength. So I had an excellent machine-gun, a first-class Number 2, plenty to shoot at but poor quality ammunition [by 1943 most German bullets had steel rather than brass casing due to shortages and they tended to jam the barrel]. I heard a noise to my right and saw that my Number 2 had fallen back in the trench, just as he was lifting a full ammunition box. He had been hit in the left temple and killed instantly.

Over in the Nordland one of the new draftees was Hans Hedrich:

I was born in 1924 in Mediasch, Siebenbürgen, and volunteered for the Waffen-SS in 1943. I believed I had to make my contribution to the German people's fight for existence – that was how the war was portrayed to us at that time. There was also a moral pressure from the 'German People's Group of Rumania' and from friends and family.

Assigned to the SS Armoured Reconnaissance Battalion Nordland, I was trained in Grafenwöhr. I found the training to be excessively hard. Despite all the chicanery in the training, it seems to have been strictly forbidden for the native German trainers to use denigrating expressions that hinted at the origins of the ethnic Germans. Generally there were no problems between the native Germans, us ethnic Germans, and the Scandinavians.

This view was echoed by the Norwegian volunteer John Sandstad:

After the DNL was disbanded I was sent to the SS Armoured Grenadier Training and Replacement Battalion 11 in Graz. There I took NCO training along with nine other Norwegians. After a home furlough and several weeks as an instructor in an ethnic German recruit company in Graz, I was sent to SS Armoured Grenadier Regiment 23 Norge in Croatia on November 2nd, 1943. Many of the Norwegian volunteers were disappointed because there was no exclusively Norwegian unit like the Legion or the Norwegian SS-Ski Battalion in Finland. The ethnic Germans came in a group in August and made up about 50% of the unit's strength. Basically we got on well with them.

The Swedish 'specialists'

Away from the volksdeutsche issue, the establishment of the Nordland made a huge difference to the smallest of the Scandinavian Waffen-SS contingents – the Swedes. Overall, Waffen-SS attempts to recruit Swedes were a disaster. Official Swedish government hostility to the idea and a preference among volunteers to serve with the Finns, were the main reasons why only about 180 native Swedes enlisted in the Waffen-SS during the war. They were joined by some 50 ethnic Swedes from Estonia, and around 100 others from the Swedish Ukrainian community, bringing the grand total to almost 350. Another 15 or so went into other branches of the Wehrmacht including the Swedish Army officer, Nils Rosen, who served for two years as a panzer commander with the Army's Panzer Regiment 6.

The Swede Sten Eriksson was a journalist before the war and served in the SS's own regiment of war reporters, the Kurt Eggers. (James Macleod)

Of those that did join the Waffen-SS, more than 80 per cent were members of Far Right parties or had family connections to Germany. On enlistment they tended to be spread across a wide range of units with no real 'home' unit. Berger wanted to form a purely Swedish battalion, the *Tre Kronor* – the 'Three Crowns' after Sweden's royal emblem – but the plan was abandoned due to an obvious lack of manpower. Ten Swedes served as war reporters in the Kurt Eggers – among them were Carl Svensson (ex-Swedish Navy and anti-aircraft gunnery specialist and one of only six pre-war professional officers who joined the Waffen-SS), Gösta Borg (ex-SSS leader, friend of Sven-Olov Lindholm and Winter War veteran), Thorolf Hillblad, Hans-Caspar Krüger, and Thorkel Tillman (who was killed in action in July 1944 while serving with the Hitler Jugend in Normandy). Svensson and Borg were also two of the almost twenty Swedes who graduated from Bad Tölz, one of whom, Wolfgang Eld-Albitz, came top of his class. Two other Swedes, Robert Bengtsson and Lars Blom (the latter held dual Swedish-German nationality) served with the Leibstandarte, while one Swede, SS-Oberscharführer Sven-Erik Olsson, even served throughout the war as Heinz Harmel's (the Frundsberg's divisional commander) personal radio operator, and ended up winning the German Cross in Gold as well as both classes of Iron Cross. The advent of the Nordland changed all of this and ushered in a very different era.

The designated flag bearer for the Swedish Waffen-SS was to be none other than the Nordland's Armoured Reconnaissance Battalion. A handful served in the Hermann von Salza panzer battalion itself; the Adjutant, Bad Tölz luminary and Iron Cross 1st Class winner, Per-Sigurd Baeckland being one, but the majority served under Rudi Saalbach and his Adjutant Georg Erichsen. Erichsen, of course, was one of 1,292 ethnic Germans from Danish North Schleswig serving in the Waffen-SS at the time. Within the Recce Battalion the Swedes were then concentrated in the 3rd Company. Their influence was such that it was nicknamed the *Schwedenzug,* even though most of the men were actually Rumanian volksdeutsche – a fact not universally popular with all of the Swedes, as Erik Wallin recounted:

'Old' Ragnar Johansson was among us [an ex-Swedish Army sergeant from the Skövde-based Skaraborgs Regiment]. He was an extremely strong Swede, in front of whom the whole company shivered. Under the influence of strong drink and with a wild look in his eyes, he would go looking for *Mussulmen,* as he called the ethnic Germans from Rumania and whom even in a sober state he found it hard to accept.

The 3rd was one of five companies in the battalion; two of which were equipped with half-track armoured personnel carriers (the ubiquitous SPW), one with wheeled armoured cars, one with half-track armoured cars, and the last with anti-tank and infantry guns as well as flame-throwers. The Schwedenzug was 160 men strong and one of the two SPW companies. It had four platoons, the first three composed of volks-deutsche grenadiers, and the fourth comprising SPW's armed with heavy weapons, manned by 5 Swedish NCOs, about 35 Swedish rank-ers and some 20 ethnic Estonian-Swedes. The prevailing thinking in the Waffen-SS was that Swedes were heavy weapons experts. The Swede Walter Nilsson led the platoon and there were four other Swedish offic-ers in the Company; Rune Ahlgren, Gunnar-Erik Eklöf (who would go on to serve in the SS-Main Office in Berlin before becoming a member of Otto Skorzeny's special forces unit the SS-Jagdverband Nordwest in 1945), Hans-Gösta Pehrsson, and the Germania Regiment veteran Heino Meyer. Meyer was twice declared officially dead during the war, before turning up on both occasions wounded but alive in field hospitals. The Swedes were overwhelmingly Wiking old-boys, and even though they were the minority they dominated the Company. It was the closest the Swedes ever came to having their own 'national' unit in the Scandinavian Waffen-SS.

The unit flag of the Norwegian SS-Police Company. (Erik Wiborg)

The Norwegian 1st SS-Police Company drawn up in three ranks and ready to be inspected on 17 May 1942. (Erik Wiborg)

The SS-Ski Battalion Norge and the SS Police Companies

Where were the Norwegians? The Norge was intended as *their* regiment, Quisling was fully behind the project, and the Norwegians of the DNL and the Wiking were a ready-made cadre. Despite this, recruitment was slow and there were always far more Danes in the Nordland than Norwegians. Granted, just as with ex-Frikorps members, there was a number of DNL legionnaires who felt they had done their bit and would not sign on again, and overall the recruiting pool at home was getting shallower as time and combat emptied it out. But even so, new Norwegian volunteers coming forward for the Nordland were far thinner on the ground than in Denmark; was there another reason? The answer was Finland.

Back in 1939 the Winter War had shocked Scandinavia and cast the Soviet Union in the role of bogeyman. Many would-be volunteers felt the attack on Finland was an attack on them all, and that by fighting alongside the Finns they would be directly protecting their own homelands. This was powerful motivation indeed. Most of those who signed on thought that they would be fighting the Red Army on the Finnish front, and when this did not happen it caused widespread resentment, Bjarne Dramstad testified to that. But the Norwegians did not forget Finland and when a generation of units were established in the spring of 1943 that satisfied this need, they drained recruits away from the Nordland. These new units were the SS-Ski Battalion Norge and the 2nd, 3rd and 4th SS-Police Companies (the SS-og-Polit Kompanies).

The 1st SS-Police Company had been formed and led by Jonas Lie, and served alongside the DNL of course, and the concept had proved its worth. Further companies were then either planned or raised over the next two years. When it was confirmed that these units would serve in Finland, and not with the Nordland, they proved very popular. The 2nd Company was the first to be formed, and was led by the ex-Norwegian Army engineer captain, SS-Hauptsturmführer Reidar-Egil Hoel. Its 160 men were sent to Finland to serve alongside the Reconnaissance Battalion of the 6th SS-Mountain Division Nord. Aage-Henry Berg, quite an unpopular 'parade ground' officer even though he was ex-DNL, was given the task of raising a 3rd SS-Police Company to join them in the summer of 1944, but by then the situation at the Front would have changed dramatically. As it was, some 11 ex-DNL and Wiking veterans did sign on for the 3rd Company, including the ex-French Foreign legionnaire August Amundsen, and the veteran DNL anti-tank gunner Bjarne Dramstad:

After I came back from the Front the first time, I joined the *Germanske SS Norge* [this made Bjarne one of only two GSSN men in the anti-tank company], the Norwegian version of the Allgemeine-SS. I participated in a three-week course at Kongsvinger, and was then given a black uniform to keep at home, that was about it really.

After the Legion was disbanded I stayed home until I signed up again for the 3rd SS Police Company. This unit was supposed to serve as an independent reconnaissance company directly under the 6th SS-Mountain Division Nord in Finland. This was in March 1944. Even though I had seen the war, the bad leadership, and was sick and tired of it all, it was better to be among comrades than in my village where there were a lot of people with sympathy for the other side. And this unit was guaranteed to go to Finland, which was my motivation in the first place. Besides, I felt that the war wasn't over yet and I had to do my share.

Three of the Norwegian Waffen-SS's most influential commanders, from left, the middle-aged former police officer Oscar-Olsen Rustand, Frode Halle, and Verre Lyngstad. (Erik Wiborg)

Recruits were hard to come by in Norway, the exception was for the SS-Ski Battalion Norge, which in this picture is parading through Oslo. (Erik Wiborg)

In August, Bjarne and their 148 comrades would arrive in Finland only to find themselves retreating back towards Norway, along with the rest of the Wehrmacht's forces in the Arctic circle. Eventually the Company would end up holding the unique record in the Norwegian Waffen-SS of never losing a man in combat.

Before the Company was deployed, Berg was replaced by Oscar-Olsen Rustand, an elderly ex-Norwegian Army NCO and police officer. However, veterans always describe their German Company Sergeant-Major Otto Kuhnle as the 'real' company commander during the withdrawal, and once back on home soil Rustand formally departed to try and recruit a 4th Company to carry on the fight. That plan came to nothing as the war ended before the new force was ready to join the fight. But the numbers tell their own story, overall more than 400 volunteers, who would have significantly strengthened Norge's Norwegian roster, chose instead to fight as SS policemen in Finland.

As it was these men were joined in the frozen north by an even larger body of Norwegian Waffen-SS men led by a Danish-born skiing expert and Professor of Physical Education – Gust Jonassen's SS-Police Ski Company, which would become in time the SS-Ski Battalion Norge (SS-Schijäger-Bataillon Norwegen in German). Jonassen, the NSUF's Sports Leader, was a subordinate and close friend of Bjørn Østring, but rather than join the DNL he proposed instead to form and lead a group of ski specialists to fight in the trackless forests of Finnish Karelia. The intent was for a purely Norwegian unit that would be engaged in long range patrolling, deliberate ambushes (i.e. planned long term ambushes perhaps lasting for days), and behind-the-lines attacks. The Germans acquiesced to the plan to smooth ruffled Norwegian feathers after the DNL was sent to Leningrad and not Finland, and in no time at all some 120 eager volunteers were training at Sennheim in the Alsace. Many of these men, mostly idealistic young NS members, would doubtless have ended up in the Nordland. As it was, Jonassen himself was packed off to Bad Tölz to earn his rank of SS-Obersturmführer, while his men ended up being put through their paces by a team of instructors led by the Finn, Jouko Itälä, an ex-Wiking artillery officer. Itälä ignored the order to go home and would serve in the Waffen-SS until the very end. Even more exotic was the addition to the company of the Italian SS volunteer Giovanni 'Nino' Niquille, who was assigned from the Nord as the new unit's war correspondent.

Like Jonas Lie's men, Jonassen's were officially classed as SS-Police rather than full Waffen-SS members, and so after Sennheim they finished off their training in Hallerau near Dresden at the German Police Instructional School. Highly rated by the powers-that-be, the Company joined the SS-Nord division in Karelia during March of 1943, where they quickly gained an enviable reputation for combat effectiveness. Organised into three platoons of three sections each, they travelled on foot, or on skis when there was snow. They were armed with a lot of automatic weapons including one machine-gun per section and with every other man having a submachine-gun. They had a section of mortars as 'mobile artillery' and uniquely there were two snipers in each section.

The war in Karelia was not one marked by cataclysmic battles between competing tank armadas, rather by vicious small-unit combats and almost individual duelling, as men silently hunted each other through vast acres of hushed pines. In this wilderness, air and artillery support was minimal, fields of fire were measured in metres, and dominating features like hills were few. The rarity of high ground made it hugely important and would lead the SS ski troopers to their defining battles in the summer of the following year. That was yet to come. As it was, the Company was in action for less than three months before it suffered the same fate as the Frikorps Danmark and lost its inspirational commander in action. Whilst out on patrol with his men on 26 May, Gust Jonassen stepped on a mine and was blown to pieces. Although replaced immediately by Otto-Andreas Holmen – a popular former member of the Norwegian Royal Guard, graduate of Bad Tölz and NS member – the Company went into shock, and was sent home on leave in July to recover. The furlough also signalled the end of the majority of the volunteers' enlistments, which had only been for one year. The Company had been a success though, and the SS authorities committed to reconstituting the unit if enough volunteers could be found. Timing turned out to be bad, as the call went out at almost exactly the same time as the Nordland was desperately trying to fill the Norge regiment.

Given the chance to sign up for another tour of duty in Finland, however, almost every volunteer did so. A number of other ex-DNL men did too, and they were joined by a crop of young volunteers eager to 'do their bit'. So successful was the recruiting drive, the unit expanded to a battalion strength of more than 450 men and was rechristened the SS-Ski Battalion Norge. Added together with the SS-Police Companies, the net result was to deprive the Nordland of close on a thousand Norwegians.

Where are the panzers?

Back with the Nordland, after manpower, came the all-important issue of the armoured component of the division. The original plan called for near enough a full regiment of panzers, but there were never the men nor

Nordland Regiment officers at Staraja-Blismezy on the Donetz River in April 1943. The majority would leave to join the new Nordland Division in Croatia within a month. From left: Hauptsturmführer Bergfeld, Obersturmführer Schlager, Sturmbannführer Hans-Heinrich Lohmann (who would command the Norge's 3rd Battalion), Obersturmbannführer Wolfgang Joerchel (who would command the Norge Regiment before going on to the Dutch General Seyffardt Regiment), Sturmbannführer Hans Collani (the Finnish SS battalion commander who would die at Narva), Hauptsturmführer Meyer, Obersturmbannführer Albrecht Krügel (who would command the Norge's 2nd Battalion before being killed leading a counter-attack at the Altdamm bridgehead in 1945), Hauptsturmführer Haupt (half-hidden).

the tanks to fulfil this ambition. Without doubt, Speer had revolutionised Germany's war industries (for example, he had reduced the total assembly time for a typical panzer down from 12 weeks to six days), but even so, supply could never keep up with demand. After all, Germany's entire armoured might on the eve of Barbarossa of 3,332 panzers had been reduced to 140 serviceable vehicles in just seven months of fighting. The result for the Nordland of the Reich's inability to provide the necessary hardware was the downgrading of its armoured punch to a solitary battalion, albeit equipped with the extraordinary Panther tank armed with its extreme high velocity 75mm gun and superb protective sloping armour. The separate self-propelled anti-tank and assault-gun battalions could not be equipped either, and were combined into a single unit, further reducing the division's effectiveness.

Despite all this, the Nordland still packed a big punch. The division had over 80 panzers, assault guns and tank destroyers, the artillery regiment had 18 self-propelled guns, the anti-aircraft battalion some 20-plus half-track mounted multiple guns, and the reconnaissance battalion more than 20 armoured cars with cannons. Plus the majority of the six battalions of infantry were in armoured half-tracks (about 15–17 per company, many armed with cannons and flamethrowers as well as machine-guns), and every battalion had companies of towed anti-tank guns, infantry cannons and light anti-aircraft guns. Its infantry numbers were low (the total establishment of just over 12,000 compared badly to the Wiking's pre-Barbarossa strength of 19,377), but the majority of them, be they ex-Rumanian Army volksdeutsche, national Germans or Scandinavians, had been fighting the Soviets for two years or more,. They were battle-hardened veterans armed with the very best military hardware Nazi Germany could produce at that stage of the war. Gone were the days of inadequately trained foreign units equipped with second-rate kit, now the Scandinavians had a plethora of cannon, artillery, heavy mortars, heavy machine-guns, Panthers, assault guns and even the mighty 88mm anti-tank gun. Full strength it may not have been, but it was still a formidable threat, and the Red Army would have to take it seriously.

South to Croatia

Berlin decided that the best place for the new III SS-Germanic Armoured Corps, and its Dutch and Teutonic/Scandinavian units, to form up and prepare for the inferno of combat on the Russian Front, would be the puppet state of Croatia in the former Yugoslavia. There, it was reasoned, the Corps could be married up with its equipment, carry out work-up training and keep a lid on local Partisan activity at the same time. Entraining from Grafenwöhr from 20 August onwards, the Corps arrived in its Sisak assembly area south of Zagreb (called *Agram* by the Germans) as autumn arrived in the Balkans. Stretched across the Sava, Una and Glina rivers, the troops settled into their billets, began to receive their heavy equipment and were put through their paces under a new divisional commander – none other than their old friend and former Nordland Regimental boss, Fritz von Scholz.

A major blow was dealt to the Corps when the news came through that the Wiking could not be spared from the Eastern Front. It was fighting bitter defensive battles down south on the Donetz in the aftermath of the failed Kursk offensive and the ensuing Soviet counter-offensive. So Steiner's Corps would be limited for the time being to the Nordland

and Nederland. The Wiking was one of seven Waffen-SS panzer grenadier divisions officially re-designated a panzer division at the same time, so along with the establishment of the Nordland, the Waffen-SS now contributed seven of the Wehrmacht's 30 panzer divisions and six of its 17 panzer grenadier divisions. Both sides, especially in the East, now realised that the keys to success on the ground were tanks, self-propelled artillery and armoured infantry. The race was on to upgrade existing forces; but it was a race the Wehrmacht was losing even as it was shipping the newest of its panzer grenadier divisions down south to the Balkans. As for the Wiking, the truth was that operational imperatives and the ever-worsening military picture meant it would not join the new corps during its lifetime. The two standard bearers of the Scandinavian Waffen-SS would never fight alongside each other.

Training, combat and the Italians

Officially assigned to the Second Panzer Army as part of Army Group F (von Weichs's Heeresgruppe F – the Wiking had been under his overall command for the 1942 Caucasus offensive), the Nordland began work-up training at platoon and company level, and also took part in local actions against Tito's increasingly effective Partisan army. This fighting, plus lack of equipment and fuel, prevented the Corps from training at the high level it really required to get itself up to speed. The situation worsened when the Italians surrendered and switched sides in September. The Nordland, like all other Wehrmacht units, was forced to move at great speed to disarm neighbouring Italian Army units and ensure their weapons and positions did not fall into Partisan hands. In a lightning-fast operation, von Scholz's men surrounded the northern Italian 57th Infantry Division Lombardia, took over its equipment and disbanded the men. Without Italian forces to help, the Germans and their remaining allies were stretched thin and the Partisans stepped up their attacks. The 26-year-old Norwegian Eivind Ingebrigtsen was a victim of the increasing violence, killed in Jablanica on 8 November in a communist attack. More of his comrades were to follow. The fighting, as always in civil and insurgency wars, was brutal and unforgiving.

The Danmark especially was involved in some extremely hard combat around the towns of Petrinya and Hrastovica, in the Glina area, in late November. A glimpse of the intensity of the struggle can be gleaned from a Special Corps Order issued by Felix Steiner himself following one particular action:

SS-Unterscharführer N.O. Christensen [a Danish volunteer], 1st Battalion SS Armoured Grenadier Regiment Danmark, after heavy fighting with superior numbers of the enemy on the 22nd of November 1943, fell into the hands of the Bolsheviks. Before they could search him, he reached into his trouser pockets, in which he had two hand grenades, and set them both off. The explosion shattered SS-Unterscharführer Christensen, the four SS men standing around him, and all the Bolsheviks surrounding him.

SS-Unterscharführer Christensen demonstrated the highest heroic courage and deserves to live on in the ranks of the regiment as an example of the highest bravery, scorn of death, and proper Germanic attitude. In the units of the Germanic Corps, his death will be a symbol of the great Germanic ideal to all young soldiers, a sign of soldierly manliness to inspire emulation and live on in the history of the Corps.

Although it is more than likely that the Partisans would have shot Christensen and his fellow SS men out of hand, it is still incredibly difficult to imagine the level of commitment needed to carry out this last act of self-destruction.

Christensen and Ingebrigtsen were not the Nordland's only casualties. In the space of just 10 weeks, when the division was meant to be focusing on training and preparing for the cauldron of Russia, two officers and 41 men were killed in action, and a further two officers and 109 men were wounded. One of the dead was the Dane, Viggo Christophersen, whose brother Egon would go on to become a Knight's Cross winner at Narva. A total of 48 Iron Crosses were awarded to divisional members during their time in the region. Croatia was no picnic for the Nordland.

The SS-Wiking in southern Russia

The Nordland had now become the mainstay of the Scandinavian Waffen-SS, but that did not mean the Wiking was now 'free' of its Nordic heritage. Well over 200 Danes, Norwegians, Swedes and Finns (and even one Icelander – Grettir 'Egidir' Odiussen) remained in the division along with Dutch, Flemish and Swiss volunteers. For these men 1943 had been a year of desperate defence. They started the year by escaping potential encirclement in the Caucasus and ended the year fending off further Red Army assaults. In between, the division did not take part in the titanic, and ultimately disastrous, Kursk offensive in July, but was subsequently caught up in the huge Red Army counter-punch that followed. With the cream of Nazi Germany's panzer forces burnt out in the Kursk fighting, élite units like the Wiking were desperately needed to try and stem the tide. (Though 'burnt out' may be an exaggeration. For an analysis of the actual panzer losses at Kursk consult *Zitadelle* by Mark Healy.) From mid-July until just before Christmas, fighting every inch of the way, the Wiking was relentlessly pushed back from the Donets and Mius rivers to the great Dnieper bend. Two accounts from opposite ends of the year recall the intensity of the combat. Firstly the Germania's Ornulf Bjornstadt:

I returned from leave in Norway to my unit on the Kalmyk steppe in the Ukraine, and it was bitter cold, [February 1943] and difficult for both sides because our weapons were frozen stiff. Our mortars were more or less alright, but our machine-guns were hopeless. Luckily we were well-served with warm clothes but nevertheless there were inevitable casualties from frostbite.

We were no longer in a defensive position, but were urged forward and ordered to attack constantly because of the threat from Popov's forces [an armoured group comprising four tank corps, two independent armoured brigades, a ski brigade and three rifle divisions] who were trying to drive a wedge between us and some neighbouring Italian and Rumanian troops. When we reached the Donets we dug in at a point on the river bank with the Russians on the other side directly opposite us, but theirs was a partly-wooded area and we couldn't see them properly. We sent out recce patrols, but the Germans weren't natural hunters and seemed incapable of moving silently. We did take prisoners though, among them were four Tartar renegades who said they would be willing to work for us and so we set them to digging trenches. They shared the same bunker as an Army artillery group whose loaded machine-pistols were hung on a post. Overnight the Tartars seized the weapons and slaughtered everyone in the bunker. Then they melted back to the Russian lines. We were forbidden to have any more prisoners in the frontline after that.

We had to deal with a command post and billets in a nearby village, but as we advanced we were puzzled by what we thought was a half-hearted Russian defence. Their troops seemed content to hit us with a bit of light artillery but nothing else. When we got within attack distance – some 100–200 metres – we found out why. Around a dozen tanks came roaring out to hit 2nd Company on our left. Our comrades had no chance, the tanks simply drove over them and they were crushed to death. My company only survived because we happened to be in a hollow on the right. Soon though our 88s were in position and got many of those tanks through their turrets.

We peeled away from the tanks and made to attack an enemy machine-gun post, firing all the way from a small dry culvert before capturing it. I have two abiding memories of that fight. One was the sight of a junior officer of ours running like hell and shooting at the same time. Then he got a bullet through the head. He spun round 180 degrees before he fell, but he didn't stop firing until he hit the ground. Then there was the gigantic haystack in our path. There would have been nothing unusual in it if the haystack hadn't started to move, and from it emerged a T-34. The tank drew level with the village cemetery and it was from there that a young SS-Obersturmführer appeared, suddenly rushing forward and slapping a magnetic mine on it. A bit later I was crouching in a culvert with my mortar in position behind me and through my binoculars I could see the enemy bunched ahead. They made a fine target, particularly one cannon I had my eye on. I was just about to line up on the cannon when there were a number of loud 'pings' by the side of me and, thinking they were Russian, I rolled over to get out of the way as fast as I could. Then I saw the muzzle of this 75mm anti-tank gun, but not before I took the full force of the muzzle blast on my cheek. The gunner had concentrated solely on the target and hadn't seen me. I was angry because he had shot up the gun I wanted and also because I was stone deaf for a long time after that.

Next we could see the Russians retreating at speed up the slope of a hill, so we moved into the now-abandoned village and had a brief rest. Then one of our SS-Obersturmführer's appeared asking to see me. After congratulating me warmly he told me that I had been granted a place on a special officers training course at Bad Tölz. But I told him that I had had enough, having originally volunteered for one year and having stayed on for two and a half. He protested that I would be leaving some good comrades behind and maybe we could discuss the whole thing over a bottle of cognac. When we finished the bottle, he gave me a broad grin and, confessing his joke, produced a sheaf of documents from his pocket. They were my discharge papers.

As soon as I was able, I made the difficult journey home via Germany and on to Norway, but not before I learnt that we had helped to stop General Popov's advance.

Bjornstadt was right about Popov, not only was he stopped but his entire force, including 251 tanks and 198 guns, was destroyed in Erich von Manstein's masterly operation that saved the southern wing of the Ostheer, and became known as 'the miracle on the Donets'. It was the end of the road for Bjornstadt, but not for Jan Munk, who was still with the division in November:

Our positions were still in the Dnieper area but were rather exposed. There were lots of bushes and undergrowth, but only a few trees. The Russians tried several attacks in what was, for them, very favourable terrain, but we managed to stop them every time. During their night attacks for example it was almost impossible for them to move without making a noise, so we had no problems in that respect.

On 2nd November 1943, we knew something was up because we heard the enemy singing and making a lot of noise. In other words they had had their ration of vodka to boost their courage prior to an attack. Sure enough, at about 1800hrs we received information that an attack was imminent. At that time I commanded a squad, and I sent them all out of the bunker we were in to take their positions in the trenches. They all went except for one, a Rumanian volksdeutsche, who told me that someone had taken his steel helmet and the one left behind was too small for him. He wanted to stay behind and guard the bunker. I told him what I thought of that and gave him my own helmet. It fitted. I went out wearing my camouflaged field cap. Then I joined my number two on the machine-gun.

The attack came, a bit fiercer than usual, but we managed to beat it off again. As always, that was the time when our own artillery started shelling, in front of the retreating enemy, catching them in between our shells and machine-gun fire. This time the barrage was very close by. I heard one gun in particular, the rounds from which landed short and to our left, then the next one was again to our left but nearer still. The one following was a bull's-eye. It landed right in front of us and destroyed our machine-gun. We had been a split-second too late in taking cover. It felt as if an enormous weight had pushed me down violently. My number two started to splutter that the bastards had blown his nose off. It wasn't quite that bad though. A tiny splinter had pierced his nose from one side right through to the other, and he was bleeding like a stuck-pig. We decided to go back to the bunker so that I could bandage him properly. To my surprise I found that I couldn't move. I thought I had merely cut off the blood supply to my legs by squatting on my haunches. When the next shell came I was pushed, or so I thought, through the trench so fast that I could not keep upright, and I scraped my face on the ground. I shouted to my comrade not to be so bloody stupid and to calm down. He helped me to the bunker. Once inside, however, he told me that he hadn't touched me, let alone pushed me. It dawned on me that something wasn't quite right. My legs were still useless, so I undid my belt and the lower buttons of my tunic and felt along my back, but found nothing. I loosened my trousers and inspected that area too, still nothing. I dressed again and went back to bandaging my friend. We both had a smoke and then I began to feel hot and sweaty. I took my cap off and blood poured down over my face. With my fingers I could feel where the blood was coming from, a small cut right on the top of my head. Now I knew why my legs wouldn't work. After a while I was carried through the trenches to an area where it was wide enough to use a stretcher. I was then brought to a collection point to wait for proper transport. Quite a few men were there, some on stretchers, some badly injured and others not quite so bad.

Then the Russians attacked again, and all the wounded who could walk were told to man their positions again. Those of us remaining were left behind to fend for ourselves as best we could. We were given some grenades and machine-pistols and wished 'Good luck'. We fully understood. More than a dozen men would have been needed to carry us away, and they couldn't be spared.

The Russians appeared and shot at us – we shot back. They threw hand-grenades and we replied. Fortunately the Wehrmacht counter-attacked with the support of some light tanks. We did not lose a single wounded man, although some of us, including me, collected a few more wounds, though nothing serious. I was then taken by stretcher again to a bunker. It was deep, with a well-protected entrance and a very thick roof. Inside were tables and easy chairs. A radio was playing, and it looked almost like something from a propaganda picture. A doctor examined me and said: 'When did you last have a piss?' As far as I could remember that was noon the previous day, a good 17 hours before. Before I knew what was happening I had a catheter inserted. I didn't feel a thing, though the doctor was pleased that he had done it in time.

During and after the German counter-attack several Russian prisoners were taken. These were used, as usual, for carrying ammunition and, on this occasion, to carry the stretchers. To go back to the dressing station we had to cross a rather bare, flat field. The Russians were directing some artillery fire on this area and every time a shell landed the Russian carrying the foot of the stretcher I was on would drop it and take cover. The one at the head end was more careful and lowered me gently. By this time I had a splitting headache and all the dropping wasn't helping. I told the one holding my feet that if he dropped me again I would shoot him. I had to warn him twice more. After each warning he would initially lower his end, but soon went back to just dropping me. Eventually I got my pistol out and fired a shot over his head. Everything went fine after that.

The long road to capitulation

The failure of the Wehrmacht to land a knock-out blow on the Red Army in 1943 condemned Nazi Germany and its allies to eventual, bloody defeat. Germany was only ever geared up for a short war and the battle of attrition it was now facing in the West and East was one it could never hope to win. It was rapidly losing the vital armaments production race and was starting to get very near the bottom of the manpower barrel. By contrast, its opponents were really starting to come into their own. The Ostheer had managed to kill and capture Soviet soldiers at a ratio of almost five to one in 1941; that had now reduced to two to one. The old-style lumbering masses of the Red Army, herded mindlessly onto Wehrmacht guns or into Wehrmacht prison camps, had been replaced by a behemoth that was now not only more mobile than the Ostheer, but was equipped with firepower on an unheard-of scale. The future looked bleak for the Wehrmacht.

As for the Waffen-SS, it had finally addressed its shortcomings regarding the treatment of its foreign volunteers. Consequently their training and military effectiveness had come on in leaps and bounds, and they were now an established and valued part of the growing Waffen-SS world. For the Scandinavian Waffen-SS this had meant the establishment of their own division. The Nordland had drawn together the bulk of the Nordics in the black guards, but it had failed in its purpose. The Finns had gone home en masse and many volunteers were still spread across half a dozen formations, most notably the Wiking, the SS-Ski Battalion Norge and the SS-Police Companies. But the Nordland as a gesture had failed. There was no new avalanche of recruits and thousands of Balkan volksdeutsche had had to fill the gaps. With the war clearly turning against Nazi Germany, there would be even fewer willing to take the plunge – from now on the Scandinavian Waffen-SS would only get smaller.

The Nordland may have failed in mass recruiting but it had succeeded in concentrating the cream of the Scandinavian Waffen-SS in a new, powerful force equipped with panzers, assault guns, self-propelled artillery, armoured cars and armoured personnel carriers. Their military proficiency was recognised not only in their equipment tables, but also in their growing prominence in technical arms and most importantly, in command positions. Across the new division, hundreds of corporals, sergeants, platoon, company and even battalion commanders could speak Danish, Norwegian or Swedish together and talk of home. Together they would defend the Third Reich back to the very gates of Hitler's bunker itself, 18 months later.

V

1944: Bled White in the East – the Wiking at Cherkassy and the Nordland at Narva

The time for grand-style operations in the East is now past.

Adolf Hitler to Erich von Manstein after sacking him as Army Group South's commander in March 1944.

Since the launch of Barbarossa, the Wehrmacht had lost just over 3,000,000 men killed, wounded or missing in the East. In effect, this was the entire strength of the original invasion force. True, the Ostheer still stood at a total of 140 infantry, 24 panzer, nine panzer grenadier and 36 allied divisions (16 Finnish, nine each from Rumania and Hungary, and one each from Slovakia and Spain), but this was not the magnificent war machine of 1941. The infantry divisions lacked men, while the panzer units would never fully recover from Kursk. Equipment, like the new Panther and Tiger tanks, was undoubtedly of excellent quality in terms of firepower, but the tanks were unreliable, and fuel was in short supply as Allied Bomber Command systematically destroyed Germany's synthetic gasoline production. The Germans were becoming increasingly reliant on horses and boot leather to move around. The men themselves were not the same either. The incredibly well-drilled officers, NCOs and men of the 1941 Wehrmacht were long gone, buried under Russian soil across hundreds of battlefields. In their place were often hastily-trained conscripts, eager just to survive the war. Germany's greatest strategist of the day, Erich von Manstein, said that the Army's divisions had been burnt out beyond repair.

While the Wehrmacht was now a shadow of its former self, facing it was a Red Army well on its way to becoming the dominant military force on the planet. Even after its millions of casualties, its strength had actually risen to 5,989,000 men in the army, 480,000 in the air force and 260,000 in the navy (mainly used as ground troops) – 6,729,000 men all up. The Soviets fielded 5,600 tanks and assault guns, 8,800 aircraft and a jaw-dropping 90,000 artillery pieces. The thousands of sturdy, American-made, Lend Lease trucks provided real mobility, while the factories and plants poured out munitions and fuel on a prodigious scale to drive it all forward.

This was what faced the Scandinavian Waffen-SS of the Nordland and Wiking at the dawn of the new year. For the Nordland it would bring a first taste of action, while for the Wiking it was a third year of struggle. For both, the year would always be remembered for two of the great battles of the Russo-German war – the Narva and the Cherkassy Pocket.

Oranienbaum

The Oranienbaum Pocket, to the west of Leningrad on the shores of the Gulf of Finland, was centred on the powerful Soviet naval base of Kronstadt, and surrounded by the flat and swampy Ingermannland. A thorn in Army Group North's side since their failure to overwhelm it back in 1941, the area had served as a staging post for Soviet attacks ever since. The Norwegians of the DNL had fought off just such an assault at Urizk in 1942. Since then depressingly little had changed in the northern sector of the Russian Front. Leningrad was still holding out, the Finns had not moved, and the Red Army was still launching offensives from the Volkhov River and the Valdai Hills to try and relieve the beleaguered city. Neither side had been strong enough to defeat the other; and both were pre-occupied with far grander battles farther south. Thousands had still died though, in brutal infantry fights and artillery duels among the forests, low hills and marshland. The front was now approaching a turning point as the Red Army grew in strength and the Ostheer's combat power ebbed away into the snow and mud.

Anticipating a series of Russian winter offensives up and down the frontline, any available troops across Europe were transferred east by the OKW. Among those sent to Russia were Steiner's III Germanic SS-Panzer Corps. Allocated to the Oranienbaum sector, as part of General Georg Lindemann's Eighteenth Army, the Corps arrived in the last weeks of November and the first half of December. It also took under command a battlegroup of the SS-Polizei division, and two weak Luftwaffe Field Divisions, the 9th and 10th. These latter were not élite paratroopers, but mainly unemployed ground crew whom Goering had grouped in formations still under his arm's nominal command. Rather than train them properly and then send them as much-needed replacements to tried and tested Army units, which would at least have given them a fighting chance of survival, an increasingly drug-dependent Goering had left them semi-trained and poorly equipped and led by officers with little if any combat experience. The exceptions to this latter rule were the divisional commanders of the 9th and 10th, Colonel (*Oberst*) Ernst Michael and Major General (*Generalmajor*) Hermann von Wedel respectively. Both men were professional officers and holders of the German Cross in Gold and the Knight's Cross. Both would die in the coming battle. Despite the presence of these two gallant officers Steiner was not happy with his Luftwaffe charges, but needs must, so he set about positioning his troops as best he could. He placed the Luftwaffe troops to the east to soak up any attack, with the Nederland farther west, and the Nordland holding the south of the salient in depth and providing some sort of reserve. Unfortunately his most powerful armoured unit – the Nordland's Hermann von Salza Panzer Battalion – was still marrying up with its Panther tanks and carrying out necessary familiarisation training, it would not rejoin the division for some time.

Coincidentally, the very first Frikorps Danmark commander, Christian Peder Kryssing, was stationed just to the east of the Corps as commander of Battlegroup Coast (*Kampfgruppe Küste*), a collection of naval, army and coastal defence units totalling 9,000 men. Promoted to SS-Brigadeführer on 1 August 1943, Kryssing's battlegroup was almost as strong as the Nordland, with von Scholz's Christmas strength return reporting 341 officers, 1,975 NCOs, 10,146 men, and 106 Hiwis – 12,568 men. This put it almost exactly 2,500 under establishment, with half of the shortfall being officers and NCOs.

The Red Army's winter offensive

Just as in 1942 and 1943, the STAVKA had decided to launch a winter offensive against the Germans in the north of Russia. But whereas those attacks had been met by resolute defence and beaten back, this was a different time.

At 0700hrs on the morning of 14 January 1944, huge concentrations of Soviet artillery began pounding the German lines around Oranienbaum. Even as the guns shifted their fire to deeper targets, the assault troops of the Red Army's 2nd Shock Army downed their hefty ration of vodka and threw themselves forward with their customary '*Urrahs!*' Their attack was aimed squarely at the Luftwaffe divisions and, despite their commanders' best efforts, the air force men were simply swept away by an enemy that outnumbered them by more than four to one. Michael's 9th Division was even attacked from behind, as the Soviet 42nd Army broke through the Army's neighbouring 126th Infantry Division and swung into the rear. The Nordland was immediately thrown into combat to try and stem the tide as the Germans attempted to rebuild a line to the south running northwest from the coast, down to the southeast below Leningrad. For an entire week von Scholz's men were Steiner's 'fire brigade', constantly switching battalions to halt Soviet breakthroughs and seal up holes in the line. The fighting was bitter, Fritz Bunse's SS-Assault Engineer Battalion (SS-Pionier Bataillon 11) lost 100 men killed and wounded in just one day's combat near the village of Malkunova. The DNL veteran John Sandstadt, now serving in the Norge's 1st Battalion, recalled that time:

On the day of the major Soviet attack our company (the 1st) had a strength of 118 men: seven reichsdeutsche NCOs, 34 volksdeutsche soldiers, 1 Flemish Unterscharführer and 76 Norwegians (the largest number in the battalion) with two officers, 15 NCOs and 59 men.

On the night of January 15, 1944, the first enemy movement took place, and our counter-attack in the morning completely collapsed under Soviet crossfire. We immediately lost 13 dead and many wounded. It was the same for the 2nd and 3rd Companies. All the same we were finally able to hold our positions for some ten days, with our three companies reduced to the strength of just one company.

My brother Olav, born in 1921, had also enlisted in the DNL on April 28 1943 and served in the heavy platoon of our company. He fell in the Kosherizy area after five days. His last resting place was in the former divisional cemetery near Begunizy, between St Petersburg and Narva.

When we had some rest on January 27 1944, our company consisted of one Obersturmführer, 5 NCOs and some 35 men. Our Battalion Commander, Fritz Vogt, appeared and handed several soldiers – including me – the Iron Cross 2nd Class. Less as a recognition for brave deeds, but more as a 'premium' for having survived the previous 12 days.

In the end there was nothing else for it – Army Group North would have to retreat. Abandoning the positions they had held for more than two years, the Sixteenth and Eighteenth Armies were more or less bundled back southwest to rudimentary positions on the Luga River, rather grandiosely called the 'Panther Line'. As the Eighteenth Army headed back west, an eerie silence hung over the miles and miles of trenches that had been home to so many soldiers for so long. Then, in an outpouring of joy, the citizens of Leningrad realised they were free at last and every bell in the city tolled. The longest continuous siege in the history of warfare was finally over. The city was safe but the fighting continued, with surviving enclaves of the Luftwaffe's 9th Division and the Army's 126th Division lying surrounded to the southwest near Ropsha, and in danger of being left behind. The Nordland lunged forward and broke them out in a last offensive effort, before streaming back to the relative safety of the river defences. Without the panzers of the Hermann von Salza, the Nordland's most powerful armoured component was Rudi Saalbach's far more lightly equipped Armoured Recce Battalion with its volksdeutsche recruits and Swedish veterans. Increasingly used as a rearguard, the battalion held Gubianzy covering the division's withdrawal to the Luga crossing point at Jamburg (also called Kingisepp). Nilsson's Schwedenzug especially was involved in bitter fighting, and was decimated at Volossovo and Orlovo. A Soviet night attack in the area on 26 January was crushed by Saalbach's men, leaving 34 Red Army tanks burning in the snow. The young Dutch volunteer, Kaspar Sporck, distinguished himself while commanding a troop of half-tracks fitted with 75mm anti-tank guns. The Recce Battalion volunteer, Toni Ging, remembered the withdrawal:

> I was trained as a driver and given an SPW with a turret and a 2cm cannon, the commander was an SS-Rottenführer and the gunner was a Swedish comrade, unfortunately I have forgotten both their names.
>
> We were near Volossovo and were assigned to recce a village. We were accompanied by an SWP with panzer grenadiers. Since no enemies were to be seen, the other SPW went back and I turned to go back also. Scarcely were the grenadiers at our level when we came under heavy infantry fire from the village. I drove into a heap of stones, which had been hidden under the snow, and thus got stuck. The fire got heavier and heavier and we had to leave the vehicle. First the commander up in the turret, then the Swede, and then me. Ducking down we ran to the other SPW which was waiting for us. But before we arrived the Swede was hit. We crept to him and pulled him into the SPW. We went to the main dressing station but unfortunately our Swedish comrade died of his wound. Our 3rd Company still had a fighting strength of 25 men at that time.

Reaching Jamburg the Nordland safely crossed to the western bank of the Luga, but it was too late. The Red Army, in a clear sign of its growing mechanization, had actually reached the river to the north and south of Jamburg before a lot of the retreating Germans. The river was now useless as a defensive barrier, and the retreat had to continue back west to the old Estonian/Russian border at the River Narva. Meanwhile the Norge held onto the eastern bank of the Luga while much of Army Group North crossed over, with the 1st Battalion and its Norwegian component bearing the brunt of the rearguard fighting.

The Narva – the Battle of the European SS

At last the German retreat outpaced the Soviet advance, and the Narva was reached by the Nordland in early February. Von Scholz gathered his dispersed troopers and threw them into a hasty defensive line based on the river and the cities of Narva and Ivangorod on the east and west banks. The battered Norge crossed to the west bank and took up position in the swamps to the southwest of Narva city itself. This time it was the Danmark and Nederland that stayed on the eastern bank to form a bridgehead. The Soviets were just days behind, and no sooner had the Corps dug in than the Red Army stormed across the river to the south and tried to cut them off from the rear. Again the Norge bore the brunt of the fighting, it managed to pin them back into two pockets with their backs to the water – the Ostsack and Westsack – but it was not strong enough to throw them back over the river. The Norge lost its highly decorated commander, Arnold Stoffers, who died while personally leading an assault, plus two of its three battalion commanders; Hans-Heinrich Lohmann who was seriously wounded, and Albrecht Krügel who went to take over at Danmark when Graf Hermenegild von Westphalen was killed.

With the line somewhat stabilised, both Steiner's Corps and Kryssing's battlegroup were grouped together with Knight's Cross winner General Anton Grasser's XXVI Infantry Corps, to form the new Army Group Narva. Kryssing's force had to fend off an amphibious assault on the night of 13 February as Soviet marines stormed ashore at the town of Merekuela. Assisted by the Nordland, Kryssing's men held and the landing was thrown back into the sea. Steiner's command was then given a real boost by the arrival of the newly formed 20th SS-Estonian Division (20th Waffen-Grenadier Division der SS estnische Nr.1). The Estonians were almost all former members of various Schuma Battalions (militia and self-defence units set up and organised by the Wehrmacht from local volunteers, mainly to combat the partisan threat.), or the Wiking's own Estonian Narwa Battalion and its Waffen-SS Estonian Legion brethren. As such the majority were combat veterans eager to defend their homeland against the advancing Red Army. They were immediately caught up in the fighting, but it was clear that the Soviet advance was finally running out of steam after six weeks of action. That did not mean the fighting stopped. The Red Army was strong enough to be able to rest large parts of its order of battle while still feeding in fresh formations to keep up the pressure on the Narva. Using the Ostsack and Westsack as jumping off points, the Soviet 8th Army tried again to cut the main Narva-Reval road and isolate the Corps. The whole of March was taken up by this see-saw fighting as

Above left: Johan-Petter Balstad, born 24 September 1924 in Norway, was an officer candidate in the Norge Regiment's 7th Company during the 'Battle of the European SS' at Narva in 1944. He became an expert at destroying Soviet T-34 tanks with hand-held panzerfausts, hence his three tank killer badges on his right upper arm. He survived the war and passed away in Oslo in 1985. (James Macleod)

Above right: The Narva battleground today. This view shows the Danmark Regiment's positions east and south of Orphanage Hill towards Auwere, specifically the ground held by the then-depleted 2nd and 3rd Battalions. (Paul Errington)

The Narva battleground today. The rebuilt fortress stands on the western bank and the photograph shows the Danmark Regiment's bridgehead on the eastern bank. (Paul Errington)

the Germans attempted to smash the pockets and restore the river line, even as the Russians sought to expand their bridgeheads. One such Red Army thrust threatened to split the Nordland from its southern Army neighbour, the 11th Infantry Division, and the two divisions had to launch no less than three co-ordinated counter-attacks along with Heavy Tank Battalion 502 (Schwere Panzer Abteilung 502 – an Army unit equipped with hugely powerful Tiger tanks) to finally smash the Westsack on 30 March. The Norwegian volunteer SS-Untersturmführer Kare Brynestad won the Iron Cross 1st Class for his bravery during the fighting. There was no such success against the Ostsack though, as it continued to hold out.

Eventually the spring thaw brought a temporary halt to large-scale operations as the low-lying land of the area became waterlogged and impassable for vehicles. Even though their trenches were now full of water, the surviving Scandinavians of the Nordland breathed a huge sigh of relief. The Corps could now take stock and lick its wounds. Casualties had been extremely heavy. The Nordland's baptism of fire had cost it a third of its total strength, with 24 officers and 788 men killed, 58 officers and 2,708 men wounded, and nine officers and 216 men missing. Only nine Hiwis survived the retreat. The Nordland was not exceptional. The Nederland, for instance, had lost an astonishing 3,300 men, some 60 per cent of its

The Swedish volunteer and war reporter Sten Eriksson, during a lull in the fighting at Narva, looks across the river from the west bank towards the imposing Russian Ivangorod fortress. (James Macleod)

strength, while Eighteenth Army as a whole suffered 20,000 casualties in the first two weeks of the offensive alone. The race was now on to try and plug the gaps before the Red Army renewed its offensive; von Scholz had some real concerns about the combat value of his division as it strove to recover, which he detailed in a report to Berlin:

> The fighting value of the Division was decisively influenced by high losses of officers and NCOs, which is all the more serious because of the few officers and NCOs available when it was established. In the composition of the Division (Germanic volunteers from Denmark, Norway, Sweden and the south-eastern area) the fighting value rises or falls depending on the elimination of this shortage.
>
> The meagre motorised capability (25% of the full vehicle numbers) along with the available weapons and equipment on hand at formation, has in the withdrawal led, despite the highest discipline, to drive the men to the borders of their physical limits and to extraordinarily high weapon and equipment losses.
>
> The training level of the replacements arriving has not allowed their inclusion in the Division as frontline troops. Further training with the Replacement Battalion (four to six weeks) has been necessary. However the physical condition and morale of the replacements is good. The mood of the troops is good, even though political developments in Denmark and Norway have had a negative effect on the Germanic volunteers from those countries.
>
> Until sufficient filling out with capable officers and NCOs, the Division has only limited capability for defence.

Hans-Gösta Pehrsson, the most decorated Swedish SS volunteer of the war at Mummasaara in Estonia in April 1944. (Lennart Westberg)

As for equipment, at the end of March the Corps' armoured punch was badly lacking, with the Nordland only mustering a negligible 10 assault guns, and the Nederland about the same. Von Scholz did manage to grab some 710 men from the now-defunct 9th and 10th Luftwaffe Field Divisions, which were unsurprisingly disbanded. The new men were given Waffen-SS camouflage smocks and distributed around the 2nd and 3rd Norge and Danmark Battalions. The 1st Battalions of each of the Nordland's two grenadier regiments were also broken up, having suffered crippling casualties. The majority of survivors were used to help fill the ranks of their sister battalions, while a cadre was sent to the Hammerstein training area, back in the Reich, to take on new recruits and ready themselves for a return to the division. As it turned out they never rejoined their comrades. By the time they were in any sort of shape to fight again, Nazi Germany was in a spiral of increasing chaos, and they were sent to reinforce the Wiking instead. Without them the Nordland would become, in effect, a model of the Wehrmacht 1945-pattern division with only four grenadier battalions and not the previous six. In those reduced four battalions there were still 1,089 Danes including 37 officers, but only 338 Norwegians (21 officers), as volunteers drained away to the Finnish front. As for the Schwedenzug, Walter Nilsson had been killed at Rogowitzky on 25 January during the retreat and was replaced by his fellow Swede, Hans-Gösta Pehrsson – an old-stager affectionately known as 'GP' by his men. Transferred to Mummassaara in the rear, the Schwedenzug was reinforced and re-equipped in preparation for the battles to come.

The Wiking at Cherkassy

By mid-December 1943 the Ostheer had been pushed back west from the mighty Dnieper River along its entire length – except for a short stretch, near the city of Cherkassy, centred on the town of Korsun. Two and a half years earlier the Wiking, in its first major operation of the war, had charged through exactly the same area as it raced to cross the Dnieper and head ever eastwards during the heady days of Operation Barbarossa. Then the division had been, numerically, the strongest formation in the whole Waffen-SS, and was the standard bearer of the Scandinavian Waffen-SS with hundreds of Germanic volunteers filling its ranks. By late December 1943 the Wiking was a very different division. It was now one of the Wehrmacht's 30 fully-fledged panzer divisions with the Wiking old boy, Hans Mühlenkamp, in charge of an entire regiment of panzers (although only one battalion was present at the time), and it had earned a superb reputation for military efficiency and combat élan.

As part of the reorganisation of the Waffen-SS in 1943 it also had one of the new SS-Assault Brigades grouped under it to provide extra combat power, in the Wiking's case it was the Walloon Belgian 5th SS-Volunteer Assault Brigade Wallonien (5. SS-Freiwilligen Sturmbrigade Wallonien) commanded by the ex-regular Belgian Army officer Lucien Lippert. Along with the Nederland and the Wallonien, two more brigades were created, the French SS-Frankreich serving with the Hungarian volksdeutsche SS-Horst Wessel Division and the Flemish SS-Langemarck with Das Reich.

Felix Steiner had moved up to Corps command of course, but in his place was the Wiking's previous head of artillery, the highly decorated and extremely experienced SS-Brigadeführer Herbert Otto Gille. Gille was tall, bespectacled, silver-haired and immensely respected by his men. Some of his Army commanders questioned his tactical skill at divisional level, but none doubted his bravery. The division, though, was not the multi-national force it had once been. Most of the Scandinavians and Dutchmen had been combed out the previous year to fill the Nordland and Nederland and their places taken by native Germans. Even so, there were still well over a thousand foreign volunteers scattered across the unit, with several hundred Scandinavians prominent among them. The Wiking was no longer the totem of the Scandinavian Waffen-SS, but nevertheless *its* story is still part of *their* story.

Wiking grenadiers and some of the division's few Mark IV panzers advance across the desolate Ukrainian plain at Cherkassy, 1944.

Above left: A tired Norwegian Wiking NCO well kitted out for the cold of Cherkassy, 1944.

Above right: Herbert Otto Gille – initially Wiking's artillery commander, then overall divisional commander and finally IV SS Corps commander – with his trusty walking stick.

A Wiking Mark IV panzer at Cherkassy. The Mark IV was outdated by the time of the battle but was still the workhorse of the German panzer formations. This one sports wide armour skirts to counter anti-tank shells.

Another Stalingrad? The December offensive

'No respite for the Fritzies', was the new clarion call from the STAVKA. The Red Army was well on the way to mastering all the technical arts of a modern military machine and had unprecedented resources. Their doctrine now emphasised a never-ending series of attacks and offensives, up and down the frontline, maintaining the initiative and never allowing the Ostheer either to recover its strength or effectively switch forces from sector to sector. Hitler's stubborn insistence on holding the line on the Dnieper, with a view to a wholly improbable future German offensive, presented the Soviets with a golden opportunity to trap a large part of Army Group South against the river. The STAVKA eyed the multiplicity of formations on the Dnieper, XI and XLII Corps from Hans Valentin Hube's First Panzer Army and Otto Wöhler's Eighth Army respectively, with barely concealed glee. Surely here was the opportunity for another Stalingrad? For once however, Soviet intelligence was off-beam. The order of battle for the two Corps might have looked impressive on paper, but in reality they were phantoms. Colonel Schmidt of the Bavarian 57th Infantry Division (part of XI Corps) said of his division at the time:

> The division's fighting strength has been weakened by the months-long battle against an enemy superior in men and material. The infantry battalions are only at 20 to 30 per cent strength. Fighting morale has sunk. Within the unit is an apathetic indifference. The troops have been living under conditions in which the most primitive essentials of life have been lacking ... harsh words of embitterment and lack of faith in the High Command are voiced by the troops.

Only the Wiking (again part of XI Corps) was still at anything approaching full-strength, and it was down to 14,000 men. Most significantly, with Hans Mühlenkamp absent reforming a second armoured battalion, the division's panzer component was just 25 Panzer IVs, a dozen obsolete Panzer IIIs, and six assault guns led by Hans Köller. The Soviet plan envisaged an encirclement trapping more than 100,000 Germans, as it turned out the number would be more like 56,000.

Following the by-now usual thorough Soviet preparations, the 1st, 2nd, 3rd and 4th Ukrainian Fronts launched an all-out offensive on Christmas Eve 1943 from Ovruch in the north, all the way down to Zaphorozye in the south. Some 29,000 artillery guns and 2,360 aircraft pulverised the German frontlines, paving the way for 2,365,000 men to throw themselves at the shelled units of Army Group South and its 1,760,000 troopers. Within days the Front had disintegrated and over 2,000 Russian tanks poured through to cause chaos and effect a link-up behind the Wiking and its fellow formations.

The Wiking and two Corps are trapped

By 28 January the men of the 6th Tank Army and the 5th Guards Tank Army shook hands at the village of Zvenigorodka on the little Gniloy Tikich River (pronounced 'neeloy teekitsch'), and the Wiking was surrounded. It joined its comrades in the Wallonien, and a half-dozen Army infantry divisions, now officially entitled Group Stemmermann after the most senior commander present, General of Artillery Wilhelm Stemmermann.

Moving with commendable speed, Koniev and Vatutin's men established two rings between the Pocket (*Kessel* in German), and the main German lines. The outer would face any relief attempt, while the inner would frustrate any possible breakout. Simultaneously the 27th and 52nd Armies attacked the encircled landsers and SS grenadiers from east and west to smash the Pocket apart, amply supported by massed artillery, which worked backward and forward over the diminishing terrain still in German and allied hands. In frightening echoes of Stalingrad a year earlier, Hitler forbade Stemmermann from any breakout and instead insisted on a relief column advancing and reaching them. The Nazi dictator would simply not give up his last toehold on the Dnieper. Erich von Manstein, in charge of Army Group South, launched a hasty two-pronged attack on 1 February with the majority of five panzer divisions involved (his entire Army Group only fielded nine including the Wiking). Two years before, such a force would have shaken the Soviets to their core, but now they could counter the assault with no fewer than six tank corps, one mechanised corps and four infantry corps of their own. The attack was halted in a week, even as the Wiking and the Wallonien were being roughly pushed off the Dnieper. The Walloon veteran, SS-Standartenoberjunker Raymond Lemaire had only just rejoined his unit after specialist assault pioneer training in Dresden:

> We pioneers had to occupy some of the infantry positions to maintain the line. After numerous actions and battles, I was the only NCO left in my platoon. The Soviets attacked our sector again on 30 January, but in two hours of hand-to-hand and close-quarter fighting we managed to beat them off. However, I was seriously wounded by grenade splinters in both legs in the process. Being unable to walk after a few hours I was evacuated by plane out of the Pocket.

Lemaire was one of the lucky ones; of his 2,000 comrades only 632 would eventually walk out alive from the Pocket. The Wiking's Scandinavians fared little better. Still concentrated in the grenadier companies, especially in the Germania, dozens of the remaining Danes, Norwegians and Swedes were killed or wounded in the constant Soviet assaults. It wasn't just the fighting that was bitter either, the weather was horrendous. All veterans remark on it. The open Ukrainian steppe was swept by freezing winds and blizzards that saw the thermometer plunge to twenty degrees C below zero. Just as at Demyansk, two years before, the Red air force tried to flatten every building to deny the trapped men any shelter. Again, just as at Demyansk, the crews of the Luftwaffe's overworked transport fleet landed their ageing Junker Ju-52 planes onto improvised airfields to bring in supplies and ferry out the injured. In the 19 days of the battle they would fly in almost 868 tons of ammunition and 82,949 gallons of fuel, while flying out 4,161 wounded soldiers. Doing so would cost dozens of aircraft and their crews, and gut Germany's remaining air transport capability. The Belgian Walloon volunteer and prominent pre-war leader of the Cristus Rex Party, Léon Degrelle, wrote: 'Every day our "Auntie" Ju's [Junkers Ju-52] were shot down after a few minutes of flight, they would fall down in flames amid the screams of the wounded who were being grilled alive.'

When the snow stopped a thaw would set in and turn the roads, already poor, into mud baths. Panzers would sink up to their side armour in the morass, to become stuck as if on flypaper. One of the Leibstandarte troopers in the relief columns said:

The fighting began in mud literally knee-deep. The heavy Ukrainian earth had mixed with snow to create a sticky mess. Even with a light nocturnal frost it hardened to hold vehicles tight and killed any chance of moving them again. Even tracked vehicles got hopelessly stuck in this lava-like mud.

Bad as things were for von Manstein's relief troops, conditions inside the Pocket were even worse as the battle neared the end of its second week. Degrelle:

The tanks hadn't come. The surrounded troops had held out as long as there was hope. Now everything was falling to pieces. We were down to our last cartridges. Since Sunday the quartermasters hadn't any food. The wounded were dying by the hundreds from exposure and loss of blood. We were suffocating under the enemy pressure.

One last effort

Refusing to give in, von Manstein planned one last throw of the dice. Gathering all eight of his available panzer divisions; the 1st, 3rd, 11th, 13th, 14th, 16th, 17th and the 1st SS-Panzer Leibstandarte, he launched them northeast towards Lysyanka and its precious bridge over the Gniloy Tikich. At the same time, Stemmermann had moved his entire force south-west in a 'wandering pocket' formation to the village of Shanderovka, and there stubbornly held a perimeter waiting to break out. The village and its environs quickly became a hell-hole, crammed with desperate soldiers, more than two thousand wounded, hosts of Ukrainian camp-followers and all the detritus of an army in disintegration. SS-Unterscharführer Schorsch Neuber of the Wiking's Signals Battalion (SS-Panzer Nachrichtung-Abteilung 5) recalled those last days: 'We were tortured by hunger. For days we hadn't anything to eat. Snow was our only sustenance. The last ration we received was laughingly small and was a small frozen-together lump of rice for eight men.'

But finally, after almost three weeks of the bitterest fighting, salvation was close. Battling through horrendous conditions and massed opposition, the armoured might of Army Group South was at last approaching the Pocket. The same Auntie Ju's supplying the Pocket were also flying just feet off the ground near the relief columns and literally pushing 50 gallon drums of fuel out the doors to fall into the snow and mud to keep the panzers rolling.

Inside the Pocket all was action, as the divisions were moved and assembled in preparation to head west. Stemmermann placed the Wiking, as his only armoured force, in the vanguard of the break-out, and on 16 February, with von Manstein's panzers less than five kilometres away, he gave the order to attack. But first he gave the order every commander dreaded – 'leave the wounded.' It had to be done, yet every soldier railed against it – after all it could be them, and those men were their friends. Every member of the Ostheer feared what would happen to them if they fell into Soviet hands, and especially if they were wounded, such an order was seen as tantamount to a death sentence. Most units disregarded it, including the Wiking, whose Chief Medical Officer, Dr Thon, put more than 130 seriously wounded men onto *panje* carts (local Russian sleds usually pulled by steppe ponies) for the trek west.

Between the beleaguered grenadiers and their would-be saviours was a dominating feature, a prominent hill with long gently sloping sides and called by its spot height, Hill 239. Control of the hill was vital. With it, the trapped Group Stemmermann could withdraw in relative safety to Lysyanka and its vital bridge. Without it, everybody would have to try and escape through a wall of Soviet fire. Unfortunately, after capturing it in a daring assault, it had had to be given up by Captain Walter Scherff's small battlegroup from the 1st Panzer Division. His few remaining Tigers and grenadiers weren't strong enough to hold the feature against the massing Soviets. The end result for Stemmermann's men would be slaughter.

On being given the command, 'Password Freedom', the Wiking's remaining panzers and assault guns thrust southeast out of Shanderovka to establish the escape corridor. Having succeeded in smashing a hole through the Russians, in an act of inconceivable bravery, Köller then turned his men round and headed back into the Pocket to cover the withdrawal. Not a single panzer would make it back to German lines. Léon Degrelle, who himself would be awarded the Knight's Cross for his actions at Cherkassy, witnessed the about-turn:

> The faces of those young tankers were admirable. Clothed in short black jackets with silver trim, their heads and shoulders protruding from their turrets, they knew they were going to die. Several proudly wore the tricolour ribbon and the large black and silver Knight's Cross around their necks, a glittering target for the enemy as they ploughed up the snow with their treads and departed through the tangle of our retreating army.

In unforgettable scenes, close on 45,000 Army and SS men almost stampeded the few kilometeres to Lysyanka and safety. The Soviets realised their prey might elude them and flooded the area with tanks, cavalry, artillery and infantry. In a little over 24 hours thousands of men were butchered in an area of less than four square kilometres. Soviet tanks ran amok over anything they saw, crushing the wounded in ambulances and carts, and the Germans had almost nothing to stop them with. Red Army horsemen from the 5th Guards Cavalry Corps joined in the carnage, hunting down groups of stragglers desperate to reach the river. Chaos reigned and command broke down. It was something no one who saw it, like Degrelle, would ever forget:

> A wave of Soviet tanks overtook the first vehicles and caught more than half the convoy. The wave advanced through the carts, breaking them under our eyes, one by one like boxes of matches, crushing the wounded and the dying horses … We had a moment's respite when the tanks got jammed in the procession and were trying to get clear of the tangle of hundreds of vehicles beneath their tracks.

Dr Thon and the Wiking wounded were part of this convoy; a bare dozen survived the slaughter. Even the Russians were awed by the sheer scale of the horror. One of Koniev's own staff, Major Kampov wrote of that day:

> Hundreds and hundreds of cavalry were hacking at them with their sabres, and massacred the Fritzies as no one had ever been massacred by cavalry before. There was no time to take prisoners. It was the kind of carnage that nothing could stop till it was over. I had been at Stalingrad, but never had I seen such concentrated slaughter as in the fields and ravines of that small bit of country.

Some of Stemmermann's force made it to Lysyanka and its bridge, but most did not, and found themselves on the wrong side of a very fast flowing, icy cold, eight-metre-wide river – the Gniloy Tikich. Gille, leading some 4,500 Wiking soldiers and a host of other troops, was among those who did not reach the bridge. In an attempt to cross over he ordered an armoured personnel carrier driven into the river to form a breakwater, but it was swept away by the current. Undeterred, he organised human chains as well as using any horses that could be found. Striding up and down the river bank in his fur jacket with walking stick in hand, he and his staff organised and encouraged the men and somehow got the vast majority to safety on the western bank.

Aftermath

As the survivors from the Pocket streamed into Lysyanka they were met by the welcoming arms of their comrades from the 1st Panzer and the Leibstandarte. However, there was no immediate rest as they were sent plodding on farther westwards in their sodden uniforms, which were rapidly freezing to their starved bodies. The bridgehead was too weak, and all too soon the relief column would have to withdraw. Having thought their ordeal was over, the sense of disappointment among survivors was palpable. Nevertheless, tens of thousands of men had indeed cheated death and capture. Of the 56,000 soldiers encircled at the beginning of the battle just over 40,000 had gotten out, either in the Ju's or on foot. Their commander, the monocled Wilhelm Stemmermann, was not among them. In the breakout he had commandeered a Wiking staff car driven by SS-Rottenführer Klenne, which had then been hit by Soviet anti-tank fire. He was lacerated by shrapnel and killed instantly. When his corpse was found by the Soviets they described him as 'a little old man with grey hair'.

The Danish Knight's Cross winner Sören Kam celebrating his award with a drink. Kam was a veteran of the Winter War and the Frikorps Danmark before joining the Wiking. He won the Knight's Cross in 1945 for bravery during the Wiking's battles in Poland's 'Wet Triangle' in front of Warsaw. (James Macleod)

As for his command, *Graf* von Rittberg's Bavarian/Austrian 88th Infantry Division was reduced to just 3,280 troopers, while Kurt Kruse's Hessian 389th Infantry Division suffered even worse and could only muster 1,932 men. As for the Wiking, its roll call had been almost halved to 8,278 after all the wounded were evacuated. This total included the remnants of the Wallonien, but not its commander Lucien Lippert, who had died after being shot in the stomach by a Soviet sniper in the fighting at the village of Novo Buda on the 13th. As for the Scandinavians, three Norwegian NCOs – the Germania's Alf Fjeld and Helge Tollefsen, and the Westland's Inge Martin Bakken – were all awarded the Iron Cross 1st Class for their part in the battle. Several Danes also distinguished themselves including the Winter War veteran Robert Hansen, who would become a company commander after the battle, and the Danish NCO, Sören Kam, who went on to become one of the three Danes to win the Knight's Cross during the war.

The battle of the Cherkassy Pocket was now over. The Ostheer had avoided a mini-Stalingrad, but had suffered thousands of casualties and lost huge amounts of equipment. Army Group South had been pushed back even farther west, and more importantly its entire panzer force had been bled white. Von Mainstein's panzer-arm had not yet recovered from the defeat at Kursk the previous summer, and had now lost more than 300 precious tanks lying wrecked and abandoned around Korsun, Shanderovka and Lysyanka. The battle was almost Erich von Manstein's last hurrah. He gave one last masterclass by saving Hube's First Panzer Army from annihilation following its encirclement in March at Kamenets-Podolsk; and then Hitler had had enough of a man who stubbornly failed to agree with his every idiocy. The architect of Germany's victory on the Meuse in 1940, the conqueror of Sevastopol in 1942, the magician who performed the 'miracle on the Donets' in 1943 and now the saviour of Cherkassy and Kamenets-Podolsk, was told a few weeks later by his commander-in-chief that his services were no longer required. He would play no further part in World War II.

No rest at Kovel

The same could not be said for the Scandinavians of the Wiking. Unlike their German comrades they were allowed some home leave following their escape from Cherkassy, an exception which did not go down well in the division. However the situation at the Front was so grave, the shattered Wiking could not be sent to the West to reform. Instead it was mustered to the north in Lublin, in Poland near the Soviet border, and then sent straight back east to the Russian city of Kovel in the Pripet Marshes to try and hold it against the still-advancing Red Army. Most of Wiking's panzer regiment, and two armoured infantry battalions, had missed Cherkassy as they were away being refitted, they now hurried eastwards to rejoin their comrades. In the meantime, Gille led his remaining emaciated grenadier battalions to the endangered city. Gille himself had been awarded the Swords (the *Schwerter*) to his Knight's Cross following Cherkassy, and would soon become only the 27th man in the entire Wehrmacht to be awarded the Diamonds (the *Brillanten*) as a further honour. The only other recipient in the Waffen-SS of this coveted decoration was the black guard's most senior commander of the entire war, Sepp Dietrich himself.

Gille's plan at Kovel was to defend the city through a defensive blockade out to the east, trading space for time to allow Wiking's heavy troops to catch up. But he had no such luck. The Red Army was advancing too quickly, and the Wiking arrived to find itself being surrounded once more. One of his staff officers, SS-Hauptsturmführer Westphal who had witnessed Stemmermann's death in the Pocket and had ended up swimming the Gniloy Tikich to escape, observed the unfolding situation: 'As evening fell we gradually realised that we were sitting in a city which was slowly but surely being surrounded on all sides by enemy forces.'

Belatedly the panzers arrived, and SS-Obersturmführer Karl Nicolussi-Leck led his brand-new Panther company on a drive to reach the besieged city on 30 March. Despite being ordered to turn back owing to ferocious resistance, Nicolussi-Leck pressed on and reached his beleaguered comrades. He was awarded the Knight's Cross for his leadership and courage. It was to no avail though, the city was still cut off and once again the Wiking was having to be re-supplied by air.

The calm and the storm

Along with elements of the 4th and 5th Panzer Divisions and the 131st Infantry Division, the Wiking stubbornly held the city against its Red Army attackers for the best part of the next three months. The Soviet's Ukrainian offensive had driven a huge wedge into the Ostheer's front, and Hitler feared the salient would be used as a launch-pad for the inevitable Russian summer assault. Such an attack could drive north to the Baltic and cut off both Army Group Centre and Army Group North in the biggest encirclement in history. If this happened, the war really would be over by Christmas and Nazi Germany defeated. Kovel stood at the northern hinge of the bulge, and OKW was determined to hold it so any Soviet assault could then be hit in its vulnerable flank. Desperately needed equipment was shipped to the Wiking to ready it for the anticipated offensive, and almost all of the Ostheer's precious panzers were concentrated nearby in preparation. But the Germans got it wrong. The blow came not in the south in the Ukraine, but in Belorussia against a weakened Army Group Centre. The Wiking could initially do nothing but watch, horrified, as the Red Army juggernaut tore a full quarter of the Third Reich's total military strength to shreds to their north. As the full scale of STAVKA's Operation Bagration became clear, the OKW transferred units from Army Group North Ukraine (AGNU) to try and stem the tide. (Army Group South had been split into Army Group North Ukraine under Walther Model and its southern neighbour Army Group A under Ferdinand Schörner.) In so doing they weakened the North Ukraine just as Koniev launched his enormously powerful 1st Ukrainian Front onto the offensive. With 1,600 tanks, supported by 15,000 artillery pieces and 2,800 aircraft, the Soviets crashed into the Wiking and its compatriots, who could only muster around half the Red Army force.

Maciejov and Ulf-Ola Olin

Right on the frontline, an armada of Soviet tanks pressed westwards from Kovel towards the Polish border. Reaching the tiny village of Maciejov on the Bug River, the Russians followed their doctrine and carried out a reconnaissance in force, sending a number of T-34 tanks forward to sniff out any lurking Germans. They were right to be watchful. Ahead of them lay a company of Wiking Panthers commanded by one of the last Finns serving in the Waffen-SS, SS-Obersturmführer Ulf-Ola Olin. Getting his panzers into protected hull-down positions with barely their turrets showing, the Panthers long-barrelled, 75mm high-velocity guns had a panoramic view of the ground in front of them. Hours of training on the tank firing ranges would now pay off, as Olin ordered his crews to let the recce tanks past and tempt the main body out of the village and into the killing ground in front of the Wiking guns. Reassured that all was well, the mass of T-34s streamed out of Maciejov to continue their headlong advance northwest. Olin gave the order 'FIRE!' and the Panthers' guns barked. Tank after tank was hit, turrets were blown off, ammunition exploded, burning crewmen ran screaming from their wrecked vehicles to die horribly in the oil-slicked grass. The Soviet tanks were not equipped with radios, all messages were relayed by commanders using flags just like in old-fashioned warships, and so were unable to respond effectively to the hail of armour-piercing rounds slamming into them. Olin's company was joined by other panzers from the 4th and 5th Panzer Divisions, and together they mercilessly pounded the Russians. The Wiking's artillery was called in to add to the carnage and cut off any Soviet retreat, and in a few hours of battle the attackers were cut to ribbons. A few T-34s managed to escape back east, but the majority lay burning on the plain at Maciejov, victims of the Germans' superlative gunnery. The best part of an entire Red Army tank corps, 103 tanks in all, had fallen to Olin and his men. They were not alone. All in all some 295 Russian tanks fell to German guns as they tried to cross the River Bug. But the cruel truth was that actions like this were less than sideshows that summer.

By now the Wiking could barely muster a hundred Scandinavians in its ranks, Olin being one. Some more would return from convalescence, others from specialist courses or leave, and even a tiny number of new recruits would arrive, but overall the Wiking was no longer a heartland for the Nordic Waffen-SS. However, it would fight on to the bitter end, as would the Danes, Norwegians, Swedes and Finns in its ranks. The focus was now firmly on the Nordland and the epic summer campaign about to start.

The celebrated Finnish SS volunteer and hugely successful Wiking panzer commander, Ulf-Ola Olin.

North on the Narva – Egon Christophersen

For the Nordland and its men, far to the north, spring had brought a welcome respite. The Red Army was content to sit on the Narva's eastern bank carrying out patrolling and the occasional snap artillery shoot, and nothing more. The Danmark and Nederland maintained their toehold in Russia at the far end of the bridgehead, while the Corps worked feverishly to strengthen the defences for the next Soviet offensive. The two sides also continued to probe each other, search out potential weak spots, take prisoners for interrogation, and all in all make life difficult for each other.

Danmark had built a strongpoint, Outpost Sunshine, at the far southeastern end of their positions to facilitate just that. An extensive earthwork fortified with logs and firing points, the regiment's whole 7th Company garrisoned it. The Russians launched a surprise attack on 12 June that overwhelmed the position, killed most of the defenders and sent the remainder tumbling back to the main line. One of the survivors was the Danish ex-Wiking NCO, SS-Unterscharführer Egon Christophersen, who rallied a handful of men and immediately counter-attacked. Such was the ferocity of the assault the Russians upped and fled leaving Sunshine back in Danish hands. Christophersen was commended for his bravery and leadership and on 11 July 1944 became the first ever Scandinavian winner of that most coveted award, the Knight's Cross. Only two other Scandinavian SS men, both Danes like Christophersen, would join him in that exclusive club of Knight's Cross winners (the *Ritterkreuzträgers* who have a members association all of their own) by the end of the war.

Men like Christophersen could hold for now, but having already lost the river as a defensible barrier, a new line had to be established about 20 kilometres back linking the Gulf of Finland all the way down south to Lake Peipus. Historic features, such as the aptly-named eighteenth-century fortification the Swedish Wall, were incorporated into the fortifications dubbed the 'Tannenberg Line'. Part of the Tannenberg Line were three hills of the Estonian Blue Mountain range; from east to west they were Orphanage Hill (so-called because of the deserted orphanage on its summit), Grenadier Hill, and lastly, Hill 69.9, named after its spot height and sometimes also called Love's Hill (in German – *Kinderheim-Höhe, Grenadier-Höhe,* and *69.9-Höhe* or *Liebes-Höhe*). These hills, with their gentle slopes and wooded tops, would be the key battleground in the coming struggle. They dominated the main Narva-Reval road network, as well as the railroad, as they emerged from the woods near the river. To the north was the Swedish Wall and to the south, swamps. Both would greatly hinder the movement of armour. If the Red Army could achieve a break-through on the road, they could get behind the whole Corps and cut off large parts of Army Group North from any retreat. The Russians could see it and so of course could Felix Steiner. The Norge's two battalions held the sector from the far south, where they linked in with the Army's veteran 58th Infantry Division, up to and including Grenadier Hill which it jointly garrisoned with the Danmark. The Danmark, and Estonian SS men from the 20th SS-Division, also defended Hill 69.9. To hold Orphanage Hill, as well as provide extra muscle for Grenadier Hill, Steiner asked for rein-forcements and was sent a 500-man battlegroup (*Kampfgruppe Rehmann*) from the reforming Flemish SS-Assault Brigade Langemarck equipped with three 75mm anti-tank guns.

More than 340 years earlier a young and bullish Tsar Peter the Great faced a Swedish army and its Estonian and German allies on the Narva, as the Russians sought to invade Livonia (as the country was then known) and destroy the powerful Swedish empire in The Great Northern War. The result was bloody humiliation, as the heavily outnumbered Swedes thrashed their Russian foes and captured their entire artillery park. Livonia was saved from Russian occupation for another decade. This time round the forces involved were of an altogether different magnitude, the Swedes numbered in their dozens and not thousands, but the parallels were still there. Would history repeat itself, could the Russians be held?

A Norge Regiment anti-tank gun crew during the Narva fighting, 1944. (Erik Wiborg)

Nordland officers at the Narva 1944, from left; unknown, the Norwegian Olaf Wahlmann, the German Hans Hoff, and the Norwegian Frode Halle. (Erik Wiborg)

In the meantime the Nordland's achievements during the early spring battles were recognised firstly by the award on 12 March to Fritz von Scholz of the Oakleaves (the *Eichenlauben*) to his Knight's Cross, and then by his promotion to SS-Gruppenführer on the occasion of Hitler's birthday on 20 April.

The Tannenberg Line

On 22 June the main Red Army summer offensive hit Army Group Centre like a tidal wave and swept it away. Over the next six weeks Operation Bagration liberated all of Belorussia and swathes of Poland inflicting the largest ever defeat on German arms in recorded history. Some 35 divisions, more than 350,000 men all told, would be wiped off the Wehrmacht's order of battle. The losses even dwarfed Stalingrad, and the Germans would never recover. As the Wiking and other formations from Army Group North Ukraine were sent north, so OKW also pillaged Army Group North units to send south to try and stem the Russian advance. Again as with AGNU, this left the North severely weakened. Grasser, Steiner and von Scholz looked across the Narva with trepidation as they saw the Soviets remorselessly build up their strength in the first days of July. The failed bomb attempt on Hitler's life on the 20th exacerbated the situation as command and control across the Wehrmacht seemed paralysed in a welter of recriminations.

An order from the Corps to withdraw the Nordland to the Tannenberg Line was cancelled by Steiner's Chief-of-Staff, Joachim Ziegler, as the Danmark was caught up in beating off battalion-sized Soviet incursions into its lines. Having done that, and taken 71 casualties into the bargain, Ziegler finally gave the withdrawal order and at 2330hrs on the night of 24 July the Germans, Scandinavians and Dutchmen of the Nordland and Nederland began to move back from the city and its river to the pre-prepared defences of the Tannenberg. The Russians guessed what was happening immediately and threw themselves forward. The result was a disaster. A withdrawal in contact, as an operation of war, is recognised among professional soldiers as the hardest thing to successfully carry out, with calamity never more than a heartbeat away. That night the Germanic Corps was unlucky. The Scandinavians managed to find their way through the woods in the dark and reach their allotted trenches but the Dutch SS-Panzergrenadier Regiment 48 General Seyffardt was not so fortunate. Caught in the open by the Soviet advance guard it was butchered along with its commander, Richard Benner. Only around 20 per cent of its members escaped. Just days later the Finnish SS Battalion's old boss, Hans Collani, would be wounded and take his own life, leading General Seyffardt's sister regiment, the De Ruyter. At the Line itself, all was confusion as men and equipment arrived pell-mell. With the Russians hot on their heels, troops were hastily marshalled into the defences and became hopelessly mixed-up.

The climax of Narva

Up until then the fighting at Narva had resembled more a campaign that had gone on for several months rather than a 'conventional' battle that was won or lost in days. That was about to change over the next four days as the fate of Army Group North was effectively in the hands of the Nordland and its Dutch, Flemish and Estonian allies. The Scandinavian Waffen-SS was now at the very fulcrum of Hitler's war with the Soviet Union.

As the General Seyffardt was being wiped out on the 25th, the Nordland was preparing itself for battle. The summer nights that far north are short and it had been light since 4am on the 26th, but the Russians did not begin their assault on Orphanage Hill until gone midday. When they did, the fighting was savage. The Flemings' German commander, Wilhelm Rehmann, took himself to the rear with a 'wound' that Steiner himself dismissed as trivial. The young Flemish nationalist, Georg D'Haese, took over in time to see almost every other Flemish officer killed including his two fellow company commanders, Frans Swinnen and Henri Van Mol. Despite this the defenders held on, but the next day the Soviets launched a massive assault on the heights that threw the Flemings off Orphanage Hill. Steiner ordered an immediate counter-attack, and the Norwegian company commander Thomas Hvistendahl led his Norge men forward to try and retake the hill, reinforced by D'Haese. Some sixty Flemings were stranded in the abandoned orphanage itself, and they willed their rescuers on as they twice tried to reach them in the teeth of Soviet fire. It was no use. The grenadiers were not strong enough and during the night the beleaguered SS men were wiped out to the last man.

As dawn broke on the morning of the 28th, everyone sensed this was to be the decisive day. The Soviet Front Commander, Govorov, concentrated troops from no less than six tank brigades and 11 rifle divisions in the lee of Orphanage Hill ready to sweep west and take Grenadier, then 69.9 and finally break III SS-Germanic Panzer Corps's resistance. The Russians carried out their usual huge artillery barrage to soften up the defenders and then poured forward. In front of them stood a lone, five-foot-four-inch railway worker's son from Kemptich in Flanders, Remy Schrijnen, and his 75mm PAK gun. In the next hour Schrijnen single-handedly destroyed seven Soviet tanks, including three mighty Joseph Stalin

JS-2s (Joseph Stalin tanks had very thick armour and a truly enormous 122mm main gun, the shells of which weighed 25 pounds) and success-fully stalled the whole attack. Schrijnen was badly wounded and knocked unconscious when his gun was finally wrecked by a tank round, but he had saved Grenadier Hill and was awarded the Knight's Cross for his bravery. During the same morning's fighting, Fritz von Scholz was hit in the head by a shell splinter. Rushed off to a field hospital, there was noth-ing the doctors could do and he died the next day from his injuries. He was posthumously given the Swords to his Knight's Cross.

Govorov would not give up and on 29 July he once more sent his tank-ers into battle to break the Nordland's line. By now the trenches were filled with dead Scandinavians, Estonians and Dutchmen, and the survi-vors were exhausted. Just as all seemed lost, the ex-Wiking artillery officer, SS-Obersturmbannführer Paul-Albert Kausch, led every last one of the Hermann von Salza's panzers in a desperate counter-attack. Supported by Norge's grenadiers in particular, the von Salza's Panthers, Mark IVs and *Sturmgeschütze* (turretless self-propelled assault guns) charged forward. At the end of the day 113 Russian tanks were left blazing around the three hills; and a badly wounded and barely-conscious Remy Schrijnen was res-cued from his wrecked gun-pit.

Knight's Cross winners from the Narva at the award ceremony on 23 August 1944. From left, the Estonian SS officer Harald Riipalu, the commander of the Nordland's Hermann von Salza panzer battalion Obersturmbannführer Paul-Albert Kausch, Schluetter and Hans Collani's Adjutant from the Dutch SS De Ruyter Regiment, Karl-Heinz Ertel. Ertel also served alongside Collani in the Finnish SS Battalion. (James Macleod)

Narva was held and the Red Army frustrated. The Ostheer might have been in the process of losing Belorussia, the remainder of the Ukraine and swathes of Poland, but in the far north the Front was safe, at least for a while. In recognition of the magnificent performance of all of his men, Felix Steiner was awarded the Swords to his Knight's Cross. Ferdinand Schörner, who had left Army Group A in the south to take over Army Group North, wrote the recommendation:

> SS-Obergruppenführer Steiner has achieved with his III Germanic SS-Panzer Corps a defensive success for the entire Eastern Front. With his two weak divisions and one brigade he held the front in Narva unbreakable against the storming 2nd Russian Shock Army and 8th Army with 11 divisions and six tank brigades. More than 1,020 tanks were destroyed. The enemy suffered heavy losses. His personal decisiveness, and his brave and versatile battle leadership, deserve special recognition.

Old Fritz's successor

With von Scholz dead, his place was taken by the Corps Chief-of-Staff, the impressively tall 40 year old Spanish Civil War veteran, Joachim Ziegler. Ziegler was a career Army officer, and had only officially been transferred to the Waffen-SS a few days before he was appointed to lead the Nordland. Promoted to SS-Brigadeführer, this experienced and courageous officer would command the division almost to the very end of the war.

Scandinavian recruitment dries up

Having been through two of the most savage battles the Russian Front had witnessed, both the Nordland and Wiking were desperate for fresh blood. The grenadier companies in particular were threadbare, and although men returning from leave and injury would do a little to fill the gaps, it was more of a sticking plaster. What was really needed was a new wave of volunteers from Scandinavia. No such wave was forthcoming. No amount of propaganda could hide the fact that the Third Reich was losing the war, and after almost five years of occupation, unrest was growing in Denmark and Norway.

Denmark's so-called 'model occupation' was falling apart. The King made no secret of his loathing for the Nazis and led a dignified, passive opposition to the Germans. Many of his subjects took matters further and industrial sabotage in particular became commonplace. Civil disturbance reached its height in June of 1944 with the Copenhagen General Strike called after the Germans imposed a curfew. In a hitherto unheard of gesture, the working population of Denmark's capital downed tools and went onto the streets to protest. The authorities were helpless to stop it and chaos reigned for days. The result was more severe repression, and needless to say this did not encourage recruits to come forward. Pro-Nazis were now openly vilified, support for the DNSAP had collapsed, and recruiting pools such as the party's youth wing had been mined out. Frits Clausen, frustrated in his ambition to lead his country, had increasingly turned to drink. He enlisted in the Waffen-SS, was admitted to hospital for alcoholism and subsequently stepped down as Party leader in May. His fall from grace would be complete that November when he was expelled from the Party. The Danish armed forces had already been disbanded earlier in the year, and they were followed by the police in September. From now onwards public order would be kept by the Hipo Corps (*Hilfspolizei Korpset* – a new uniformed force based on the intelligence sections of Knud Martinsen's Schalburg Corps). The Corps would wage an increasingly bitter war against the Resistance in the dying days of the conflict, with arson attacks and vicious tit-for-tat murders.

Up in Norway the situation was similar, with the Resistance growing in strength and the Germans becoming more and more heavy-handed to keep order. Quisling had taken over government, as Minister President, only to fail spectacularly, with clumsy attempts to radicalise the population falling flat, especially when he clashed with the unions and the teachers. Again, this adversely affected recruitment among the general population, while the barrel of the Far Right had just about been scraped. The SS recruiting office in Oslo reported that the GSSN, for example, had 1,247 registered members at the end of September, but 330 were already at the Front, 245 were in the police and 511 were in emergency units at home. That left just 161 men uncommitted. It also stated that of the 4,133 Norwegians it had recruited already, only 1,434 remained in service, 606 had been killed and 2,043 discharged at the end of their contract term. The recruiters went on to say that 1944 had been a very slow year with only a handful of men coming forward. The well, never deep, had just about dried up.

The Wiking on the Vistula

Ulf-Ola Olin and his men had bloodied the Red Army's nose on the Bug, but the Red Army's massive 1st Ukrainian Front pressed on regardless and succeeded in crossing the Vistula (*Weichsel* in German) at Baranow and Sandomierz about 100 miles south of Warsaw, and Magnuszew just 20 miles southeast of the city. The Reich's response to this deadly threat was to create the *IV SS-Panzer Corps*, comprising the 3rd SS-Panzer Division Totenkopf and the Wiking, under Gille's command. His place with the Wiking was meant to be taken by the 35 year-old Bavarian Knight's Cross winner, Dr Eduard Deisenhofer, but the ex-Totenkopf man went instead to the 17th SS-Panzergrenadier Division Götz von Berlichingen, before being killed in action in Arnswalde in 1945 whilst on his way to take command of the 15th Latvian SS Division. In his absence, leadership of the Wiking went to one of its most distinguished old boys, Hans Mühlenkamp. The Luftwaffe's Hermann Goering Panzer Division and the Army's 19th Panzer Division were then combined with the new Corps to establish a formidable armoured force. Together, they pinned the Soviets back into their bridge-head at Sandomierz, although they could not destroy it, and then switched north to savage the Soviet 2nd Tank Army in front of Warsaw itself in the so-called 'Wet Triangle'. The battle saw the Russians lose more than 170 tanks, 3,000 men killed and 6,000 taken prisoner.

Wounded during the fighting was the young Norwegian SS-Untersturmführer, Fredrik Jensen. Commanding the Germania's 7th Company, the tall, blond Jensen had already earned the Iron Cross 1st Class in the Ukraine the previous summer. His bravery in front of Warsaw won him the German Cross in Gold, confirmed in December, and although his injuries prevented him from returning to the Front again, the award would be enough to make him the highest-decorated Norwegian Waffen-SS volunteer of the war. His place with the 7th Company would be taken by yet another Norwegian Bad Tölz graduate and old Nordland Regiment veteran, Arne Gunnar Smith, who would be killed himself five days later.

The Warsaw Uprising

Behind the Corps, Warsaw rose in revolt on 1 August. After years of brutal occupation, the Polish Home Army (the *Armija Krajowa* or AK for short) under the leadership of General Duke Tadeusz Komorowski, codenamed Bor, attacked key points across the capital. For the next 63 days some of the most horrific fighting of the war would rage in one of Europe's most beautiful cities. Under the leadership of the head of Nazi Germany's anti-partisan forces, Erich von dem Bach-Zelewski, a mixed force of Army and Waffen-SS (which included Azeris, Cossacks, Ukrainians and Oskar Dirlewanger's convicts) forsook every accepted rule of war and butch-ered, raped and burnt their way to victory and infamy.

Above left: A portrait of the most highly decorated Norwegian Waffen-SS volunteer of the war, the Germania Regiment's Fredrik Jensen. (James Macleod)

Above right: The Norwegian Wiking volunteer Fredrik Jensen relaxes in the sun. He won the German Cross in Gold as well as the Iron Cross. Today he lives in Spain. (James Macleod)

Controversy has raged ever since as to whether Stalin left the Polish patriots to their fate so as to prepare the ground for a post-war communist takeover, or if he had no such intent. On the balance of evidence it is absolutely clear, and Norman Davies's work on this is extremely powerful, that although the Red Army was exhausted, the Soviet dictator did indeed abandon Warsaw and watched with glee as thousands of potential Polish foes died manning the barricades.

The Wiking, the 'Wet Triangle' and Sören Kam

As for the Wiking, and its new stable mate the Totenkopf, the two SS panzer divisions continued to defy two entire Soviet armies in front of the city throughout the autumn and into the winter. In early October, Mühlenkamp left the Wiking to become the Inspector of the Waffen-SS Panzer Troops, and was succeeded by the Knight's Cross winner and ex-Das Reich and Totenkopf officer, Karl Ullrich. Ullrich would lead the Wiking for the remainder of the war. At the same time, to help keep the division up to strength, the reformed 1st Battalions of both the Norge and Danmark Regiments, now almost entirely made up of teenage German

Left: An earlier photograph of the Danish Waffen-SS volunteer Sören Kam, in the uniform of the paramilitary Schalburg Corps back in Denmark. Following the end of the war he settled in Germany, like many other foreign veterans, to escape persecution at home. (James Macleod)

Right: Unterstumführer Wolfgang Eldh, Swedish Adjutant of a German Battlegroup during the Latvia battles in July 1944. Eldh was badly wounded in the fighting at Dünaburg later the same month. (Lennart Westberg)

conscripts and unemployed Luftwaffe ground crew, were shipped from their Hammerstein training ground to the Polish front. Incorporated into the Wiking they would never serve with the Nordland. About 80 Danes and Norwegians were in the two battalions, evenly split between them, many of them by now being NCOs or officers.

Two such volunteers were the 19-year-old Norwegian Karl-Aagard Østvig, an officer in the Norge's 3rd Company, and the Danish platoon leader and ex-Frikorps veteran Sören Kam. Both were heavily involved in the vicious struggle in front of Warsaw, with Kam briefly having to take over command of his entire battalion when every other officer was either killed or wounded. He would become the second Dane to be awarded the Knight's Cross for his actions. Østvig too distinguished himself, but was not so lucky and died in the fighting.

Army Group North cut-off

Such was the strength of the Red Army in 1944, and the weakness of the Ostheer, that the STAVKA could resource constant attacks along the entire frontline from Narva in the north to the Crimea in the south, which the Germans could do little to stop. The destruction of Army Group Centre was the key, as with no available reserves it forced the OKW to draw troops from every other army group, so creating weak points. The Wiking may have helped halt the flood in front of Warsaw, and the Nordland had stopped the advance on the Narva dead in its tracks, but in the huge expanses of the Russian Front élite units, like those containing the Scandinavian Waffen-SS, were few and far between and the Red Army was everywhere. To Steiner's south, the Soviet 2nd Guards, 6th Guards and 51st Armies found just such a weak point and punched west taking Daugavpils, Panavezys and finally Siauliai before turning north where Colonel Kremer led his 8th Guards Rifle Brigade to the shores of the Baltic itself at Klapkalnice, to the west of Riga, at the end of July. The III Germanic SS-Panzer Corps had only just beaten the Russians at Narva (and won a staggering total of 29 Knight's Crosses doing so), and now found itself cut off in a giant pocket. That pocket was all of Estonia and most of Latvia, and in it were the 27 divisions and 500,000 men of two whole German armies – the Sixteenth and Eighteenth – basically Army Group North in its entirety. Without delay, the Germans had to push west to avoid disaster.

Estonia is abandoned

In the way that only Adolf Hitler could, a decision to order Army Group North to leave Estonia and rejoin the German frontline was delayed seemingly endlessly. Without doubt there was a moral dimension in leaving Estonia to its fate, for the Waffen-SS that would visibly manifest itself in its 20th Estonian Division, an excellent formation that would now effectively lose its *raison d'être*. But it was clear that the immorality of abandoning Estonia to Soviet brutality was not even on Hitler's short list. Absurdly, it was his old cry of 'to the last man and the last round', that had already cost Germany so dear, which framed his thinking. Only a personal plea from Schörner as the Army Group's commander could save it. Schörner told Hitler:

> The Front is undoubtedly broken at several places. The Estonians have run away again. They're simply going home, we have now lost two-thirds of the infantry force and we are deceiving ourselves if we think we are just going

to depend on the courage of the troops to take care of everything again. That cannot happen time after time! We are talking about the fate of an entire Army Group here!

It worked and Hitler relented. The go-ahead was given for Operation Aster, the break out from Estonia and withdrawal west into Latvia.

Carrying out a fighting retreat the III Germanic SS-Panzer Corps 'crabbed' south-westwards, elements went by sea from Pernau, but most of the men crammed onto any vehicle they could find and drove to freedom – albeit temporary. The Red Army desperately tried to take Riga, Latvia's capital, and cut off the retreat but in the end the corridor was held open for most of September and the Army Group survived. A new defence line was now set up in Latvia stretching from the base of the Courland peninsula south-west to Memel (now Klaipeda) and to the borders of the Reich itself. In the teeth of heavy Russian attacks, during which the ex-DNL veteran Peter Thomas Sandborg was killed commanding Norge's 11th Company, the Red Army reached the Baltic yet again and Army Group North was isolated once more: this time in the Courland peninsula.

The Courland Pocket

Courland, called *Kurland* in German and *Kurzeme* in Latvian, is Latvia's westernmost province and sticks out in a bulge into the Baltic Sea. A prosperous, fertile area, its traditional 'capital' was the city and port of

Six Swedish Waffen-SS officers at Mummasaara, Estonia, April 1944. From left: the war correspondents Untersturmführer Gösta Borg and Untersturmführer Hans-Caspar Krüger, the Nordland men Obersturmführer Hans-Gösta Pehrsson and Untersturmführer Gunnar-Erik Eklöf, and the war correspondents Untersturmführer Carl Svensson and StandartenOberjunker Thorkel Tillman. Tillman held joint German/Swedish nationality and would be killed in action in July of that year while serving with the Hitler Jugend Division in Normandy. (Lennart Westberg)

Liepaja (*Libau* in German) at its south-western corner, with its other major town being Ventspils (*Windau* in German) to the north at the mouth of the Venta River. Like much of the Baltic coastline it had been conquered by the Teutonic Knights, a medieval Germanic crusading order. The conquest had been followed by migration, and ethnic Germans dominated the local land-owning classes. Now this area would become the scene of no less than six separate battles, which would only stop with the surrender of the surviving 180,000 German troops on 8 May 1945.

Finland had now made peace with the Russians and was out of the war, so the Red Army in the north could concentrate all of its offensive power on the hapless men of Sixteenth and Eighteenth Armies. As the leaves fell across the Courland forests in October, the Germans and Scandinavians of the Nordland withdrew across the Daugava River, blowing its bridges and taking up position in the east of the peninsula, basing their defence on the villages of Bunkas and Jaunpils. Riga fell on the 15th as the Soviets instigated what became known as the First Battle of Courland. The 1st Shock, 6th Guards and 51st Armies pushed west from Riga, capturing Kemeri, and were then halted by determined resistance. The Nordland's own line was threatened on 27 October at Trekni, when the assaulting Soviets overran a nearby hill that dominated the surrounding landscape. Ziegler called on Pehrsson and his re-equipped Schwedenzug to re-take the hill immediately and secure the defence. Charging forward in their SPWs with all guns blazing, the Swedes and volksdeutsche roared into the assault. Soon the fighting became hand-to-hand as the SS grenadiers cleared the trenches of Red Army men. The charge was successful, but the Soviets counter-attacked time after time to take it back. The attacks were repelled for four days, but on the fifth day the Swedes were forced to retreat. Pehrsson's headquarters bunker was only a hundred metres behind the Front, and when he saw that the line had broken he grabbed every man he could find and charged. There were just 12 of them. The Soviets were dumbstruck, and retreated in confusion. Pehrsson and his men took more than a hundred prisoners that day. For his bravery and example the young Swede was awarded the much-sought after Roll of Honour Clasp of the German Army (the *Ehrenblattspange des deutschen Heeres*). But the price was high – half of all the Company's Swedish speakers were either killed or wounded in the fight. From now on the Swedish Waffen-SS numbered some 20 men all told. Pehrsson was not the only Scandinavian Waffen-SS man to distinguish himself during the first two battles of what became the Courland odyssey. The two Danes, Alfred Jonstrup and Per Sörensen, also earned the Roll of Honour Clasp for their bravery during a counter-attack. It cost the ex-Frikorps man Jonstrup half his jaw.

Overall, during the autumn fighting, casualties were very heavy on both sides. During September and October the four Red Army Fronts, (each roughly equivalent to a German Army in size) facing Army Group North's two armies, lost a total of 56,800 men killed and 202,500 wounded. Broken down, the Leningrad Front lost 6,000 killed and 22,500 wounded, the 1st Baltic 24,000 killed and 79,000 wounded, the 2nd Baltic 15,000 killed and 58,000 wounded and the 3rd Baltic 11,800 killed and 43,000 wounded. German casualties were not on that scale, but tens of thousands had been killed, wounded or taken prisoner, and unlike the Soviets, their losses could not be replaced.

In late October and mid-November the Red Army launched further attacks on the trapped Germans, the Second and Third Battles of Courland. The fighting was intense, with the Nordland's ever fewer panzers, armoured cars and half-tracks shuttled around the Pocket sealing off breakthrough after breakthrough. A German volunteer, SS-Rottenführer Albert Sudhoff, described some of the fighting:

> When I walked around a shed I was suddenly standing in front of a T-34 that was pointing its gun at me. Frightened, I fired my panzerfaust and rushed into a shed. Outside there was a tremendous noise and I landed in the midst of some guys. At first I couldn't see clearly but then I felt a sword-belt and a sidearm. I groped further and felt a sticky mess on my hands. It was a short while before I realised that comrades had gone into hiding before me and had not survived a direct hit ... two Russians appeared at the door and I threw myself beside my comrades and played dead. The Ivans shot blindly into the heap and disappeared. A shot had struck me in the upper thigh, and my leg went its own way and shook around.
>
> Then suddenly two SPW and a *Sanka* [German military ambulance] were outside ... I was unnoticed and crawled out of the shed as best I could. The Sanka was filled to the roof with wounded men, and about 100 metres away from me – then it took a direct hit and I saw with horror how the bodies flew through the air.

Another German volunteer, SS-Unterscharführer Eduard 'Edi' Janke, recalled the Third Battle of Courland especially. Janke was a platoon commander in the 4th Company of the Armoured Reconnaissance Battalion and knew Pehrsson and his Schwedenzug well. He was a combat veteran and already held the Infantry Assault Badge, the Wound Badge and the Close Combat Clasp:

> One day in December 1944 a heavy snowstorm began. I informed the whole platoon that the Russians would come in white camouflage and they should

The German Nordland Recce Battalion veteran, Eduard 'Edi' Janke. (James Macleod)

all be especially watchful. In the evening I lay down but was awakened by the shout of one of the machine-gunners; 'Unterscharführer, the Russians are here!' As I fired a white flare some 30 Red Army men stiffened at once. Immediately I shot off a second flare, then the machine-gunner on my right swung his gun round and fired a whole belt into them. When I fired my third flare we could see the Russians running away. Afterwards we found one wounded and nine dead Russians who had broken through our wire and had just planted a mine in front of us. I made a report and the company commander gave the alert gunner his own Iron Cross 1st Class. The name of the gunner was SS-Sturmmann Konrad.

Even as the fighting went on, civilians, the wounded and some designated units were taken out of the Pocket and back to Germany by sea. The latter included most of the Nordland's remaining armoured complement, who left their panzers to other units and headed back to Germany to be re-equipped. This, and combat attrition, reduced the Army Group's strength down to 250,000 men by year end. The Ostheer desperately needed those men to defend eastern Germany, but the Nazi dictator would not countenance withdrawing them, despite pleas from his own Chief of the General Staff, the panzer legend Heinz Guderian. In Hitler's own fevered imaginings, Schörner's men not only tied down huge numbers of Soviet troops that could be better used elsewhere, but also safeguarded Swedish iron ore imports, enabled the Kriegsmarine to test new designs of U-Boats in the Baltic, and held out the prospect of launching a future grand offensive. This was beyond self-delusion, it was a kind of madness.

The Scandinavian Waffen-SS in 1944

1944 had been a seminal year for the Wiking and the Nordland, with vital roles in two of the bloodiest battles of the Russo-German war – Cherkassy and the Narva. Transfers and casualties had eaten away at the Germanic character of the Wiking so that by year end it was essentially a German SS division. Men like Ulf-Ola Olin continued to fly the flag for the Scandinavian Waffen-SS in their former 'home' formation, but to all intents and purposes the Nordland was now the heart of the Nordic SS. That division had been tempered in the fire of Estonia and Latvia, and had proved itself a worthy successor. Both of these units were emblematic of the Norwegians, Danes, Finns and Swedes in the ranks of the black guards, but they were not the whole story. Far away in the frozen north there were hundreds of Norwegians wearing the double *sig* runes and fighting the Red Army, and they were part of the Scandinavian Waffen-SS as well.

Norwegians in the Nordland may have been pretty thin on the ground, but there was no such problem in manning the ranks to fight in Finland, as a member of either the SS-Ski Battalion Norge or the SS-Police Companies, which were designed to serve alongside the SS-Nord division. The end of 1943 had seen the old SS-Ski Company Norge reorganised and strengthened into a roughly 450-man battalion commanded by the decorated German SS officer, Richard Benner. Benner led his men through their work-up training in Oulu, Finland and organised them into an upgraded version of the original unit, with three infantry companies and a headquarters company that included platoons of combat engineers, signallers, supply troops and medics. What they did not have, unlike the other battalions in the SS-Nord, was a heavy weapons company as it was not considered necessary for their stated role of mobile warfare and long-range patrolling.

They were joined in Oulu by the 160 volunteers of Hoel's 2nd SS-Police Company, although Hoel soon handed over command to another ex-Norwegian Army officer, Lothar Lislegard. All too soon both units were sent north, to Karelia in north-eastern Finland, where they took up position on the Nord division's left flank near Lake Tiiksjarvi in January 1944. They were now part of Germany's 85,000 strong Twentieth Mountain Army (XX

Gebirgsarmee) led by the victor of Narvik, Edouard Dietl. Alongside them were the Finnish Army numbering barely 180,000 frontline soldiers – the lines were thin indeed. Opposing them was the Finns' old enemy from the Winter War, General Kirill Afanasievich Meretskov, and his Karelian Front comprising the Soviet 14th and 19th Armies, and farther south the much larger Leningrad Front. What became clear to the Norwegians very quickly was that this was not the Winter War anymore; the Red Army had changed and was now better led, better equipped and better trained. What had not changed was the Soviets' ability to field massive forces. Facing the Finns, Germans and their Norwegian allies were 450,000 men, 11,000 artillery pieces (including 1,000 of the dreaded Katyusha rockets), 530 aircraft and 800 tanks. The Germans lacked any and all of these resources. It was going to be a long, hard spring and summer in the far north of Europe.

Back with the SS-Police and the Norge, the men began to settle into their new positions and role, and their expertise on skis and natural affinity with both the few locals and the terrain, made them a very welcome addition to Lothar Debes's division. In the forested vastness of the landscape the Norwegians played an endless game of cat and mouse with their Red Army counterparts as both sides aggressively patrolled against each other. The men were quartered in huts and tents and even in wooden bunkers, but spent most of their time silently gliding through the forests on their skis looking for any Red Army troops bold enough to probe their positions.

Struggle at Schapk-Osero

The few pieces of high ground in the whole region were overwhelmingly in the hands of the Wehrmacht and Debes used them as a string of strongpoints to group his troops around and so dominate the surrounding countryside. This was probably the best tactic in the circumstances, but it did mean that there was the potential to be isolated, cut-off and annihilated. Heavy weapons and strong reserves could insure against this but the Germans lacked both. As it was, the SS-Police were grouped around a major strongpoint on the top of a hill called Schapk-Osero, with a single platoon semi-detached to the north on yet another hill, the Medevara. Like everybody else, the Company was almost alone in the wilderness, and found itself facing an enemy who was determined to attack across a broad front, seize the hills and control the area. After two months of stand-off and relative quiet, the Red Army threw an entire regiment against Schapk-Osero, outnumbering the defending Norwegians by 10 to 1. But Lislegard's men had not been idle and had used their time to cut down every tree for several hundred yards, giving them deadly fields of fire. As their Finnish cousins had done some three years previously, the Norwegian SS men let the assaulting Soviets get to within a few metres of their positions before unleashing a devastating wall of automatic fire. The result was carnage. Soviet dead were piled waist high on the slopes and the attack disintegrated in a welter of blood. Having failed in their initial aim, the Red Army had to settle for repeated probing and heavy use of artillery, gradually thinning the Norwegian ranks. Over the next few weeks casualties mounted, which included two of the four Norwegian platoon commanders, SS-Unterstürmführers Erling Markvik and Øystein Bech, both killed in action. Relieved from Schapk-Osero at the end of March, the remains of the Company were sent to the strongpoint at Sennosero, where they were merged with their countrymen of the SS-Ski Battalion Norge's 1st Company under Willi Amundsen.

The Norge had not been idle either, and had already joined with a battlegroup from the SS-Nord in destroying a growing concentration of Soviet troops in front of the divisional line in the same month. The attack itself was intended as a short, sharp, shock action, but quickly developed into a major engagement as the Soviets brought heavy artillery to bear and rushed reinforcements forward. Although outnumbered, the SS troopers continued their attack until the Soviets abandoned their positions.

Kaprolat and Hasselmann Hills – the Norwegian SS fights for its life

Following the fighting in March the decision was taken by the SS authorities that a Norwegian should lead the SS-Ski Battalion, so Benner was replaced by the 38-year-old SS-Hauptsturmführer Frode Halle, flown up from the Narva front at the beginning of April. Halle was ex-Norwegian Army, who had then served in the DNL before transferring across to the SS-Nordland's Norge Regiment. A professional, dedicated officer, he was an ideal choice to lead the battalion.

On arrival he found his new command holding an extremely long section of the line on the Nord's northern flank. The main anchors were two hills; Kaprolat and Hasselmann, which were protected by log-trunk bunkers and trenches covered in thick protective snow. Fritz Grondt's 3rd Company held Kaprolat, while SS-Obersturmführer Tor Holmesland Vik's 2nd Company was based on Hasselmann (Vik had replaced Martin Skjefstad). Grondt was the only German company commander in the battalion and when he was wounded he was replaced by none other than Bjarne Dramstad's old anti-tank commander from the DNL, Arnfinn

Vik. Getting wounded in April cut Vik's tenure short, and his place was taken by another Norwegian, SS-Untersturmführer Axel Steen, an ex-Norwegian Army officer and GSSN member. Constant patrolling had worn down the ranks, but the addition of Lislegard's SS policemen had helped keep the unit in some sort of shape. However, within a couple of months everything had changed as the SS-Police finished their term of enlistment and were sent home and SS-Obersturmführer Sophus Kahrs's 1st Company (Kahrs was ex-DNL and had taken over from Willi Amundsen) were detached to shore up the line elsewhere.

Halle and his remaining 300 men were now desperately vulnerable, and with the onset of summer, the defences on Kaprolat and Hasselmann lost the snow that hid them from view, softened the blast impact from artillery shells and provided the Norwegians with their mobility. Inexplicably, during this time of utmost danger, Halle (now promoted to SS-Sturmbannführer) was sent back to Norway on a staff assignment, and over a hundred of his men were also given home leave. On Kaprolat, Steen had just 57 men to man the defences.

Above left: Axel Steen, the Norwegian SS-Ski Norge officer in command of Kaprolat Hill in Finnish Karelia, summer 1944. Surrounded and almost out of ammunition he shot himself rather than surrender. (Erik Wiborg)

Above right: The Norwegian Nordland and then SS-Ski Battalion Norge commander, Frode Halle.

Kaprolat Hill today. With hills few and far between, they were key features in the cat and mouse fighting in Finnish Karelia. (Erik Wiborg)

Norwegian SS-Ski jägers return to their bunkers on Kaprolat Hill after another patrol. (Erik Wiborg)

Norwegian SS-Ski jägers on parade, clearly some of these soldiers are little more than boys, and soon they would be pitched into battle against the Red Army. (Erik Wiborg)

Norwegian SS MG34 machine-gun crew in action on the Finnish Front; they are wearing snow-shoes. (Erik Wiborg)

The Norwegian SS-Ski jägers use a mortar on the Finnish Front. (Erik Wiborg)

Panorama of an SS-Ski jäger patrol on the Finnish Front. (Erik Wiborg)

On 22 June the news started to filter through to the battalion that a massive Red Army offensive had struck Army Group Centre far to the south. Reports were very sketchy, but it was clear that the Soviet Bagration offensive was on a massive scale. Whilst not of the same magnitude, it would soon be the Norwegians' turn. In fact, Meretskov had concentrated two of his full-strength Rifle Divisions to hit the SS-Nord, now little more than a brigade, and punch through their 'Road Position' on the Kiestinki-Louhi Corridor. The Norwegians were right in the path of the intended attack.

Three days after Bagration began to tear Army Group Centre to pieces, the Soviets launched their own offensive in Karelia. Kaprolat was targeted first. A massive artillery barrage was followed by an entire regiment of assaulting infantry who swarmed up the hill's pretty gentle slopes. Steen and his men fought back ferociously and inflicted horrific casualties on the Russians. One of the Soviet regiment's battalions was reduced from 400 to just 36 men in the fighting. But the end was inevitable. Bunkers and trenches fell throughout the day and night, until finally the Soviets reached Steen's command post and surrounded it early the following morning. Along with Steen, who was already wounded, was his fellow Norwegian, SS-Standartenoberjunker Birger-Ernst Jonsson. With ammunition running out, Steen and Jonsson shot themselves rather than surrender. Only one Norwegian commander was still alive, Jonsson's Bad Tölz classmate SS-Standartenoberjunker Kaare Børsting. He gathered the few survivors together and led them in a desperate breakout attempt. Fighting all the way, Børsting managed to guide the remnants of his Company to Hasselmann Hill where they gratefully threw themselves into the arms of the 2nd Company. Their relief was short-lived though, as the Red Army offensive rolled on and hit them later that same day. Hasselmann saw the same pattern as at Kaprolat, with massed Russian artillery being followed up by determined infantry assault. As at Kaprolat, the Norwegian SS men put up a stout defence, but the odds were stacked against them. When Kaare Børsting was killed as his stick grenade detonated before he could throw it, the heart went out of the defence and the hill fell. A handful of Norwegians escaped the disaster and fled west, where they married up with a relief column from the SS-Nord's SS-Mountain Regiment 11 Reinhard Heydrich sent to support them.

It was too late. The SS-Ski Battalion Norge had been virtually exterminated. Halle had rushed back from Norway but had been too late to save his unit from destruction. In less than three days of fighting the 2nd and 3rd Companies were wiped out, with an estimated 135 volunteers killed and more than 40 captured. Fifteen of these prisoners did somehow manage to overpower their guards and escape back to German lines but

Above left: A Norwegian SS-Ski trooper kitted out for the cold of Finnish Karelia. (Erik Wiborg)

Above right: Lonely sentry duty for SS-Ski troopers in the snowy wastes of Karelia. (Erik Wiborg)

Left: Norwegian SS-Ski troopers on another long patrol across the silent forests of Finland. (Erik Wiborg)

SS-Ski grenadiers pose in Finnish Karelia; the middle trooper is armed with a Soviet submachine-gun. Many troopers used captured Russian weapons on account of their sturdiness, reliability and ready access to ammunition. (Erik Wiborg)

it was scant consolation. For their unluckier comrades, years in the gulags awaited them. It was not until 1955 that the last Kaprolat POWs were repatriated from the Soviet Union after 11 dreadful years in captivity.

As for the dead, alongside Steen, Jonsson and Børsting, the 3rd Company lost its other two platoon commanders, Rolf Walstrøm and the SS-Wiking veteran Tor Torjussen. Second Company lost one of its platoon commanders, Sverre-Andersen Østerdal (who had been the President of the Norwegian Sporting Association), its most senior NCO, SS-Oberscharführer ('Senior Squad Leader') Ola Magnussen, and its overall commander, Holmesland Vik, who had been badly wounded. To put Kaprolat and Hasselmann in context, the DNL lost 158 legionnaires killed in more than 12 months service at the Front, and the SS-Ski Battalion Norge lost about the same in less than 72 hours.

Aftermath

The Norge had taken a hammering but its solid defence had helped the SS-Nord to stem the Soviet tide. The same was true along the line as

Wehrmacht and Finnish units held out, taking the steam out of the Russian assaults. Fighting continued for most of the next month, but without a decisive breakthrough. Kahrs's 1st Company was reunited with their surviving comrades and took a full part in the defensive battles. Halle and Kahrs were awarded the Iron Cross 1st Class for their bravery, as was Steen, although his award was posthumous. With the Front now quiet the SS-Ski Battalion set about building new defensive positions on the Sohjana River and reorganising, and one company was even sent to man an island in Lake Pundum from where it patrolled up to the neighbouring Lake Pja. Any enemy they spotted were dealt with by long-range artillery fire from the SS-Nord's guns to the south.

The return of the troopers on leave gave the battalion a significant boost, as did the recovered wounded like Arnfinn Vik who came back as a company commander. A fresh tranche of 50 new recruits also fleshed out the ranks, as did the arrival of Berg's 3rd SS-Police Company fresh from training at Sennheim. The battalion was now back up to a strength in excess of 400 men, and prepared to face further action against the Red Army. However on 4 September 1944 the situation changed dramatically.

Above left: The Norwegian 3rd SS-Police Company is inspected. (Erik Wiborg)

Above right: The Norwegian 3rd SS-Police Company take a break during training in 1944. Their generally unpopular commander, Aage-Henry Berg, is in the middle at the back wearing the peaked cap. (Erik Wiborg)

Finland capitulates

The utter destruction of Army Group Centre and the astonishing loss of 350,000 German soldiers in a few short weeks had convinced Marshal Mannerheim and the rest of the Finnish Government that Nazi Germany was beaten. Their only hope to avoid calamity was to negotiate an honourable surrender. The Red Army offensives against Karelia had been stopped but the attack out of Leningrad had not; the Soviets were now advancing north killing thousands of Finland's best troops. Moscow's peace terms were not unduly harsh, but they did demand that Finland turn her armed forces on her erstwhile ally and expel all German military personnel, by force if necessary, in a matter of weeks. The Germans had laid contingency plans for a Finnish surrender, even so, considering the vast distances involved there was no way they could comply. They had hardly any vehicles and little fuel in any case, the roads were few and generally pretty poor and the withdrawal route to Narvik was more than 1,000 kilometres long. The scene was set for tragedy.

Dietl had died in an air crash back in June, so it was the Twentieth Mountain Army's new commander, Colonel-General Lothar Rendulic, who led the retreat back to Norway. Rendulic would later go on to command the III Germanic SS-Panzer Corps and its component Norwegians. The SS-Nord was used as the Army's rearguard, and the SS-Ski Battalion Norge as the SS-Nord's rearguard. Thus they were some of the very last Wehrmacht men to cross over into their homeland some three months later after having to fight off attacks from their old allies. The irony was complete, the Norwegian SS men had volunteered to fight alongside their Finnish cousins and had ended up shooting at them. Bjarne Dramstad took part in the withdrawal as a member of the 3rd SS-Police Company:

At the beginning of September Finland capitulated, this led to mixed emotions in the Company, some were angry that they were not given the chance to fight the Russians and help the Finns, but I could really understand them, they were under enormous pressure and had to do what they could to save their country. But it was bitter, most of the Finns probably felt the same.

Well, we were given the order to walk back, thousands and thousands of soldiers retreated on the long, cold, hard march. I was given the job of being head of the Company's field-kitchen, this was a good but demanding job, as we were constantly on the move so it was hard to keep the food warm.

In Rovaniemi an ammunition train was blown up and I was thrown onto the field-kitchen, but didn't get any injuries. A lot of the NCOs and soldiers were constantly drunk in Rovaniemi, the four years of war had taken

Bjarne Dramstad (helmeted soldier shaking hands) receives the Police Honour Medal (*Politiets Hederstegn*) from Jonas Lie himself in Oslo, spring 1943. (Knut Thoresen)

their toll, and by now we knew the war was lost. Finally we reached the Norwegian border at Skibotn. Luckily the Finns never attacked us, that would have been very hard for me, I had struggled so hard to fight for the Finns, so this was an ironic end to it all. First I was fooled by the Germans and sent to the Leningrad front and not to Finland as promised, and finally when I managed to get there the Finns gave up.

Back in Norway while the Norge was sent south to Oslo, Bjarne and his comrades were kept in Narvik and used as hunting teams (*Jagdkommandos*), to patrol the far northern border, guarding against Red Army incursions and local resistance:

Service in the Jagdkommandos in Norway meant hard, long ski patrols that lasted for days, often under harsh conditions. Our squad was stationed in a farm at Dividalen National Park patrolling the border area. The farmer, as I later found out, was connected to the Resistance, and he probably warned them when we went out on patrols. This gave me a great respect for him even though he belonged to the other side. I had the pleasure of meeting him [in 2007], he was then one hundred years old, but still remembered how he fooled us during the war. This gave us both a good laugh.

Vidkun Quisling inspects men of the Norwegian SS-Ski Battalion Norge. (Erik Wiborg)

Bjarne's service finally ended early the following year when his Company was first sent south to Oslo and then subsequently disbanded. His old company commander, Oscar Rustand was trying to establish a 4th Company at the same time of course for one last throw of the dice but needless to say there were few takers.

As for the Norge down in Oslo, it was renamed the SS-Ski Battalion 506 (motorised), and ordered to prepare to combat a possible communist-inspired uprising and root out any internal resistance. That was a step too far for Frode Halle who refused to fire on fellow Norwegians, he relinquished command and the old SS-Police company commander and Iron Cross 1st Class holder, Reidar-Egil Hoel, took over. It was an inglorious end to a story full of heroism and tragedy. The specialist Norwegian SS ski troopers had joined to help Finland and ended up in Lappland fighting alongside Germans and some three hundred kilometres from the nearest Finnish unit. There, in a beautiful but forgotten wilderness, they had lost more than half their number in vicious fighting, and had then been igno-miniously cast out by the very people they had signed up to fight for. Back home they were then expected to turn their guns on their own countrymen.

VI

1945: The End of the Scandinavian Waffen-SS – the Wiking in Hungary and the Nordland in Berlin

Our mobility, which had always given us an advantage over the vast but slow Soviet formations, was now only a memory.

Guy Sajer, an Alsatian volunteer in the Grossdeustchland Division, (*The Forgotten Soldier*, Ballantine Books, 1971)

Nazi Germany in 1945

As 1945 began, Adolf Hitler's empire was fast shrinking and the end was finally in sight. His last substantial reserves were being frittered away in the Ardennes, while in the East the Red Army continued its ominous build-up all along the Front. Finland and Rumania had abandoned Nazi Germany, Slovakia was in rebellion, most of the Balkans had been lost and Horthy's Hungary was only being kept in the war by threats and kidnap – the SS commando leader Otto Skorzeny had actually taken Admiral Horthy's son hostage in a daring raid. German industry was somehow miraculously supplying the Wehrmacht with an ever-increasing amount of modern equipment, but the critical fuel shortages Guy Sajer noticed in the Grossdeutschland meant that most of this high-grade kit just sat idle. The horse was now the Army's main method of battlefield mobility, while its ranks were increasingly filled with half-trained conscripts who were no match for the military juggernauts facing them in the East and West.

The Kriegsmarine was still operating in the Baltic, but the U-Boat battle in the Atlantic was lost. High grade aviation fuel was in even shorter supply than gasoline, so when the Luftwaffe could get into the air it concentrated on trying to protect German cities and it was becoming a rarity over the frontlines.

Making for home

Against this tide it was the remnants of the old élites whom Hitler and OKW would turn to for some sort of a miracle, and they would be rushed from one sector to another in a vain attempt to keep on saving the day. The inevitable result was massive, recurring losses in the ranks of divisions like the Wiking and Nordland, and the Scandinavian Waffen-SS simply could not afford the casualties. In this sixth year of the war they only numbered just over a thousand men, with the majority still in the Nordland, a minority in the Wiking, and a handful strewn over other formations. The Allied advance across Western Europe created a last big influx of volunteers into the Waffen-SS among the likes of the Dutch, Flemish and French as those lands were liberated, but the same did not happen across occupied Scandinavia. Coupled with this, the familiar recruiting pools among

Above left: From left: the Swedish Untersturmführer Gunnar-Erik Eklöf (platoon commander in the Nordland's famous Schwedenzug – 3./AA 11), the German SS-Sturmmann Muzzi Emmerich, and the Swedish Unterscharführer Markus Ledin. The three men brew up coffee with their half-track in the background during the Dünaburg fighting in Latvia, July 1944. Ledin would later be cut off behind Soviet lines before escaping home via Finland in a requisitioned fisherman's boat. (Lennart Westberg)

Above right: Erik Wallin, helmeted on the right, with his friend and fellow Swede Karl-Olof Holm. Holm tried to desert home from the Nordland in October 1944 while serving in Courland. He was caught, tried and shot. (James Macleod)

Germany's foreign workers and the home-grown Far-Right parties had dried up. There would be no new waves of 'Vikings' into the Scandinavian Waffen-SS. So the burden fell on the thinning ranks of veterans. The Finns, bar a tiny handful, had gone home and were now mourning their country's 79,047 war dead and abiding by their peace agreement with Stalin. With the Norwegians of the SS-Police Companies and specialist Ski Battalion repatriated, it was Per Sörensen and his Danes who made up the lions share of the remaining volunteers with some 70 per cent of the total.

There were still a few dozen Swedes serving, although desertion became more common now it was absolutely clear that the war was lost. Hans-Gösta Pehrsson was still the ranking Swedish officer in the Nordland, and he intended to stay until the end, but he would not stand in the way of his countrymen who wanted to call it a day, either before or after the devastating fight at Trekni. Fighting in Estonia and Courland on the shores of the Baltic meant the Swedes could almost see home; and some went. Three volunteers, SS-Unterscharführer's Sven Alm, Markus Ledin and Ingemar Somberg (the first two were veterans of the Winter War) got trapped behind the advancing Soviets when their armoured half-track broke down. Left stranded, they repaired the vehicle and decided to head to the coast. Arriving at the fishing village of Noarootsi, they killed the handful of Red Army troopers billeted there, grabbed a boat and headed for Finland. Arrested by the Finns, Alm and Ledin's Winter War medals earned them all a quick release and they crossed over into Sweden and safety. Their erstwhile comrades Nils Berg, Elis Höglund and Knut Fagerström, followed the same path and took another boat with some Estonian refugees from a nearby port. They too made it home. Not all were so lucky though. Erik Wallin's friend, the ex-Swedish Army sergeant Karl-Olof Holm, tried to desert but was caught, court-martialled and shot.

Resistance on the Home Front

It wasn't just Pehrsson's Swedes who knew the war was lost, back in the Scandinavian homelands everyone else knew too. In Denmark and Norway the occupation, and resistance to it, was becoming increasingly violent as the two sides fought it out in the streets. On 8 February, Quisling's Chief of Police and commander of the paramilitary Hird, the ruthless and detested Sturmbannführer Karl Alfred Marthinsen, was assassinated outside his Oslo home. Acting on orders from the Norwegian government-in-exile in London, the *Milorg* resistance movement used a gun team to spray his official car with bullets, Marthinsen died instantly. In the aftermath, 29 anti-occupation Norwegians, including the leading lawyer Jon Vislie and the prominent Milorg supporter Kaare Sundby, were rounded up and shot in retaliation by the Nazi authorities. The whole of Norway went into shock at this unprecedented act of brutality. Across the Baltic things were just as bad in Denmark. The authorities tried to maintain order through repression, and the reaction was predictable. Two months after Marthinsen was killed it was the turn of his Danish counterpart, the leader of the Hipo Corps, Erik Viktor Petersen, to be gunned down in the street by his fellow countrymen.

The SS-Wiking in Hungary

While the Resistance cut down the Far Right on the home front, the Red Army was completing the task against their Waffen-SS counterparts on the battlefront. November and December had seen Hungary invaded and Budapest surrounded. Some 95,000 German and Hungarian troops ended up trapped in the city, with the core of the defence based on the cavalrymen of the 8th SS-Cavalry Division Florian Geyer and the 22nd SS-Volunteer Cavalry Division Maria Theresia. Hitler was obsessed with holding the capital and the Hungarian oilfields, which were the Third Reich's last major supplier of fuel. No matter that his entire 'Fortress' and 'hold to the last man' strategies had proved themselves to be utter failures and that the oilfields in question could not even provide Army Group South's needs let alone anyone else's. As ever, Hitler refused to accept reality and the Ostheer was ordered to expend its last strength in vain attempts to relieve Budapest and defeat the Soviets on the Magyar plains in a series of operations codenamed Konrad (there were to be three in the end). Involved from the start was the Wiking, which was dispatched south from Poland along with the Totenkopf, and sent straight into the attack from its transport trains on New Year's Day.

Advancing from Komarno, the Germans main base in western Hungary, the two panzer divisions surprised the 4th Guards Army and threw it back some 20 miles. But the Russians swiftly got over their initial shock and poured fresh forces into the struggle. The offensive slowed and casualties mounted. Unwilling to concede defeat, Hitler pulled Gille's Corps back and moved them near Szckesfehervar to try again. With Hans Dorr's Germania in the lead, the Wiking attacked again. Scandinavian grenadiers fell to mines, artillery fire and even electrified wires as their ranks were further thinned. But somehow they carried on, the Wiking's King Tigers (an armoured monster that weighed 68 tonnes and sported the superlative 88mm gun as its main armament), creating carnage among the Soviet tank ranks as the division advanced to within a mere 12 miles of the centre of Budapest. The garrison, desperately battling for their survival among the smoking ruins of the once-beautiful city, could hear the rumble of the guns as the Wiking edged forward – surely they would be saved. Then disaster struck.

Dorr called a briefing for his officers in a barn in the just-captured village of Sarosd. A lone Soviet anti-tank gun and its crew had been overlooked by the assaulting troops and had kept their heads down. Sensing an opportunity, the gun commander saw the SS officers gathering in the barn near the square and ordered his gunner to hit it. With the trademark retort that gave the Soviet 76mm gun its nickname among the Germans of the *ratschbum*, the high velocity shell shot across and slammed into the building's roof showering the assembled commanders with red-hot shrapnel. At a stroke the Germania was beheaded. Dorr, a Knight's Cross winner and Cherkassy survivor, was wounded for the sixteenth time in his brief career and would later die of his injuries. Several other men were killed instantly, and almost everyone else was wounded by the razor sharp steel fragments. The stuffing was knocked out of the Germania by the losses and the offensive ground to a shuddering halt as the Soviets threw ever-more reinforcements into a counter-attack. Within days, not only had the Germans been stopped but the Wiking itself had been surrounded.

The former Norge and Danmark 1st Battalions were heavily involved in the fighting, particularly around the town of Pettend. Fritz Vogt, now Erik Brörup's battalion commander, personally destroyed six Soviet tanks with hand-held *panzerfäuste* during the fighting that claimed the lives of several Scandinavian volunteers, including the ex-DNL veteran Fritjof Røssnaes (his elder brother Knut was also in the division) and the surgeon Dr Tor Storm, allegedly burned alive with his wounded charges after trying to surrender. The two battalions did manage to break out from Pettend and rejoin the rest of the division, but the price was astronomically high. The Danmark was effectively annihilated and was never resurrected, while the Norge could muster just 36 officers and men by mid-February. The Westland's commander, SS-Obersturmbannführer Franz Hack spoke of the ferocity of the combat:

The Soviets attacked us frontally during the day, supported by artillery and Stalin's Organs [German nickname for the multi-barrelled Katyusha rocket launchers]. The battle raged in and around the little town of Seregelyes, and somehow we captured a complete Stalin Organ with tractor and ammunition. Our artillerymen and infantry gunners, under SS-Hauptsturmführer Peter Wollseifer, turned the multiple launcher around and soon the Soviets were getting a taste of their own medicine.

The Red Army's Vistula-Oder offensive

Peter Wollseifer's success with the Katyusha was nowhere near enough to turn the tide, and Konrad 2 was abandoned. With it went a large part of the division's Nordic past as most of the Wiking's remaining Scandinavian grenadiers were either killed or wounded in the twin offensives. By now, the focus of the war on the Eastern Front, no longer the Russian Front of course, had shifted north. On the morning of 12 January the Soviets burst out of their bridgeheads on the Vistula River and struck west towards Berlin – the STAVKA plan was to end the war in just 45 days. Guderian, as Hitler's Chief-of-Staff, had warned his leader of the danger on the Vistula, but Hitler had long retreated into a military fantasy world. The dictator even called the Soviet build-up 'the biggest bluff since Genghis Khan'. His amateurish failure to recognise the obvious would cost the Wehrmacht and the Scandinavian Waffen-SS dear.

Spring Awakening in Hungary

So as the Red Army tore the Wehrmacht to pieces in eastern Germany, the Wiking was held fast in Hungary unable to influence the decisive battle being fought hundreds of miles away to the north. 'Grossfaz', a derogatory shortening of Goebbels' sycophantic public description of Hitler ('der grösste führer von alle Zeit' – 'the greatest leader of all time'), then proceeded to compound his original error massively by sending Sepp Dietrich's entire Sixth SS Panzer Army to join the Wiking to try and inflict the ever-elusive decisive defeat on the Soviets in Hungary.

Operation Spring Awakening (Unternehmen Frühlingserwachen) was launched on 18 February by Nazi Germany's strongest remaining field force. The offensive began seven days after the doomed Budapest garrison of 30,000 survivors desperately tried to escape the burning city. Forced to leave well over 10,000 wounded men to the tender mercies of the Red Army, the remaining Germans and Hungarians set off west along the Italian Boulevard and through the city's drains and sewers. The Russians were waiting and cut down the escapees in droves. Pretty soon their few panzers and other vehicles were knocked out and everyone was on foot. It became a giant hunt, with packs of Soviets ripping the German/Hungarian columns to shreds. In the end only some 700 reached the German lines, the rest were either taken captive or perished like the SS-Polizei battlegroup commander, SS-Oberführer Helmut Dörner. Joachim Rumohr and August Zehender, respectively commanders of the Florian Geyer and Maria

Theresia SS Cavalry Divisions, committed suicide during the break-out rather than face capture. Budapest is sometimes described by historians as the 'Stalingrad of the Waffen-SS', which is an overstatement, even so it was a momentous battle that wiped out the Waffen-SS cavalry arm, sealed Hungary's fate and hammered another nail in the Ostheer's coffin.

With Budapest finally lost, there was little point left to Spring Awakening, but on it went anyway. Dietrich now had the I, II and IV SS Panzer Corps under his command, but it was to no avail – fuel and ammunition were in short supply, the ground was marshy and water-logged, and the roads and bridges unable to bear the weight of the massive German panzers. Just as with every Wehrmacht offensive of the past 12 months and more, the initial breakthrough could not be exploited. Exhausted, the cream of the Waffen-SS was forced back to its start line and pushed onto the defensive. Remarkably though, there were still a small handful of Scandinavians fighting in the Wiking, one of whom was the Frikorps Danmark veteran Erik Brörup. Having served for some months in SS Parachute Battalion 500 based in Hungary, he had then been forced to watch as his old unit, the Florian Geyer, had been exterminated in the capital. Joining the Wiking's Armoured Reconnaissance Battalion, where one of the company commanders was his fellow Dane Robert Hansen, he was pretty clear that there was still plenty of fight left in the Scandinavian Waffen-SS that springtime:

My most memorable encounter took place on St Patrick's Day, 17 March 1945, near Szekesfehervar in Hungary. I was Adjutant, with the rank of SS-Obersturmführer, to SS-Sturmbannführer Fritz Vogt, holder of the Knight's Cross. Actually I had heard of Fritz Vogt's exploits in the West in 1940 during a lecture by my old tactics instructor from the Danish Cavalry when he was telling us about the Waffen-SS. Anyway the Russians had started their offensive the day before, which was also Fritz Vogt's 27th birthday. Our unit was SS-Panzer Reconnaissance Battalion 5 [*SS-Panzer Aufklärungs Abteilung 5*].

I had established a command post in a small house and set up com-munications with a switchboard and radio while shells fell around us. SS-Obergruppenführer Gille telephoned to congratulate Vogt on his birth-day and to tell him he had just been awarded the Oakleaves to his Knight's Cross. His face lit up and he said: 'This calls for a drink!' We hoisted a few, then the Supply officers showed up bearing some bottles of beer, and all the other officers found time to show up for a quick drink. All the while the war was going on around us.

One company commander was having some trouble with the enemy, so I suggested to Vogt that I go out and try to straighten things out. Vogt laughed and said: 'What's the matter with you, do you feel like a hero today?' I answered that he had just got himself a new medal and should let others have a chance to win one. He replied: 'Okay but watch what you are doing!' By that time of course we had all had a good drink and were in excellent spirits!

I got an SdKfz 250/9 [an armoured personnel carrier with mounted 20mm cannons] and went into battle. We were firing high-explosive shells and it seemed easy, like shooting fish in a barrel. Then the Russians brought up an anti-tank rifle and shot up my vehicle, forcing us to bail out. We ended up in hand-to-hand combat with them. I had a panzerfaust anti-tank rocket but it wouldn't fire. I therefore used it like a club and cracked one Russian's head with it. I was in trouble though. However Fritz Vogt then appeared with a few more armoured personnel carriers and got me out. He told me to take a couple of hours off, and later he and I went off alone on a reconnaissance behind the enemy lines. I got the Iron Cross First Class for all this. That Fritz Vogt was some character!

The SS-Nordland in Courland

While New Year's Day 1945 found the Wiking's Scandinavians getting off their trains and going into battle in Hungary, the Nordland's volunteers were in the frozen north of Courland waiting for the next Red Army assault. Having fought off the Soviets during the First and Second Battles of Courland the previous October and the Third in November, both sides were gearing up for a further trial of strength. Guderian was still pressing Hitler hard to evacuate the peninsula and re-deploy the Army Group (now renamed as Army Group Courland – *Heeresgruppe Kurland*) in its entirety to Prussia, to defend the eastern Reich, but he would not hear of it. His argument, as before Christmas, was that the soldier's presence kept the Red Fleet from dominating the Baltic, safeguarded Swedish iron ore imports and drew major Soviet forces away from the main front. While these reasons were arguably cogent, the end result was that the majority of two entire German Armies would be unavailable to the Ostheer when it needed them most.

Nazi Germany had now been retreating in the East for close on two years. For the men in the line it is hard to imagine how they kept up their morale as the ranks were continually depleted and the miles swept by endlessly. Incredible as it now seems, some still believed in ultimate victory, one such was the Swedish SS-Unterscharführer Erik 'Jerka' Wallin serving in the Nordland's Schwedenzug that new year:

We knew that a significant part of the most vital German industries had gone below ground and were therefore invulnerable from the air. We knew that even better weapons would soon be mass-produced, and that the German forces in the West, just a few days before, had started a successful offensive in Belgium and Luxembourg. Soon the terrible pressure of numerically superior forces would have to ease. We just needed some months of breathing space. Then we would hit back with annihilating power, especially here in Courland … With our toughness and persistence against the furious assaults of the Red Army, we could offer a breathing space to the reserves, who were now being organised and freshly equipped in Germany.

It is difficult to comprehend how anyone could believe this was really the case, but Wallin had been fighting the Red Army since the Winter War and final defeat was probably too awful a prospect for the NCO to contemplate. Leaving Bunkas in the east of the Pocket on 4 January, the Nordland moved south-west some 40 kilometres to the town of Preekuln, just to the east of the main port town of Liepaja. Its neighbours were the 30th Infantry Division on its left and the 11th on its right, with the experienced 14th Panzer Division covering the whole sector as the mobile armoured reserve. Wallin for one was grateful to leave Bunkas, as he described in his book *'Twilight of the Gods' A Swedish Waffen-SS Volunteer's experiences with the 11th SS-Panzergrenadier Division Nordland, Eastern Front 1944-45*:

… we were relieved and could leave Bunkas, a real death trap. It lay in the open without any connections to the rear except during the dark of night. We were lucky to get out of there before Ivan had finished with his build-up for the great assault we knew was coming. Instead our successors had to face the storm a few days later and according to what I heard hardly anyone from the relief came out of there alive.

The Fourth Battle of Courland

Unsurprisingly that far north, January 1945 in Courland was damnably cold. The snow was not metres thick, but it was there, and the nights were clear so everything froze overnight. The Ostheer had finally learnt its lessons from the eastern winters, and the kit and equipment Erik Wallin and his comrades were issued with was a world away from the dire 'jackboot and overcoat' days of 1941. The grenadiers were issued with reversible white/camouflage padded uniforms, weapons were greased with antifreeze, and heavy weapons had special lubricants to keep them working never mind the thermometer reading. But despite all of this welcome technical advancement every infantryman still froze – the weather is the weather and no soldier can beat it. Even the Scandinavians, no strangers to northern winters, felt the cold. But the Scandinavian Waffen-SS had precious little time to worry about the temperature after their move west, as the Red Army launched yet another offensive against Army Group Courland. This time it was aimed at the southwestern end of the Pocket, and designed to take Liepaja and deprive the Germans of the port. The main blow fell first on the 30th Infantry Division, and then the Nordland itself on 23 January. After resting behind the lines for a day or so, Wallin's company were back in the line when the blow struck, as usual it was preceded by an enormous artillery barrage:

> During the bombardment we received orders that our mortars had to go into action. The only thing we could do was to take a deep breath and run out into that hell. The area around us had completely changed character … ploughed away by Ivan's artillery and a new landscape created. One of the mortars had obviously taken a direct hit down the barrel, because the remains hung like an opened banana skin over the mounting. The other mortars had survived, as had the stock of shells, about 150 of them.
>
> What then followed was, for me, one of the most frantic episodes of the war. I guess it would have been too much to hope that the enemy should cease firing at our mortar position, so that we, in peace and quiet, could carry out our own action! However their fire didn't show any sign of slackening at all. Every other minute you had to throw yourself down some hole to avoid being torn to pieces by a howling shell. During this we had to keep on firing according to the corrections that the field-telephone blared to us direct from the artillery observer who was somewhere out in front of us.
>
> In that way we kept going all afternoon, hour after hour. The stock of ammunition ran out, but new boxes were delivered without any interruption in our firing. With wet blankets we ran from mortar to mortar to cool off the gleaming hot barrels. Our rounds spread a terrible destruction among the charging Russian infantry waves.
>
> For days and nights this slaughter went on at Preekuln. Only at dawn, or sometimes in the afternoon was there a pause as the yellow-brown Russian infantry soldiers started to crawl out of their hideouts and spread over the terrain in front of our lines … the first shouts of 'Urrah!' from the storming Bolsheviks were drowned by the murderous defensive fire from our mortars, from the fast-firing MG42s [the MG42 had an incredible rate of fire of 1550 rounds per minute and was nicknamed the 'Hitler Saw' because of the noise it made when fired] and from the sub-machine guns closest to the

enemy. Wave after wave of attackers poured forth, but they were all crushed to pieces or fell back and faded. Our line held.

Both the Nordland and the 30th Infantry Division were pushed back during the fighting, and the Danmark was all but destroyed, but vigorous counter-attacks by the 14th Panzer Division helped restore the line and forced the Red Army to halt their offensive. With the crisis temporarily over, Hitler agreed that Steiner's Corps should be evacuated from the Pocket and brought back to Germany to re-equip and help defend eastern Germany. When Steiner broke the news to Ziegler both men breathed a deep sigh of relief, but it was a relief no doubt tinged with guilt at the thought of the undoubted fate of the Army comrades they were leaving behind. As Steiner took his leave from General Rendulic he almost certainly knew that the Sixteenth and Eighteenth Armies were doomed. They would fight two more huge battles against the Red Army, performing magnificently, before OKW finally gave its consent to the evacuation of Courland on 3 May. Hitler himself had committed suicide on 30 April and Berlin surrendered on 2 May. In a last ditch operation the Kriegsmarine managed to bring out some 26,000 soldiers before the last remnants of the old 'Army Group North' finally laid down their arms. Over 180,000 men then marched east into Soviet captivity.

Embarking at Liepaja at the end of January on the *Karin von Bornhofen* and other transport ships, the Nordland was ferried safely to Stettin where it set foot on German soil for the very first time since its formation two years previously. As the troops recovered, and new replacements and equipment arrived, the division was recognised for its feats in Courland over the preceding four months with the award of the Oakleaves to its commander, Joachim Ziegler. His citation read:

On January 23 1945 the Russians started out for the area of Preekuln, with elements of three Armies and the mass of the 3rd Guards Mechanized Corps (eight divisions and three tank regiments confirmed). After a preparatory barrage of fire, the expected big offensive began towards Libau. Annihilating the biggest part of the troops occupying the main fighting line, the Russians succeeded in breaking through in depth in spite of the bloody defence of isolated, surviving, resistance nests. Seeing the threatened breakthrough, SS-Brigadeführer Ziegler reacted immediately. He stopped the supply services and deployed the gathered troops in blocking positions. Then, with the small divisional reserves, he himself led a counter-attack.

Only thanks to his own brave and untiring performance on the battlefield, especially on January 24–25 1945, was the situation stabilised. He personally led into action small battle-groups and reorganised the resistance in sectors of the front which had lost contact with each other. SS-Brigadeführer Ziegler prevented the breakthrough towards Libau. Through his exceptional bravery Ziegler ensured the continuation of the fight in Courland.

Operation Summer Solstice – *Unternehmen Sonnenwende*

Back on Stettin's quayside, Ziegler and his men disembarked, climbed into their vehicles and left the bombed-out city behind them. The Nordland's grenadiers drove south into the quiet Pomeranian countryside where they married up with their panzer battalion, now reformed and boasting 30 Panthers and 30 assault guns. This would be the last period of calm the division would experience before its extinction in the rubble of Berlin three months later. From this moment until the end, the Scandinavian Waffen-SS would be involved in bitter fighting across the east German landscape, being worn down by battles at Arnswalde, Massow, Vossberg and Altdamm. At each location, now all in modern-day Poland, they would leave yet more comrades behind, lying dead in the mud. For now though, the war seemed a long way off as the men spent more than a week training during the day and then relaxing at night in the local Pomeranian hostelries, eating, drinking and dancing with the local farm girls.

To the east and south the Red Army was equally happy, but for very different reasons. Having surged forward from its bridgeheads on the Vistula, the Red Army had broken into Germany and was approaching the Oder River just to the east of Berlin itself. Successful though the offensive had been, the STAVKA's plan to defeat Nazi Germany in 45 days had failed, as the troops' logistics failed to keep pace with their leader's ambitions. Having splintered Army Group Vistula, under the hapless command of a totally unqualified Heinrich Himmler, the Russians were now short of fuel and ammunition and their attack came to a natural halt. Guderian, probably Hitler's best remaining general, was the first to see the opportunity for a counter-attack to destroy Zhukov's overstretched 1st Belorussian Front, and give the Germans much-needed breathing space.

A plan was quickly pulled together that called for a double pincer movement to cut Zhukov's command in half, a thrust from Stargard in the north meeting up with a southern one from Frankfurt-an-der-Oder. Guderian also proposed that, for the first time in the war, the operation be totally controlled by the Waffen-SS. He called for Dietrich's Sixth SS Panzer Army to form the southern arm, and a new SS Army, the Eleventh Panzer, to form the northern one. This made sound military sense as it would position Dietrich's veterans to defend Berlin in the coming battle, but there was now no place at all for sound military thinking on Hitler's part. The dictator was still obsessed with Budapest and Hungary, never mind that the city had fallen and the country almost lost. He refused to sanction Dietrich's move north, and insisted the northern thrust alone would be enough.

Felix Steiner and the Eleventh SS Panzer Army

That blow would be delivered by none other than the man who symbolised more than any other the incorporation of European volunteers into the Waffen-SS – Felix Steiner. Promoted from Corps to Army command, Steiner was now given ten divisions, most of them divisions in name only, and no time to properly organise his staff. Ammunition was low, fuel desperately short and air cover non-existent. Arrayed on a 30-mile front, the attacking force was split into three columns. The Eastern Group was the weakest being made up of the 163rd and 281st Infantry Divisions and the Führer-Grenadier Division, collectively called the Corps Group Munzel after their commander. Their goal was flank protection, and to push out towards Landsberg on the River Warthe. Steiner's old command, the III Germanic SS Panzer Corps, comprising the Nordland, a Flemish SS battlegroup, the Führer-Begleit Division and the Dutchmen of the Nederland (now upgraded to a division), made up the Central Group under General Martin Unrein. Their mission was to punch south and reach Arnswalde (now Polish Choszno) before advancing further. Completing the counter-attack force was the XXXIX Panzer Corps known as the Western Group. This Corps contained the Army's Holstein Panzer Division, as well as the 10th SS-Panzer Division Frundsberg, the 4th SS-Panzergrenadier Division SS-Polizei and Degrelle's Walloons, like the Dutch, recently renamed as a division. Their role was flank protection, as with the Eastern Group, but they were also there to exploit and reinforce any success achieved by the Central Group.

Facing Steiner's new army were no less than five Soviet ones, including the experienced 1st and 2nd Guards Tank Armies, the 3rd Shock and the infantrymen of the 47th and 61st. With each Soviet Army being roughly equivalent to a German corps in size, it was clear that even if the attacking divisions had been up to strength they would have been badly outnumbered by the Soviets. As it was, their only hope of achieving the three to one ratio all military manuals lay down as necessary for an attacker to ensure success against a defender, was to concentrate all of their combat power into one overwhelming punch. This, Steiner's inexperienced staff failed to achieve. Confusion reigned in the troops assembly areas, men and vehicles clogged up the few roads, and a thaw made the ground boggy and restricted movement. As a result when H-hour came on 15 February, only the Nordland was ready to cross the start line. They attacked into the northern flank of Zhukov's 1st Belorussian Front, but right from the off Soviet resistance was bitter, and the going heavy, as the rain poured down and the ground turned to slush. It wasn't exactly blitzkrieg. Nevertheless the Scandinavians, Germans and volksdeutsche pushed on, and reached the beleaguered town of Arnswalde on 17 February. Just as with so many towns and villages across the east, the local Nazi Party hierarchy had not prepared the people for the invasion and evacuation was left far too late. Needless to say the 'golden pheasants' themselves, as Nazi Party functionaries were disparagingly called on account of their penchant for flashy baubles of rank, managed to escape in time, but for the majority of the populace the swift Soviet advance left them high and dry and at the mercy of a vengeful Red Army.

More than 2000 German soldiers, many of them wounded, had taken refuge in the town and beaten off several determined Soviet attacks while the civilian population cowered in their cellars praying for deliverance. For once that early spring, their prayers would be answered with the arrival of the Nordland's grenadiers. As the camouflaged and heavily-armed young troopers stormed into town there was a surge of relief as thousands of people poured out into the streets to greet them. Ziegler's men consolidated for the day and then surged south again, only to hit a veritable wall of Russian steel, as artillery, armour and aircraft fire deluged them. As the SS troopers struggled on, behind them the civilians of Arnswalde packed as many of their belongings as they could onto carts and their own backs and headed north to safety, saved by the Nordland's advance.

Further gains were impossible, and in a matter of days the now-deserted Arnswalde was again the frontline as the Nordland was pushed back by ever-greater Soviet attacks. On 23 February the town was abandoned. Summer Solstice had failed and the Nordland withdrew back to the line of the Ihna River. So ended the Nordland's last offensive of the war.

Ultimately unsuccessful as the operation was, Ziegler and the Nordland were commended for their part in the battle. The official report formed part of Ziegler's citation for the Oakleaves to his Knight's Cross:

On February 15 1945 the 11th SS-Panzergrenadier Division Nordland, in spite of the severe shortage of fuel and ammunition, began the planned attack to free encircled Arnswalde. Knowing that with the quickly replenished panzer grenadier regiments, the attack's objective could only be achieved by achieving surprise and leading it personally, SS-Brigadeführer

Ziegler and the regimental commanders supervised the deployment for the attack in detail. At the beginning of the attack Ziegler placed himself at the head of the foremost battalion. After breaking the first resistance of the enemy, SS-Brigadeführer Ziegler ordered his armoured group to undertake a violent breakthrough towards Arnswalde.

With further attacks of the panzer grenadier regiments, the enemy [a large part of the 7th Guards Cavalry Corps] was annihilated. Booty included 26 anti-tank guns, 18 heavy grenade-launchers and two batteries of heavy artillery destroyed.

The enemy was defeated by surprise with minimal casualties [one regiment had just seven dead and two wounded] and for the first time an encircled fortress [1,000 wounded, 1,100 troops and 7,000 civilians] was liberated.

Praise indeed, but though casualties were relatively few overall the Scandinavian volunteers were fast becoming a rarity in the Nordland. By the time of the retreat into Courland the division still counted 534 Norwegians in its ranks, this had dropped to just 64 in the Norge by the end of Summer Solstice, and barely a hundred in total throughout the formation. Their places in the ranks were taken by recently-drafted German conscripts and redundant Luftwaffe and Kriegsmarine men. Hastily kitted out, these poor unfortunates became so much cannon-fodder, with the Nordland's remaining veterans providing it with its real combat power.

Solstice had indeed failed, however the Arnswalde relief had unintended consequences for the Germans. Despite all the evidence to the contrary, Stalin and the rest of the STAVKA still feared what the once-mighty Ostheer could achieve, and they were now worried about a more general German assault from the north. They were determined to avoid this by driving to the Baltic Sea on a wide front and crushing all of north-eastern Germany. This would clear their flank, and leave the way open to take Hitler's hated capital and end the war. While this operation was being hastily planned and executed, the chastened Red Army also pushed west seeking to establish bridgeheads across the last natural barrier between itself and Berlin – the River Oder.

Prelude to Berlin

It was just east of Massow. I was ordered to take up a forward position with seven men. We were to stop Russian infantry attacks with two MG42s. In pouring rain and pitch black darkness we groped our way to our three pits. I took the middle one with Gebauer, a German farmer's son from Rumania, and brought the MG in position, hoping we would have some cover when day broke. The second MG was to our left with three boys, and the remaining three crawled into the pit to the right with assault rifles and sub-machine guns.

In the case of an attack this position was hopeless. There was no connecting trench back to the main line … For three days and nights we had to lie in these godforsaken pits, waiting, waiting, waiting. The rain started pouring again, no food reached us and any connection backwards was unthinkable as long as the artillery fire raged between us and the rest of the Company. Suddenly Gebauer shook me violently: 'They're coming!'

A quick glance through the camouflage, there, only 30 metres away, a drove of Bolsheviks were approaching – no time to panic. I could already see a second wave of infantry emerging from the haze, only 50 metres behind the first one. I got the MG going and fired for all I was worth. My fire and the screams of the wounded woke up the other boys, and our weapons spat fire and death on the brown masses.

I happened to look to the left and saw a Bolshevik working his way through a depression towards us, to get at us from behind. In the same instant he saw me and disappeared. There he was again! He aimed a burst from his sub-machine gun at me. The duel was on. The distance was hardly 20 metres. I got hold of an assault rifle [by now the Ostheer's trusty old Mauser single shot bolt action K98 rifles had mostly been replaced with the highly sophisticated Sturmgewehr 43 assault] and waited for him. Martin, the Rottenführer with the other MG could have touched the Russian if he had looked in his direction but he didn't notice the duel. Finally the Russian made a mistake, I squeezed the trigger and there, he was up again behind his weapon and before he could react he had a hole between his eyes. His head was thrown back, then sank, disappeared and his limp hand dropped his weapon.

Furious, the Bolsheviks threw themselves against us, the situation was hopeless but the boys fought formidably. While I helped Gebauer to feed the MG with new ammunition I could hear myself swearing non-stop, wishing them the worst possible tortures in hell. I let Gebauer handle the MG alone while I fired alternatively with the assault rifle and with my sub-machine gun. He forgot the danger, pushing his chest above the parapet in order to fire better. 'Down!' I screamed but he laughed, he was just 19 years old. Too late. Gebauer suddenly jerked backwards and sank to one side. I turned him around towards me. He was hit under the left eye, the bullet passing through his neck. He was still alive, blood flowing down from cheek and neck. He begged; 'Write to my mother … just a few lines …' and then I was alone.

Martin was now also alone. I called out to him to grab his weapon and come over. He came rushing with wild leaps. To the right as well only one boy was left. All the others had died with a bullet through their heads. We got him over to us. I implored them to try and keep their heads down. Of course, Martin in his eagerness forgot my advice, and he broke down seconds later with a bullet just above the nose ridge.

'Grab the gun and run!' I bellowed to my comrade, as I got hold of my MG, hooked some ammo belts around my neck and ran. Zigzagging over the field in a crazy run, we reached what was left of the protective edge of the wood. My comrade was a few leaps behind me. As I threw a quick glance behind me, I saw him grab his chest, then fall forward. From the cover of the trees I looked up once more and saw him lying there weakly waving at me. Too late, nothing doing, the Russians were already there. (Erik Wallin)

The Soviets had waited barely a week before resuming their offensive against the Nordland positions on the Ihna River. Wallin's entire section was wiped out in the fighting, as he recalled above, while his fellow Scandinavian Per Sörensen, now an SS-Sturmbannführer no less, was leading the Danmark's 2nd Battalion in a struggle at nearby Freienwalde. Edi Janke was in the Danmark's 3rd Battalion battling alongside Sörensen's men near Vossberg. He remembers the tactics they used to try and slow down the Soviets:

We usually held a village for 24 hours during the withdrawal, and then came the order – 'back to the next village'. First came the enemy tanks, we ourselves usually had just one anti-tank gun, which was set up to shoot the first tank. Then the tanks stopped and sent the infantry forward. The infantry was hit hard, then it got dark and we received the order to move back to the next village.

One day we were in a small village in Pomerania, on a reconnaissance patrol, when we discovered we were in danger of being cut off by the enemy. My commander ordered me to explain the situation to the commander of a nearby, solitary King Tiger.

The tank was commanded by an SS-Oberscharführer, a holder of the Knight's Cross, who told me to make sure our own anti-tank gun didn't open fire before he did. The King Tiger moved off towards the enemy and positioned itself behind a small hillock. It wasn't too long before the first Russian tank emerged from the wood near the village. One, two, three, four, five, six, seven tanks came out. We became increasingly uneasy.

Only after the thirteenth enemy tank had appeared did the King Tiger open fire, shooting the last one, it burst into flames, and then our PAK gun joined in shooting the first. One could see the panic break out among the enemy tanks. They turned this way and that trying to avoid the danger, but to no avail. One tank after another was hit. The panic grew as the King Tiger continued to fire. It did them no good. Soon all the Russian tanks were burning without them having fired a single shot.

All the troops who had watched the action were jubilant. The danger of encirclement was still great, however, and we had to pull out of the village later that day. Nevertheless it was a day to remember.

Not far away from the jubilant Edi Janke, Erik Wallin was busy heading west in his trusty SPW half-track when he was stopped by another vehicle from the Schwedenzug carrying a wounded man:

I looked down to see a waving hand rise up from all the blood, oh God it was my fellow countryman and friend SS-Untersturmführer Heino Meyer, the favourite of the Company.

He was almost unrecognisable. A splinter had cut his chin in two and stuck in a neck vertebra and he was few a millimetres from death. He had also been shot in the shoulder and his chest was covered in blood. His legs were pierced by an immense number of shrapnel fragments. But he was alive and even tried to tell me of his misadventure. But his voice was weak and with his damaged chin his speech was slurred … He made it of course, the doctors picked out all the iron scrap except one small piece which remained in his neck as a souvenir, but he never returned to the Company.

The Swedish Waffen-SS officer, Heino Meyer. Hugely popular with his fellow volunteers, twice declared killed in action while serving with the Wiking and Nordland, Meyer survived the war and ended up living firstly in Spain and then South America. (James Macleod)

By the middle of March the Nordland had been pushed back to Altdamm, a river port that straddled the east and west banks of the Oder with a vital bridge connecting the two halves of the town. By now they were joined at the hip with the Flemings of the 27th SS-Freiwilligen Panzergrenadier Division Langemarck, and the Walloons of the 28th SS-Freiwilligen Panzergrenadier Division Wallonien. Grand sounding as this was, both Belgian divisions were no more than a few thousand men strong by this time. Nevertheless, this truly multinational force held back the Soviets on the Oder's eastern bank for several precious days. The OKW report stated:

In the hard defensive battles in Pomerania that began with an enemy break-through to split the Front, the 11th SS-Panzergrenadier Division Nordland has stood as the focal point of resistance since March 3 1945. The Soviet units attacking the division were the 2nd Guards Tank Army, elements of the 61st and 47th Armies and parts of the 3rd Shock Army.

On March 17 after a strong artillery barrage and the deployment of newly-committed forces, the enemy once again tried to push through Altdamm towards Stettin. Ammunition was in short supply and battalions were down to below 100 men each. SS-Brigadeführer Ziegler stayed at his command post repelling sporadic enemy breakthroughs with his staff and repeatedly reorganising the resistance of his exhausted men despite the high casualties in officers. Loss of radios meant artillery fire could not be directed, ammunition was critically low, our panzers were out of action and a large number of heavy infantry weapons were destroyed. Only thanks to his exceptional bravery in this critical situation was the bridgehead held, Ziegler was the spirit of the resistance. In the period from March 3-18 1945 the 11th SS-Panzergrenadier Division Nordland destroyed 194 tanks.

Altdamm became an inferno. Wallin again:

Day and night an annihilating rain of shells of all calibres, from the heaviest howitzers, heavy Stalin Organs, 120mm mortars and infantry guns, down to 37mm anti-tank guns, beat against our positions in that narrow area. ... Our casualties were heavy. Pehrsson, our company commander, was wounded and taken back to Stettin ... We could stand the hunger, the exhaustion was worse. Our eyes smarted and our faces were stiff. There was no quiet place in that burning and exploding inferno. Everywhere the shells fell with their devastating and lacerating rain of shrapnel.

With six mortars my platoon had taken position in the yard of a house that had been completely riddled with bullets and shells. It lay a short distance outside the actual residential area of Altdamm. Our fire-controller was in a cellar in an advanced position. As long as the field-telephone worked the rounds rose in a continuous stream from our barrels.

No other platoon could have kept up their firing better, at least not under such conditions. But after all they were staunch guys, all of them. Several of them had been in the thick of it ever since the engagements at Narva and Dorpat. Even the newcomers stood up to prove themselves, inspired by their older comrades' calm and presence of mind.

Not all the Nordland men were quite so sanguine though, as Wallin observed:

In the evening I was ordered by the new company commander to go over myself to relieve our observer. He had had a nervous breakdown. That told me quite a lot about what was waiting for me over there. I left the command post to the calm and reliable Kraus, a promising NCO, then I was off.

One of Wallin's company officers who he would serve with right until the end was the Danish volunteer SS-Untersturmführer Mogens Schwarz. He had already had an eventful journey just to arrive at the Front:

At the beginning of March I was sent to a company, and was given maps and a soldier who appeared by chance to drive me. Unfortunately when we arrived the position was no longer occupied … we wanted to cross a small bridge but were instantly fired on by Russian infantry. I myself got over the bridge unharmed, my escort thought he had no chance and went back alone. Since it was impossible for me to get back across the bridge unseen, I went on in search of my company.

I only had a 6.35mm pistol and a hand-grenade, suddenly three Russian soldiers came toward me and talked to me. Naturally I understood nothing and patted a Russian amiably on the shoulder. I walked on about 100 metres when they called to me, I jumped over a ditch and found cover behind a single tree. They fired at me but I wasn't hit, then I saw them deciding what to do next, they were only about 10 metres away so I took my hand-grenade and threw it among them. Then I jumped up quickly and ran away, hiding in a pond until dark. I went on in dripping clothes and fortunately I found our troops and heard Norwegian voices, I called out, 'Same troop, don't shoot!', and when I heard the answer, 'Understood', I stepped into our own lines. At the command post they had already started to wonder where I was.

It wasn't long before the new arrival Schwarz was 'at home' among his men and the ever-worsening battlefield situation at Altdamm, as Wallin testified:

The Danish Waffen-SS officer, Mogens Schwarz. Schwarz served in the Nordland's Recce Battalion alongside the famed Swedish *Schwedenzug* right until the end in Berlin. (James Macleod)

Moaning wheezes came from two unbelievably mutilated bodies that had been laid on the floor, with a pair of shredded and bloody overcoats as their only protection from the cold floor. Neither of them could live much longer. One of them had no face. Where eyes, nose, mouth and chin used to be was only a hollowed-out, bloody mess. Out of the left corner of the other's mouth ran a stream of blood ... In contrast to this terrible scene there sat SS-Untersturmführer Schwarz, tough and unperturbed, without equal in the Company. He sat on a sugar-box beside a stinking piece of cotton waste, seemingly untouched by everything and everyone around him. He was squeezing lice. Each time Schwarz found a louse, and there were plenty of them as we never got rid of them at the Front, he lifted it with a pleased grin against the weak light, snapped it with his nails, the let it fall down in the hot oil in a tin can. He did everything with calm, almost lazy movements. Now and then Schwarz glanced at the two dying men on the floor and shook his head compassionately. He turned to the officer by the radio and said 'Do you see now that it's going to be hell for us.'

Our new company commander arrived and Schwarz rose to attention with his trousers round his ankles. The newcomer, a sympathetic SS-Obersturmführer straight from Berlin, had not yet had time to become acquainted with Schwarz, a somewhat unusual officer, but he received his report with a straight face. It was clear that he was finding it difficult not to laugh. Then he caught sight of the bloody figures on the floor and went and knelt by them. He spoke in a low voice to them but got no answer apart from moaning, he whispered a question to the medical orderly and got a shake of the head as an answer.

The bridgehead continued to hold out. Only on 20 March did the last Flemings, Walloons, Germans and Scandinavians cross over Altdamm's bridge before blowing it sky high. Berlin was less than an hour's drive away. Both sides now took a breath and readied for the final act. The Soviets built up their forces for the push to Hitler's capital, and the remnants of the Wehrmacht tried to upset those preparations and buy valuable time, though to what end now, no one knew.

Amidst the growing chaos, there were reminders of another world that were hugely unsettling in these surroundings – letters from home. Wallin was given one by Pehrsson, now back from hospital even though still bandaged up:

The first letter from home for more than a year, from a girl who still kept thinking about me. It was a little bit strange – I felt ashamed of the lump in my throat. For more than a month the letter had been on its way from peaceful Stockholm with its cleanliness and undisturbed life. There would still be neon signs and friendly shining windows, with no black-out curtains at night. Cinemas would be open and people would be strolling about. It was a letter from another world.

I tore open the envelope with hands that were now shaking more from joyful excitement than from exhaustion and the recent hardships harrowing effects on my nerves. My eyes swept quickly over the lines. Then I read it again, slowly, then one more time, then once again. Perhaps there was not very much in that letter. It was mostly about ordinary things and small events back home. But it strengthened and renewed me to think about life up north. It was all so far away and distant from the life of the frontline soldier. It helped me to indulge in daydreams as I sat down outside the barn door … Just like the others I was utterly worn out. A week of long, uninterrupted combat, without sleep, among collapsing houses, howling shells and human beings torn apart in dirt, smoke, fire and blood, had consumed all our strength … but now I was once again back home with my relatives and friends. I was back in the well-remembered streets of the Old Town and the South Side. My daydreaming went on until tiredness overwhelmed me and I fell asleep right where I was sitting, still dreaming of far-away Stockholm.

Phantom divisions

With the Oder line lost, all the enfeebled Wehrmacht forces could do was to try and delay the inevitable. Stalin was determined to take Berlin and Hitler with it, and his by now massively powerful Red Army would grind all to dust to deliver that goal. Who would the Soviets' opponents be though? One glance at the Wehrmacht's strength distribution map would be enough for anybody to realise that Berlin was almost totally undefended. Large German forces were effectively cut off in Courland and the Balkans, and a huge number of those facing the Western Allies were in the process of being surrounded in the Ruhr. The majority of the Reich's military formations were still deployed in the East, as they had been since 1941, but the biggest concentration by far was in the south on the Hungarian-Austrian border. It made no military sense, and contributed to the Allies' mistaken belief in the existence of a last chance 'Alpine Redoubt', where the diehard SS would hold out indefinitely among the high peaks. In reality nothing like that existed, but the mere threat of it worried Eisenhower immensely and presented Berlin to the Soviet dictator on a platter.

Swedish volunteer Erik Wallin in his SS camouflage fatigues. He was wounded in the Berlin fighting but managed to escape the city along with his friend and commander, Hans-Gösta Pehrsson. (James Macleod)

The OKW situation maps did indeed show a number of German divisional insignia between the Oder and Berlin, the Nordland being one, but just like all the others it was a division in name only. Casualties had continued to pile up and replacements were non-existent. From its establishment in September 1943 to the end of March 1945, the division suffered extraordinary losses – 2,937 men killed, 10,454 wounded and a further 1,278 missing – in effect in 18 months its entire original complement was gone. This is how Wallin described it:

> The struggle was furious and our losses heavy. Our division soon had the strength of a regiment. It wasn't unusual to see an Untersturmführer with a machine-gun across his shoulders, move off with an Unterscharführer and a couple of men carrying ammo boxes – and that was a whole company. What could we hope to achieve with battalions of forty to fifty men, and regiments of two to three hundred? … Our company, which had managed better than most in the division, now numbered no more than 40 men.

Ziegler's division was burnt-out. But the war wasn't finished with it yet.

The counter-atack that never was

Wallin and his comrades were granted a few days respite, and the Nordland reorganised as it was put to preparing hasty defences at Schwedt-an-der-Oder to the north-east of Berlin. Their opponents also used the first half of April to prepare for the last battle. The Red Army massed 2,500,000 men (carried in 100,000 trucks) and 6,200 tanks, supported by 41,000 artillery pieces and 7,200 aircraft. Alongside the Nordland, the Germans could only muster 300,000 men, 950 panzers, 1,500 artillery guns and 300 aircraft. However fuel was critically short, leaving many of the planes grounded and the panzers reduced to towing each other to conserve petrol.

At dawn on 16 April the Soviets went into the attack. Their strength may have been overwhelming, but not everything went their way. The Germans furiously defended the crucial Seelow Heights position, costing Zhukov's 1st Belorussian Front an incredible 30,000 men killed in just 3 days. With the Russians stalled, Wallin and his comrades were massed for a counter-attack near Strausberg on 19 April. Driving their half-tracks into an abandoned village, where they were due to meet up with some King Tigers, the Nordland's recce battalion spread out through the houses to snatch a few hours sleep before the assault began. Less than an hour later disaster struck:

A terrible thunder, as if the ground had opened up for a volcanic eruption, woke us with a violent shake and was followed by repeated close-up explosions in our immediate vicinity … The previously peaceful village had been turned in an instant into a hell beyond any attempt at description. Volley after volley from Stalin's Organs and heavy artillery created a horrible bloodbath … Soldiers jumped terrified out through doors and from windows, others came staggering with their hands on their bleeding heads or pressed against torn open bellies, where their guts came out through their fingers. Others shuffled along with one or both legs cut off. But many were left inside the burning houses, dead or dying … A bloody arm-stump hit the side of my half-track with a splashing sound and the blood spattered my face …

Of the entire force that should have been the battering ram against the Bolsheviks' bridgehead, nothing but shredded remains were left. The attack had been smashed to pieces before it had even started. Our recce battalion, an élite unit with few peers on the whole Eastern Front had had one of its bloodiest days of the war. Of the mortar platoon's ten half-tracks there were just four left with reduced crews. All of this had happened in only about 30 minutes.

The Soviets had anticipated the Nordland's counter-attack and reacted with crushing force. Among the casualties was the Danmark's commander, Rudolf Klotz, who was killed in a direct hit on his vehicle at Strausberg airfield. His place was taken by the 31-year-old Per Sörensen. Finally the Danmark Regiment was led by a Dane, even though Danes now numbered less than a hundred in its depleted ranks. In turn, Sörensen handed his 2nd Battalion over to his fellow countryman, SS-Obersturmführer Rasmussen. The Danmark's other battalion, the 3rd, was still led by the highly decorated and hugely experienced, SS-Sturmbannführer Rudolf Ternedde, while the Norge's two battalions were under his fellow German, Richard Spörle.

Following up the massed artillery strike, Soviet tanks charged forward and splintered the division. In the chaos, some parts of the Nordland were isolated, cut-off and destroyed, while others were shoved to the north. One of the latter was Rasmussen's 2nd Battalion. Unable to rejoin their comrades they were integrated into Felix Steiner's command and retreated westwards to safety. Eventually the battalion would reach the Elbe River and cross over into American captivity.

For the rest, somehow Ziegler managed to restore some semblance of order; Wallin:

In the midst of this bloody confusion the staff of the Nordland were stunned but chilled. The scattered battalions and companies were gathered and made ready for action. The Front had really come into being and it wasn't long before we were in contact with the Red Army again.

Those Nordland men Ziegler and his staff could gather were now more or less in the suburbs of greater Berlin, the very heart of Hitler's 'Thousand-Year Reich'. Most of them would never leave it.

Berlin: the end

Berlin's last defenders were a true reflection of the sad, hopeless and bizarre place the Third Reich had become by that late spring. The ranks were filled with children, grandfathers and foreigners. Fourteen- and fifteen-year-old Hitler Youth boys stood alongside old men in their fifties from the Volkssturm, the German equivalent of Britain's Home Guard. The Nordland's Danes, Norwegians and Swedes were joined by a battalion of Latvians from the 15th SS, and a battlegroup of French SS men from the 33rd Charlemagne. Trying to exercise command of this pathetic garrison was the artillery general, Helmuth Weidling. Dividing the city into sectors, he split the Nordland up and used its various parts to stiffen his rag-bag of defenders. On 23 April, Wallin and the rest of the Recce Battalion were based in Neukölln in the south-east of the city, Per Sörensen's Danmark held a bridgehead at East Cross, with the last of the Nordland's assault engineers in Treptow Park and Plänterwald. The Norge defended the three main bridges over the River Spree in Schöneweide, while the Anti-Aircraft Battalion was in Adlershof using their few remaining guns in a ground role. All of the Nordland's artillery were concentrated in Britz to provide fire support anywhere in the city. For once, ammunition was plentiful as the grenadiers found stockpiles pretty much all over the place. This was now street-fighting. All war is savage, but there is something about combat in the rubble of peoples' houses and lives, amidst so many signs of otherwise normal life, that somehow makes urban battle the worst there is. The choking smoke and dust, the flames and claustrophobia of a city-scape are all horrible, and made far worse by the immense noise. Noise may not seem to be anything other than a nuisance, but in urban fighting it is a massive factor. Explosions and shots are amplified by the constricted nature of the buildings, all communication soon comes down to endless shouting and even your own weapons are truly deafening. The effect is disorientating and exhausting. The brain struggles to make sense of its surroundings and often just blanks them out instead, making men sluggish and despondent. Overall, men burn out quicker and need to be rotated out of combat after no more than a couple of days. Prolonged exposure to street fighting, with no time out of the line to gather oneself, will turn a unit into so much human rubble in a matter of days. This is exactly what awaited the Nordland, whereas there was an opposite feeling amongst the Soviets – no-one wanted to die now with victory so close – as Wallin observed:

> There was no limit to their tank forces. The infantry we saw less and less of though. Time after time we realised that the forces ranged against us were exclusively tanks, assault guns and entire battalions of Stalin Organs. There wasn't an infantry soldier amongst them. The motorisation of the Red Army had reached its peak, and the infantry were mostly transported in American trucks following in the tracks of the tanks.

Berlin was surrounded and dying. Neukölln was lost, despite a French counter-attack, Gatow airfield was destroyed and Tempelhof airfield threatened, with Soviet tanks on the edges of its runways. The attempt to hold this last link to the outside world led to a bitter-sweet moment for Erik Wallin:

> We were suddenly pulled out of the battle and sent urgently southwards down to Tempelhof and Mariendorf where the Soviets had managed to make a dangerous breakthrough. The half-tracks were driven at a raging speed southwards along Frankfurter Allee, Skalitzer Strasse, Gitschiner Strasse and Belle-Alliance Strasse.
>
> The Company arrived at a petrol depot among the airfield's administrative buildings to refuel, and among the comrades I met there was Ragnar Johansson. During the hard fighting of the last few weeks we hadn't seen each other even once. He was amazed to see me. 'You're still alive?' he asked incredulously. 'Yes of course I am.' I replied. 'But the boys said you got it at Küstrin.' Ragnar couldn't believe his eyes, then he smiled broadly and declared, 'Come on, let's celebrate.' He pulled me over to his half-track and pulled a bottle from the back. 'Danziger Goldwasser, great stuff, it's the company commanders but I borrowed some, he can't take too much anyway.' Ragnar said beaming. We each took a big gulp from the bottle and then quietly enjoyed a cigarette. He was a fine man and soldier, and ever since most of the Swedes in the Waffen-SS had been gathered in our unit he had been the connecting link. First as a motorcycle dispatch rider, then as GP's half-track driver, and in this role he had been a link to all of us, bringing us news and letters from home.
>
> That was the last time I saw Ragge Johansson.

The fight at Tempelhof was over before it really began and the place was abandoned. The fighting was confused, there was no real frontline, and it was incredibly difficult to keep any sort of control among the wrecked and burning buildings. Unable to get a clear picture of what was going on around him, Sörensen shinned up a telegraph pole, clinging on precariously with one hand, while holding his field-binoculars with the other. It was too good a target to pass up, and a Soviet sniper put a bullet right into him. He was dead before he hit the ground. His men buried him the next day in Plötsensee Cemetery, in a makeshift coffin made from old ammo crates. The Norge's Richard Spörle was killed at pretty much the same time, leaving both the Danmark and Norge Regiments leaderless. With all three remaining battalions mustering barely a thousand men all together, Ziegler amalgamated them under the command of the Danmark's Rudolf Ternedde. Gathering up the exhausted grenadiers, Ternedde led them to the city's inner defence ring, the so-called 'Sector C'. There they established a makeshift defensive line along the over ground S-Bahn tram line from Treptow Park and through to the Sonnen Allee.

Ziegler out – Krukenberg in

The entire Nordland now numbered no more than 1,500 men, and as far as Joachim Ziegler was concerned his surviving Scandinavians, Germans and volksdeutsche had done enough, and he was determined to try and spare them more bloodshed. The tall SS general spoke to Weidling about how to best bring the fighting to a close, but the taciturn Wehrmacht man was having none of it and relieved Ziegler of his command on the spot. His replacement was an old acquaintance from service in the Baltic states – the SS-Charlemagne's Dr Gustav Krukenberg. The militarily undistinguished 57-year-old would now command both the Nordland and his own French SS men. The German Nordland veteran, SS-Unterscharführer Burgkart, was a witness to the abrupt handover:

On the morning of April 25 1945, we – SS-Sturmbannführer Saalbach and SS-Sturmbannführer Vollmar and I – were standing talking in front of the stairway entrance to the advanced command post of the division in a building of the lung hospital at Hasenheide. Suddenly we were spoken to from behind, 'Where is the Nordland command post?' I turned and said, 'Down there in the cellar.' As I said that I saw the silver-grey coat insignia and knew it was a Brigadeführer. He went past me followed by a couple of SS men with machine-pistols under their arms; they didn't say a word.

When I looked round I saw a few trucks carrying SS men had driven up, the men got out and formed a cordon cutting off the whole street. Everything was stopped. A short time later Brigadeführer Ziegler, his orderly and his driver, Hauptscharführer Emmert, came up the stairs, Ziegler walked straight up to me and said; 'Burgkart take your kit and any private belongings out of the wagon.' I asked, 'Why Brigadeführer?', and he replied; 'Take your things out, I have to go now.' Only then did we learn that the other Brigadeführer was Dr Krukenberg of the SS-Charlemagne and the men with him were French.

Emmert meanwhile had gotten into the wagon and started it. I took out my kit, overcoat and assault rifle, and Ziegler and his orderly went to get in. Before he did Ziegler turned to us, saluted and said; 'Gentlemen, all the best.' Vollmar turned to me and asked what was going on, I wanted to go into the command post but was stopped by one of the Frenchmen saying; 'No, back, no, back.' At this moment two or three armoured personnel carriers full of wounded SS men drove up. The crews were searching for a hospital for our gasping, groaning and shrieking comrades. The Frenchmen shouted at them to stop but the drivers ignored them and drove on. Suddenly one of the Frenchmen fired at the first SPW with his assault rifle. The SPW's gunner reacted instantly and fired his MG34 into the French SS men. I saw three or four French SS men rolling around on the ground yelling and thought it was time to get out of there as fast as possible.

'Boys, it's all over'

Most of Berlin was now in Soviet hands, and it was burning. The weather was warm for the time of year, and the skies were clear. With no Luftwaffe, and much of the city's air-defences knocked out, the Red air force had carte blanche to strafe and bomb anything in sight. If they could not level it from the air then the Soviets hit it with artillery or tanks. As the defenders' heavy weapons became fewer and fewer, the Russians boldly wheeled their big guns down the middle of Berlin's streets, smashing everything at point-blank range. The Nordland and the Charlemagne in particular still exacted a heavy toll from their attackers, but come 29 April their resistance was giving out. By that time the Norge was in the Spittelmarkt, and the Danmark around Koch Strasse U-Bahn underground train station. The engineers, anti-aircraft crews and the last five King Tigers of the Hermann von Salza were in the Tiergarten. Most of the Nordland's Recce Battalion were fighting alongside Henri Fenet's Frenchmen in Potsdamer Platz, with Pehrsson and the last of his Swedes and their six half-tracks defending the Reich Chancellery.

Then on 30 April, deep in an underground bunker, after a short wedding ceremony, a middle-aged Austrian crunched on a cyanide capsule and blew his own brains out with a small calibre pistol before the poison could take effect. Next to him his wife of less than an hour committed suicide too. Adolf Hitler was finally dead. Having caused millions of deaths the dictator lacked the courage to stand with his men and go down fighting. As his body was hurriedly burnt in a shallow trench outside the Chancellery bunker, the news started to leak out – it was over.

Krukenberg's men, both Nordland and Charlemagne, were pulled back to the huge Air Ministry building on Leipziger Strasse, though the Norge was still at the Spittelmarkt. A lone King Tiger stood sentry in the street outside as everyone tried to work out what to do next. Pehrsson, though, was in no doubt. He gathered his men together and told them the war was over, that their oaths were absolved and they should try and escape the city.

Breakout

Thousands of Berlin's defenders simply sat down and waited to be rounded up by the Red Army. Others drank themselves into a stupor on rivers of alcohol that seemed to appear from nowhere. A few, like Waffen-Obersturmführer Nielands and his Latvian SS recce company, stayed in their positions and prepared to die – there would be no POW Camp for those Stalin regarded as traitors. Several thousand though were determined to try and break out of the city to safety. Their officers took them to the Weidendammer Bridge over the Spree at Friedrichstrasse. There they waited for nightfall to try and cross the bridge and head west out of Berlin.

In the waiting throng, private soldiers rubbed shoulders with generals like Ziegler and Krukenberg, and high-ranking Nazi Party officials, even Hitler's deputy Martin Bormann was there. A few of the Nordland's last armoured personnel carriers and panzers managed to reach the bridge by draining fuel from the rest, which were then disabled and abandoned. As night fell, the mass of would-be escapees prepared to make the dash over the couple of hundred metres of open bridge and road. The Soviets were waiting.

Just after midnight on 1 May, a group of men stormed forward onto the bridge, only to be cut down by shell and machine-gun fire. The next wave were undeterred and after marshalling the armour, they charged. After that it was more or less a free-for-all, as chaos reigned. The Soviets were determined to stop anyone from getting away and they poured steel and high explosive into the hordes of Army and SS men. It is impossible to calculate how many men died at Weidendammer Bridge, except to say it was carnage. No panzers made it beyond the far side, and neither did any half-tracks. Erik Wallin's friend, Ragnar 'Ragge' Johansson, was driving one of the latter when it got hit on Friedrichstrasse. Johansson dived out, only to be caught and killed in a shell blast a few yards away. He was perhaps the very last member of the Scandinavian Waffen-SS to die in combat in World War Two. Some Nordland men did make it across the bridge though, and they swiftly dispersed and struck west. Among the lucky ones were two of the Norge's Norwegian panzer grenadiers, Lage Søgaard and Kasper Sivesind from the 12th Company, and the Danish officer, SS-Obersturmführer Birkedahl-Hansen, who led a group of fellow Danes from the Danmark out through Spandau. Birkedahl-Hansen was suffering from jaundice at the time and several of his men were wounded, but somehow they managed to keep going north until they reached the Baltic Sea port of Warneminde. There the SS men half-begged and half-bullied a local fisherman to take them to Denmark. By mid-May they were home. As for Ziegler and Krukenberg, the two SS generals got over the Weidendammer and then split up. Just short of the Gesundbrunner U-Bahn station in the Humboldthain district, Joachim Ziegler was hit by a ricochet and killed instantly. Krukenberg managed to lay low in the ruins for a couple of days before being discovered and captured by a Red Army patrol.

Among the ruins, the columns of weary prisoners, and the sudden eerie silence, Vasily Ivanovich Chuikov, the victor of Stalingrad and now the conqueror of Berlin as commander of the Soviet 8th Guards Army, wrote in his diary on 2 May: 'Everything was quiet in Berlin.'

As for the Swedish Waffen-SS contingent, only Hans-Gösta Pehrsson and Erik Wallin made it out of the city alive. Wallin had been wounded in the left leg by a shell blast on 27 April, and tried to find shelter in the crumbling city:

> I remembered that one of my Swedish comrades, Untersturmführer Gunnar-Erik Eklöf, an officer from our battalion, recently had a command in Berlin as the city became the frontline. Perhaps he was to be found in his apartment at Getraudenstrasse. I went in that direction towards Wilmersdorf. Every street crossing had a tank barricade, it was difficult to get through. When I finally reached my destination, it was clear the house was empty. On again.

Wallin was lucky, and found shelter and medical care in an overflowing first-aid centre in a school in Nikolsburger Platz. He was still there when the city surrendered. Abandoning his uniform, he moved around Berlin for the next few weeks hiding out with other Swedes, mostly

The Swedish Waffen-SS officer, Gunnar-Erik Eklöf, who served in the Nordland's famous Schwedenzug, then the SS-Hauptamt in Berlin, before ending up with Otto Skorzeny's commandos in the special forces unit, Jagdverband Nordwest. (James Macleod)

civilian workers, trying to find a way home. In a stroke of pure luck, he then met up with Eklöf, who was also in touch with Pehrsson. Pehrsson told Wallin about the death of his friend Ragnar Johansson on Freidrichstrasse during the break-out, and the two of them then resolved to escape the city as soon as practicable. On 2 June, with Wallin's wounds healed, the pair of ex-grenadiers started out north on foot. En route they heard of an official crossing-point for displaced foreigners trying to get home, over the Elbe River at Wittenberge. Trekking to the site, alternately dodging and bluffing their way through the Red Army, the two Swedes posed as Italian refugees and smuggled themselves onto a ferry.

> The feeling of having at long last got out of the range of fire from the Red Army was overwhelming. We reached the other bank and were greeted by laughing British soldiers, with the words, 'Welcome back to civilisation!'

The end of the SS-Wiking

Away to the southeast, and following the failure of Spring Awakening, the Wiking had been steadily pushed out of Hungary and into Austria. Along with the rest of Dietrich's men, the Wiking was caught up in the defence of Vienna and the fighting around Stühlweissenburg. In the chaos and confusion the division splintered, with much of the Westland separated from its compatriots. Some fell into the vengeful hands of the Red Army near the River Mur, but Karl Ullrich led the majority to the American lines at Radstad, where they laid down their arms and went into captivity. After four years of constant combat, all of it in the East, and having fought in Barbarossa, the Caucasus, Cherkassy, Kovel, the Vistula and Hungary – the 5th SS-Panzer Division Wiking was no more. Tens of thousands of men had been through its ranks, with so very many of them killed or wounded in the process, but the division had established a military reputation that equalled that of the very best Waffen-SS formations, and it was not stained by tales of wanton atrocities as were so many others. Overall the Wiking had won an extraordinary 55 Knight's Crosses, of all the Waffen-SS divisions only the Das Reich (69) and the Leibstandarte (58) Divisions earned more.

Years after the end of the war, Erik Brörup emigrated to Canada and ended up serving in the Royal Canadian Armoured Corps. He is standing in front of his armoured car. (James Macleod)

Erik and Grethe Brörup at home in Canada. Erik suffered strokes towards the end of his life which left him severely incapacitated. His mind was still sharp though, until he passed away peacefully on 7 January 2010. (Erik Brörup)

The Wiking had always been majority-manned by Germans, despite its name and the intent of its founders, but until the advent of the SS-Nordland it had proudly carried the banner of the Scandinavian Waffen-SS and several thousand Danes, Norwegians, Finns and Swedes had worn the Wiking cuff-title. The establishment of the Nordland had effectively brought an end to the Wiking's Nordic heritage, although even then a few Scandinavians continued to be found in its ranks – when Erik Brörup surrendered to the Americans on 8 May, just south of Fürstenfeld, he was not the only Scandinavian. Having surrendered, the men were well treated and sent to a detention camp in Upper Bavaria at the beginning of June. A hasty 'de-nazification' process was declared complete by September, and from then on men were released in batches and sent home. For those Germans from the now-lost eastern Länder (roughly translated as 'regions') there was no home to go to, and they started again among their comrades from western and central Germany. Things were not so easy for the foreign volunteers, who went home to face their vengeful countrymen.

VII

Homecoming – Retribution and Legacy

Behold the cruel Danish, Norwegian and Swedish races, who in the words of the holy Gregory 'did not know except how to grind their teeth like barbarians, but who can now already intone a Halleluja to the praise of God.' Behold that race of pirates who used to raid the coasts of Gaul and Germany but who are now satisfied with their own lands. Their ferocity has gone.

Adam of Bremen on the Vikings from his *History of the Bishops of Hamburg*

When the Third Reich officially surrendered in the West, Norway and Denmark were still occupied by substantial German forces. There was no resistance, and all Wehrmacht personnel laid down their weapons and marched silently into captivity. Amongst them were thousands of Scandinavians, either in uniform or not, who had served alongside the occupiers and who were now joined by survivors from the Wiking and Nordland as they returned home. Whilst the Germans were allowed to leave in peace, 'retribution' was the watchword for those deemed by their own countrymen to have collaborated. In the East the process was simple and brutal. All those who had sided with the Germans, in whatever capacity, were rounded up and either shot or dispatched to the infamous gulag slave labour camps. There they were worked, starved and beaten to death. In France, Belgium and the Netherlands, a judicial process followed hot on the heels of an 'unofficial' reckoning and settling of scores that left several thousand dead. Scandinavia was distinct in not suffering a wave of revenge killings, but even so Denmark and Norway were convulsed in the aftermath of occupation.

The Dutch volunteer Jan Munk at a reunion with his comrades from the Wiking in 1996. (Jan Munk)

Denmark

The Danish Government had a legal conundrum. The original Frikorps Danmark had been officially sanctioned, and Danes had received limited but still significant encouragement from their own State to serve with the Germans. The Frikorps' very first commander, Christian-Peder Kryssing himself, had only taken up the role after being asked to do so by Copenhagen. The Danish solution was a law rushed through at the end of May 1945 which revoked the original decision to allow volunteering, and retrospectively criminalised it. Danish officers who had served in the Wehrmacht were banned from re-admittance into their own armed forces, and in November the first trials of Danish SS men began. Altogether 15,724 Danes were arrested for some sort of collaboration, with 1,229 acquitted and the rest convicted; 3,641 received prison terms of more than four years each, of which 2,936 also lost all their civil rights on a permanent basis. The death penalty, abolished years earlier, was reinstituted with 112 sentences handed down and some 46 carried out. Among those executed were two of the earliest and best-known Danish Waffen-SS volunteers; Knud Börge Marthinsen and Tage Petersen. Marthinsen was convicted of murdering a fellow Waffen-SS officer whom he suspected of having an affair with his wife. He was shot by firing squad on 25 June 1949, but was rehabilitated by a shamefaced Danish Parliament several decades later. Kryssing's family suffered terribly. His wife was crippled in an Allied air-raid while serving as a Red Cross nurse, and two of his sons were killed in action serving with the Waffen-SS. He himself, to his absolute horror and disgust, was disowned by King Christian X, tried and sentenced to five years behind bars. Appalled at his treatment he moved to Haldersleben in North Schleswig after his release, dying on 7 July 1976. As for Frits Clausen, he died of a heart attack in prison while awaiting trial. The Knight's Cross winner, Sören Kam, moved to Germany after the war and received citizenship in 1956. On 21 September 2006, 85 years old, he was detained in Kempten, Bavaria in accordance with a European arrest warrant issued by Denmark. Wanted in connection with the murder of newspaper editor Carl-Henrik Clemmensen in Copenhagen, he denied the charge and Germany refused to extradite him. Nevertheless, as late as November 2009 he was named as a wanted war criminal in a list published by *The Times* in the UK. Kam's fellow Knight's Cross winners, Johannes Hellmers and Egon Christophersen, survived the war as well and went into quiet retirement in Denmark. Christophersen lived in the small town of Køge and worked in Ørum Hansen's machine factory for over thirty years before dying in January 1988, while Hellmers lived another 11 years, finally passing away in late 1999. The Honour Roll Clasp winner Alfred Jonstrup, permanently scarred after losing half his jaw in Courland, died in 1983 aged 67.

Brörup was released from an internment camp in Germany, went back to Denmark but quickly decided to make a new life abroad. Emigrating to Canada, he ended up serving in the Canadian Royal Armoured Corps and then became a qualified bush pilot and forest ranger before retiring. He died in January 2010 after suffering a number of strokes. Paul Hveger, by 1945 an Unterscharführer still serving in Copenhagen, was drafted into the Wiking's Replacement Battalion (Ersatz Bataillon) and sent to Ellwangen prior to transfer to the Front. It turned out he and his new company commander had a history, and not a good one, and as a result Hveger was sent home. That decision almost certainly saved his life. The Replacement Battalion was wiped out in the last months of the war, and almost every Danish volunteer was killed. After the war ended he was arrested and given a 12-year prison sentence, and was released in 1949. Three of his friends did not fare as well; one committed suicide, the other two (both officers) were sentenced to death. Sturmmann Vagner Kristensen served with the Danmark Regiment until the end of the war and survived. Back home he too was tried and sent to prison, and on release was drafted into the Danish Army. He ended up serving two tours in the 1959-60 UN-mission (UNEF) and was awarded the UN medal. One night he had a few drinks and started singing forbidden Frikorps songs. This didn't go down well with his superiors and he was discharged and sent home.

Above left: The first ever Danish Waffen-SS Knight's Cross winner, Unterscharführer Egon Christophersen. Christophersen won his Knight's Cross for leading a successful counter-attack during the savage Narva battles in the summer of 1944.

Above right: The teenage Danish Frikorps and Danmark Regiment volunteer, Vagner Kristensen, at home in Germany. (Vagner Kristensen)

Left: The Danish Knight's Cross winner Sören Kam at his home in Germany. (James Macleod)

Finally, a postscript on Iceland: it had lost its independence to Norway way back in 1262, and since then had 'swapped' rulers so that by the outbreak of the Second World War it was part of Denmark. Occupied by the Allies as an essential North Atlantic base, the island and its people were so remote that the Scandinavian Waffen-SS passed it by. Even so, two Icelanders were known to have served in its ranks; Björn Björnsen went to Bad Tölz, did not graduate but became an SS war reporter instead in the Kurt Eggers Regiment, while Grettir 'Egidir' Odiussen served as a panzer grenadier with the Wiking. He was captured by the Russians and sent to the gulags. He never returned.

Norway

For Norway, the German occupation had lasted five long years, and in the form of Vidkun Quisling the people had a focus for their anger. Quisling himself had refused to flee; even when Albert Speer offered him his personal plane and pilot, the Norwegian Minister-President turned him down (the Walloon SS leader Léon Degrelle used it instead to escape to Spain). In the early hours of 9 May he asked Bjørn Østring, as the head of his personal bodyguard at Gimle, to telephone Oslo's Central Police Station and inform them he was on his way there to surrender himself. On arrival he was arrested and quietly led away. Just as in Denmark, Norway had also reinstated the death penalty especially to deal with its collaborators. Convinced of his own rectitude, Quisling defended himself during his three-week trial. Found guilty of treason on 3 September, he was tied to a post in the grounds of the Arkerhus in Oslo and shot by firing squad. Three- and-a-half years earlier he had been appointed as the country's Minister-President in the very same building. He was one of 25 Norwegians executed for treason and collaboration.

Again in common with its neighbour Denmark, the new Norwegian Parliament passed a Penal Code Amendment on 1 June 1945 which criminalised volunteering. The trials began immediately. But unlike in Denmark, apart from Quisling the 'hydra' largely decapitated itself – Jonas Lie (so long Quisling's opponent) died at Skallum on 11 May; suicide was suspected but unconfirmed. The Hird leader, Henrik Rogstad, did kill himself, as did Josef Terboven and Himmler's representative in Norway, Wilhelm Rediess. In a bizarre pact both men got drunk in a bunker at Skaugum, then Rediess shot himself, before Terboven blew them both up with a mine. Lie's old comrade from their days as Leibstandarte war correspondents, the Justice Minister Sverre Riisnaes, was judged to be mentally ill and committed to an asylum, while the SS-Ski and Police commanders, Frode Halle and Reidar-Egil Hoel, were both imprisoned. Hoel passed away in 1971, Halle at the beginning of 1995. In total a staggering 90,000 Norwegians were investigated for collaboration (out of a population of just three million), with more than half being tried and convicted. Some 28,000 were deprived of their civil rights or fined, and a further 18,000 were sent to prison. Six hundred of those were sentenced to more than six years each. For a comparison, given respective population sizes, this would have meant some 300,000 Britons imprisoned for collaboration. Ornulf Bjornstadt, the SS-Germania veteran, was arrested, tried, convicted and sentenced to five years hard labour. Fredrik Jensen, as an officer and the most highly-decorated Norwegian SS man, was lucky to receive just three months in jail and the loss of his citizen's rights for 10 years. Even so, on release he moved to Sweden and worked as a foreman in fabrication machinery. Still registered by Interpol as a 'war criminal', he was arrested and deported from the USA during a holiday in 1994. Today he lives in Malaga in southern Spain, but is under investigation accused of assisting Mauthausen Concentration Camp's 'Dr Death', Aribert Heim, to escape, a charge he vigorously denies. Olaf Lindvig, as an officer and GSSN leader, was handed down 12 years. He died in 2007. Bjarne Dramstad first had his front teeth kicked out by former Resistance men during his interrogation, before being given five-and-a-half-years hard labour.

Bjørn Østring, as a prominent Norwegian Waffen-SS volunteer and close friend of Quisling, was definitely in the firing line:

> Like all my comrades I was tried and convicted. A retroactive law declared the mere membership of the NS as criminal, as was volunteering for front-service with the Germans. I was given a seven-year sentence (NS membership plus front-service plus 'political activity') and served two years of it. I also lost my civil rights, later restored, but I never considered leaving Norway, although I did help some comrades and others make their way to Argentina.

Even 65 years on Bjørn Østring is still an admirer of Quisling – note the photo of Vidkun Quisling on the wall over his shoulder. (Chris Hale)

When the trials finished, Norway did its best to move on, but bitterness still persisted. Bjarne Dramstad did several jobs after finishing his prison term, mainly in the construction industry, and by the mid-1970s he found himself working on an oil rig out in the North Sea. He never hid his past, and in the confined space of the rig he became the victim of sustained harassment from leftwing union members. Eventually he was forced to quit. As for Østring and Lindvig they gained a certain notoriety for their trenchant views later in life. Østring, married towards the end of the war, stayed in Oslo and founded the Institute for the History of the Norwegian Occupation (the INO, of which Dramstad became a member), dedicated to preserving the memory of the volunteers and their experiences. There was no formal national veterans group, as with the Flemings for example, but many ex-Waffen-SS men continued to meet up as the years went by for conversation, a coffee and sometimes something stronger.

Sweden and Finland

Sweden, alone of all the Nordic lands, saw no battles or occupation. It remained strictly neutral, and so had no collaborators or any interest in retribution against the few surviving Waffen-SS volunteers. Only those men who had first deserted the Swedish armed forces before enlisting abroad, or had committed some other minor infringement, were put in front of the courts. Erik Wallin was one of the latter; his crime was to have supposedly 'stolen his Swedish Army uniform'. He was tried and sentenced to several months behind bars. Whilst inside he was repeatedly beaten by other inmates, owing to his service, as the guards looked on. On release, he recounted the story of the last year of his time in the Nordland to his fellow countrymen and former Waffen-SS war reporter, Thorolf Hillblad. The resulting book is an extremely rare firsthand testament from a Scandinavian volunteer. Wallin continued to meet up with Hillblad and other veterans on a regular basis until he suffered a heart attack at a reunion in Berlin and died.

Hillblad's fellow correspondent and prominent Swedish SS man, Hans-Caspar Krüger, could not settle back in Sweden after the war and like many others found his way to Argentina after the war. The two most decorated Swedish Waffen-SS men; Hans-Gösta Pehrsson and Sven-Erik Olsson, were not arrested and lived out their days in peace. Pehrsson became a salesman in Stockholm and passed away in 1974 aged 64, and Olsson 11 years later in 1985.

The Finns were very different; well, what else would they be? Having effectively fought three wars in six years, they at least ended up on the winning side and managed to avoid becoming a Soviet satellite. Waffen-SS service was in no way considered a crime, indeed it was often a career advantage. Of the 1,200 or so men who survived their service, 282 went on to become officers in the Finnish Army, several of them of high rank. One, Sulo Suorttanen an ex-Bad Tölz graduate and SS-Untersturmführer, even became the Defence Minister in a subsequent national government.

'Daddy, what did you do in the war?'

The Waffen-SS remains one of the most controversial military bodies to have ever existed. On the one hand its military achievements deserve to stand as examples of martial excellence, but there is no getting away from the fact that as an organisation it was intimately connected with the vileness of Nazism. The verdict of the Nuremburg Tribunal on the Waffen-SS summarises the criminal aspect:

> The SS was utilised for purposes which were criminal under the Charter involving the persecution and extermination of the Jews, brutalities and killings in concentration camps, excesses in the administration of the occupied territories, the administration of the slave labour program and the mistreatment and murder of prisoners-of-war … The Tribunal declares to be criminal … those persons who had been officially accepted as members of the SS as enumerated in the preceding paragraph (members of the Allgemeine SS, members of the Waffen-SS, members of the SS Totenkopf Verbände …).

Erik Wallin at a reunion of his Nordland comrades in Germany after the war. He died from a heart attack at one of these reunions. (James Macleod)

Thus membership of the Waffen-SS was condemned as a crime in itself, yet this seems ill-judged given the complexity of events and circumstances. Waffen-SS soldiers committed the atrocities at Le Paradis, Oradour and Malmédy, amongst others, and of that there is no doubt whatsoever. Even as late as 2009 a 28-year-old Viennese student, Andreas Forster, stumbled across the alleged massacre of 58 Hungarian Jewish slave labourers just before the war ended. The 90-year-old Wiking veteran, Adolf Storms, has been charged with murder and is now awaiting trial.

Does that mean all of those who wore the same uniform should be condemned? In essence should we condemn the Scandinavian Waffen-SS? The volunteers' own views are revealing. Bjarne Dramstad:

We felt sorry for Russian civilians, and gave them food and other small things when we could spare them. Some Russian women had to clear roads of snow, they were brutalised by the Germans if they didn't work fast enough and I felt sick when I saw this happening. On our way to the Front, on our first day in Russia, we found a dead Russian woman shot in the head, probably by the German gendarmerie for breaking the curfew of something.

I didn't see any atrocities myself, but soon after arriving at the Front I was on guard duty at an ammo dump in Duderhof West with some old German policemen from the 16th Polizei-Regiment I think. They openly bragged of how they had been getting rid of Jews in Poland. For example how they had dragged married couples out of their beds at night and shot them. We were shocked and felt sick, this was terrible. I never had any negative feelings towards Jews, the only ones I ever met went round the villages back home selling clothes and we gave them food whenever we could. Long after the war I went to Auschwitz, it was terrible, but it opened my eyes. I believed in Hitler during the war, I was wrong – he was a madman.

I believe that everyone is responsible for what they have done, and if anyone committed atrocities they should answer for it. There is a difference between a soldier and a murderer in uniform; I look upon myself as a soldier.

Bjørn Østring said much the same:

In the internment camp I was trained as a professional painter and later on at the earliest possible opportunity I gained my Master's Certificate, founding a company of my own with several employees. My trade expertise then provided me with good jobs in leading companies, one founded by Alf Bjercke the WWII Spitfire pilot. I am and always have been proud of my commitment to the cause that I fought for, and I have never concealed it from anybody. I was genuinely relieved that WWII had come to an end, but I wasn't glad we lost as I was scared of Stalin taking over Europe. I never witnessed any atrocity of any kind, and nothing of the kind has ever been alleged to have taken place in our sector, but as time went on and much came to light of which we knew nothing, I was enraged that it soiled our honour.

Yet it is also clear that the war was not fought in parallel worlds, in the Russian campaign in particular it is tremendously difficult to separate out the 'niceties' of normal combat and the very nature of the Nazis' war in the East, which was based entirely on the concept of racial extermination. Paul Hveger witnessed a Ukrainian militia unit shooting unarmed civilians in 1941 and was appalled. He did not commit any crimes himself, but neither could he claim ignorance. Christian von Schalburg, who has never been accused of any atrocity, wrote a letter to his wife in late August 1941 during his service in the Wiking, where he discussed the treatment of Jews during Barbarossa:

> Jewish rule in the Soviet Union was far greater than even I believed. The population hates them more than Aage H. Andersen himself could dream of [editor of the Danish anti-Semitic newspaper, *Kamptegnet*]. These people … are so damned passive, despite all their hate. Many lives would have been saved, most of all their own, if they cut down the Jews before they fled from us. I think that that will come.

The Scandinavian Waffen-SS and its legacy

Himmler's ambition to create divisions of Scandinavian Waffen-SS troops failed. Overall around 10,000 Danes, 6,500 Norwegians, 1,500 Finns and a few hundred Swedes enlisted. At any one time there was never more than two to three thousand serving at the Front, and though they fought well (especially when they had gained some combat experience – the Nordland Division won the fifth highest number of Knight's Crosses of all the Waffen-SS divisions, 25) they never achieved the size necessary to turn the mammoth battles of the Russian Front in their favour.

Recruited from the need for manpower as well as racial kinship, it soon became clear that the martial traditions of the ancient Viking societies had long since disappeared. The best card the likes of Terboven had to play was the 'Red Threat', and having seen what had happened to Finland this was a powerful draw for some. This anti-communist sentiment was combined with the usual attractions to youth of potential glory and bold action, creating a heady mix that appealed to a number of individuals. Even then, most recruits came from Scandinavia's small Far-Right movements, and the Nazis 'model occupations' did not convert the masses into adherents of German National Socialism. That naïve ambition very soon hit the buffers of strongly independent Nordic populations with solid democratic foundations and distaste for extremism of any kind. As such, the likes of Erik Brörup, Vagner Kristensen, Paul Hveger, Bjarne Dramstad, Ornulf Bjornstadt, Bjørn Østring and Erik Wallin were always a minority, both at home and in the Waffen-SS as a whole. Hausser and Steiner's creation was never a European army, but it became an army of Europeans.

Perhaps it is best left to the veterans themselves to have the last word on the Scandinavian Waffen-SS. Erik Wallin:

> What a road we had travelled … once, we had stormed forth victoriously over the boundless plains of east Europe. With the fighting excitement of youth we had thrown ourselves into battles that have gone down in history. Many of us, after the assault over the Kuban and Terek Rivers by Maglobek and Maikop, could even have imagined Asia beyond the cloud-topped, snow-covered Caucasus.

Bjørn Østring:

> We, the Norwegian and other foreign volunteers, did not fight for Hitler or his regime, but alongside his country. Just as Britons didn't fight for Stalin but alongside the Soviet Union, it's a sad truth but in war you can't pick your allies. If people are really interested in what actually happened then they should find out for themselves. They will see that it was not so easy at the time to choose a course of action, but it was then that a choice had to be made.

APPENDIX A

Wehrmacht Bravery Awards

Not one of the champions … was able to deliver us from
the tyranny of the foreign hordes … because of the greatness
of their bravery and ferocity.

Early tenth-century Irish chronicle, 'Wars of the Irish with the Vikings'.

As with all things in the Wehrmacht, when it came to bravery awards there was a thorough system and process in place. Courage, and the citations and medals that went with it, were taken very seriously and based on a pyramid structure, with the Iron Cross being the standard basis of measurement, along with a series of specialist awards such as the Close Combat Badge, the Wound Badge etc. Up the pecking order from the Iron Cross was the German Cross, the Honour Roll Clasp and then finally on to the pinnacle, the Knight's Cross. Most of the awards had at least two grades, with the Knight's Cross having four; the Knight's Cross itself, then awarded with Oak Leaves, then Swords and finally Diamonds.

Close Combat Day – (Nahkampftag)
A Close Combat Day was designated as fighting the enemy hand-to-hand. These days were acknowledged in a soldier's individual *Soldbuch* by his superior officer and noted as such. The Norwegian volunteer, SS-Unterscharführer Sverre E.H Larsen, who also won the Iron Cross 1st Class and lost an arm during the retreat from Oranienbaum, was known as '*Sverre Nahkampf*' due to his combat proficiency and the many close combat days he achieved.

Iron Cross – (Eisener Kreutz)

Awarded in two classes, the Iron Cross 2nd Class was authorised for a single act of bravery in combat beyond normal duty, some 2.3m were awarded during the war, including 214 to Finnish volunteers.

The Iron Cross 1st Class required you to already have the 2nd Class award and a further three to five additional acts of bravery; some 300,000 were awarded. Thirty-eight Norwegians, 16 Finns and 10 Swedes were among the recipients including Heinz Harmel's personal radio operator, SS-Oberscharführer Sven-Erik Olsson.

Honour Roll Clasp of the German Army – (Ehrungsblattspange des deutschen Heeres)

The Honour Roll Clasp required the recipient to have both classes of Iron Cross as a prerequisite, and was then awarded for an additional act of unusual bravery which just fell short of deserving a Knight's Cross. Some 166 Waffen-SS soldiers won this prestigious award including five Scandinavians – the Swede Hans-Gösta Pehrsson for his leadership and courage in the fighting for the hill at Trekni in 1944, the Danes Alfred Jonstrup and Per Sörensen in Courland, and the two Finnish machine-gunners Kalevi Kønønen and Yrjø Pyytia in the Caucasus.

German Cross – (Deutsches Kreuz)

Awarded in two classes, the lower being Silver, the higher in Gold. This award was instituted by Hitler personally as a median award between the Iron Cross and a full-blown Knight's Cross. It only required the winner to already have the Iron Cross 2nd Class, and was awarded for repeated acts of exceptional bravery in combat that did not merit a Knight's Cross. One thousand and sixteen Waffen-SS soldiers won this award, including Fredrik Jensen who in so doing became the most decorated Norwegian Waffen-SS volunteer of the war.

There were 20 men in the Waffen-SS who held both the Honour Roll Clasp and the German Cross in Gold; seven were in the SS-Wiking Division (one then served in the Nordland in the 1st Battalion the SS-Norge Regiment), and two in the SS-Nordland Division (one having served in the Horst Wessel Division first) and the other being Per Sörensen.

Knight's Cross – (Ritterkreuz)

Highly coveted, this was the highest award for bravery available to members of the Wehrmacht. Worn on a ribbon around the neck it was colloquially known as 'curing your throat ache'. While it could be earned by all ranks for exceptional acts of courage, it was also awarded to officers as recognition of the deeds of the units under their command; hence many were earned by battalion, regimental and divisional commanders. No Norwegians, Swedes or Finns won the Knight's Cross, but three Danes did; SS-Unterscharführer Egon Christophersen for his bravery at Narva, SS-Untersturmführer Sören Kam on 7 February 1945 while serving with the SS-Wiking, and SS-Obersturmführer Johannes Hellmers (who also won the German Cross in Gold) on 5 March 1945 while serving with the Dutch SS-Nederland Division during the Fourth Battle of Courland. Hellmers was commanding the De Ruyter's 6th Company when it was dug-in around the town of Kaleti. Subjected to furious attacks from large formations of Russian infantry and armour, Hellmers personally led counter-attack after counter-attack to keep the Soviets at bay. As a direct result the line held and a major disaster was averted.

Waffen-SS Formation Organisation

SS Section – (Gruppe)

Commanded by a junior NCO, such as an SS-Rottenführer or an SS-Unterscharführer. Made up of anywhere between 6–12 men, depending on casualties, the section was the foundation and the building block of the Waffen-SS fighting formations, as in all armies. When a man passed his Waffen-SS recruit training, he would be posted to a division, which would then send him internally to a regiment and a named battalion. In the battalion he would be detailed to one of the companies and a specific platoon within that company. He would then finally be allocated to a section in the platoon and that *Gruppe* would become his home and sanctuary until killed, wounded, captured or told otherwise. If Sections in a unit don't work then nothing else does either. All unit cohesion and performance rested on them within the Waffen-SS.

SS Platoon – (Zug)

Commanded either by a junior officer such as an SS-Untersturmführer, an officer candidate such as an SS-Oberjunker or a senior NCO such as an SS-Oberscharführer. The platoon had its component sections, usually 3–4 depending on casualties, with a young officer commander and a veteran platoon sergeant who would act as second-in-command. The platoon sergeant would also control the platoon's supplies (ammunition, food, water etc) and provide a steady hand and voice of experience to his young officer. In SS panzer formations a platoon would comprise five tanks. A soldier's closest friends were his section, but his home was his platoon.

SS Company – (Kompanie)

Commanded by a more senior and experienced, though usually still young, officer such as an SS-Obersturmführer or an SS-Hauptsturmführer.

In the British Army a company is commanded by a Major, around early thirties in age and no less. Normally consisting of three platoons, the company was the lowest tactical unit that external attachments were made to, including forward artillery fire observers and forward air controllers. In panzer formations the company would comprise four tank platoons, and two command and control tanks.

SS Battalion – (Abteilung)

Commanded by an older and more experienced officer such as an SS-Sturmbannführer. An average battalion would be made up of four companies and could have sections of specialist troops such as assault engineers attached as necessary for a particular operation. A battalion would be numbered with a Roman numeral in front of its parent regiment's designation, such as II/SS-Panzergrenadier Regiment 6 Theodor Eicke, which denoted the 2nd Battalion of the Theodor Eicke Panzergrenadier Regiment number 6.

SS Regiment – (Standarte)

Commanded by a senior and very experienced officer such as an SS-Oberführer or SS-Standartenführer. Equivalent to a brigade in British Army parlance, the regiments were a division's major sub-units and as such would have their own integral staff as well as supporting elements including at the very least a heavy gun company, an anti-aircraft defence company, a combat engineer company and its teeth arms of either three foot-borne infantry, armoured infantry battalions or two panzer battalions, depending on its designation as an infantry, panzer grenadier or panzer regiment respectively. This was a major difference between Army and Waffen-SS regiments with Army formations having the same number of panzer battalions but crucially only two infantry battalions in each panzer grenadier or infantry regiment. This heavily reduced the unit's combat power and meant that Army units tended to burn out far more rapidly in the battles of attrition so prevalent on the Russian Front. However, due to manpower shortages later on in the war many Waffen-SS regiments raised in late 1944 and 1945, including those in the Flemish Langemarck and the French Charlemagne, mirrored Army formations and only consisted of two-battalion regiments. This reduction in strength meant the unit's combat effectiveness could be quickly eroded in periods of intense fighting. The regiment would be described by type, Roman numeral if it had one, and then honour name if given one, so for example in the Das Reich there was SS-Panzergrenadier Regiment 3 Deutschland. If composed of Germanic volunteers the term 'Freiwilligen' i.e. 'volunteer', would be added. So in the Dutch SS-Nederland Division there were two regiments – SS-Freiwilligen Panzergrenadier Regiment 48 General Seyffardt, and SS-Freiwilligen Panzergrenadier Regiment 49 De Ruyter. Non-Germanic volunteer units were designated as 'Waffen-Grenadier der SS', i.e. 'Armed Grenadier of the SS', such as the Latvian Waffen-Grenadier Regiment der SS 42 Voldemars Veiss.

SS Division – (Division)

Next up the chain came the mainstay of the Waffen-SS formation. The division was entirely different from the British Army system where the much smaller regimental formation was the building block of the field army and a soldier's spiritual home. A British soldier in the Second World War would feel loyalty to the Royal Norfolk's, the Cameronians or the Irish Guards – famous regiments all, but in the Waffen-SS it was to the Das Reich or Hitlerjugend Divisions. This 'division as home' concept was a great help in maintaining morale and combat effectiveness during the frequent decimations of the Waffen-SS divisions.

There were three main types of Waffen-SS division, each with its own structure: the Panzer (tank) division, the Panzergrenadier (mixed tanks and infantry) division and the non-mechanized division (infantry, cavalry or mountain infantry).

All three types were commanded by either an SS-Gruppenführer or SS-Brigadeführer. Just as with regiments, the division would have a structure of support units and these would typically comprise a headquarters staff, military police, transport, medical support, logistics, a signals battalion, an engineer battalion, an artillery regiment and an anti-aircraft battalion (almost all entirely mechanized in panzer and panzer grenadier divisions). The teeth of the different types of divisions were as follows:

Panzer division

These were the armoured fists of the Waffen-SS and each had two panzer grenadier regiments of three battalions each and a panzer regiment of two battalions. There were seven full panzer divisions in the Waffen-SS and they comprised the crème de la crème of the Waffen-SS fighting strength, such as the 1st SS-Panzer Division Leibstandarte SS Adolf Hitler. Of the non-German Waffen-SS formations only the famous 5th SS Panzer Division Wiking attained this celebrated status, and of course is described in this book.

Panzergrenadier division

Comprising two panzer grenadier regiments of three battalions each and a single panzer battalion, these were not full panzer divisions but were still very powerful formations with their own integral armour. In the 'combat pecking order' these formations were still an élite within the Waffen-SS. There were seven panzer grenadier divisions including the only Waffen-SS division to fight exclusively on the Western Front, the ethnic German 17th SS-Panzergrenadier Division Götz von Berlichingen. Five of the divisions that attained this status were non-Reichsdeutsche formations including the Nordic 11th SS-Freiwilligen-Panzergrenadier Division Nordland (again covered in this book) and the Hungarian volksdeutsche 18th SS-Freiwilligen-Panzergrenadier Division Horst Wessel, the Götz and the Belgian Langemarck and Wallonien.

Non-mechanised divisions (infantry, cavalry or mountain infantry)
These formations formed the bulk of the Waffen-SS order of battle and the vast majority of foreign formations came under this designation. As non-mechanized units they were the least well-equipped of the Waffen-SS formations and were of widely differing quality, organisation, strength and combat effectiveness. Usually called 'grenadier' divisions, they normally comprised two grenadier regiments of three battalions each with supporting arms, but in practice this was chopped and changed to suit the availability, or not, of both equipment and manpower. In the French 33rd Waffen-Grenadier-Division der SS Charlemagne (französische Nr.1) for instance, there were only two grenadier battalions in each regiment (for more information see Book 1 in the Hitler's Legions series, *Hitler's Gauls*). Crucially, these formations lacked any integral armour and the necessary transport to give them the mobility on the battlefield that was increasingly essential as the nature of warfare, particularly on the Eastern Front, became one characterised by rapid movement. In total there were 26 grenadier divisions including two number 23s, two number 29s and two number 33s (the number being reused when the original formation was disbanded). Thus the original 29th Waffen-Grenadier Division der SS (russiche Nr.1) under Bronislav Kaminski, became the 29th Waffen-Grenadier Division der SS (italienische Nr.1) under Heldmann when Kaminski's men were absorbed into Vlasov's ROA.

There were four SS cavalry (Kavallerie) divisions, including the short-lived 33rd Waffen-Kavallerie Division der SS (ungarische Nr.3), which was overrun before formation and its number reused for the French Charlemagne division.

There were also six mountain infantry (Gebirgs) divisions including the German 6th SS Mountain Division Nord, and the Yugoslav ethnic German 7th SS-Freiwilligen-Mountain Division Prinz Eugen.

A few of these formations were excellent combat formations, especially the three Baltic grenadier divisions, plus the Nord, the Prinz Eugen, the Langemarck and the Wallonien. The majority however, were of questionable quality and many were formed as defeat loomed and were of little value at the Front. Some of these latter were the lowest of the low and deserve to be remembered with nothing more than horror and contempt at their records, which were brutal beyond belief. Probably the most infamous was the 36th Waffen-Grenadier Division der SS under Oskar Dirlewanger, whose record in Belorussia and especially Warsaw, will forever stain the reputation of the Waffen-SS order of battle.

SS Corps – (Korps)

Commanded by either an SS-Obergruppenführer or SS-Gruppenführer, the Corps was the next level up in organisational terms and consisted of a number of divisions, the minimum of which was two but could rise to three or even four. The Corps was a fully-functional field force in its own right with a full-time staff comprising complements of headquarters staff, transport, logistics, and military police, medical and signalling units of different strengths. Component divisions would then be placed under Corps command but did not 'belong' to that Corps, as it were, for any more than the specific campaign the Corps was involved in, or even for no longer than a single operation. The Wehrmacht's ability to swiftly regroup formations under differing Corps commands during often complex phases of battle was one of the reasons that the German forces held out for so long towards the end of the war. During the latter defensive stages of the Russian campaign, formations would often rapidly switch Corps control to face and close off Russian offensive threats, and its true to say that few armies have ever mastered this incredibly difficult art. During the war a total of 18 Waffen-SS corps were formed including Felix Steiner's famous III Germanic SS-Panzer Corps and the I SS and II SS-Panzer Corps of Kharkov, Normandy and Ardennes fame.

SS Army Group – (Armeegruppe)

Commanded by either an SS-Obergruppenführer or SS-Oberstgruppenführer – only Sepp Dietrich ever achieved this latter rank, (see Appendix C, Waffen-SS Ranks). These were the largest formations ever fielded by the Waffen-SS during the war, including Dietrich's Sixth SS Panzer Army and Steiner's Eleventh SS Panzer Army. This grouping would normally consist of several corps-sized units, but was extremely unwieldy to handle even for the well trained Wehrmacht General Staff corps. During the early stages of the war the separate Waffen-SS formations were distributed between the different Wehrmacht Army Groups, such as Army Group A, B or C for the invasion of Soviet Russia, and it was only when to all intents and purposes the war was lost that Waffen-SS formations were brought together in this way (in an interesting volte face often with Army formations integral to them).

APPENDIX C

Waffen-SS and Comparable Ranks

SS-Schütze
Private (this was the basic private rank; any speciality would be reflected in the title, e.g. *Panzerschütze* – tank trooper)

SS-Oberschütze
Senior Private (attained after six months' service – this may seem strange to have 'grades' of Private but in the modern British Army there are no less than 4 Private grades and it can take two years or more to move from Class 4 at the bottom to 1, with soldiers gaining greater qualifications in the process as well as higher pay)

SS-Sturmmann
Lance corporal (first NCO rank)

SS-Rottenführer
Corporal

SS-Unterscharführer
Lance Sergeant (this rank, above full Corporal but below Sergeant, is only used in the British Army in the Brigade of Guards – the Household Cavalry use slightly different rankings)

SS-Junker
Officer candidate (acting rank only, substantive rank of SS-Unterscharführer, non-university graduates hold this rank in the British Army while training at RMA Sandhurst)

SS-Scharführer	Sergeant
SS-Standartenjunker	Officer candidate (acting rank only, substantive rank of SS-Scharführer, this was a step up from SS-Junker)
SS-Oberscharführer	Colour/staff Sergeant
SS-Hauptscharführer	Warrant Officer Class 2
SS-Standartenoberjunker	Officer candidate (acting rank only, substantive rank of SS-Hauptscharführer, yet another step in the process of becoming a fully-fledged officer in the Waffen-SS)
SS-Sturmscharführer	Warrant Officer Class 1 (could only be achieved after fifteen years' service)
SS-Untersturmführer	Second Lieutenant
SS-Obersturmführer	Lieutenant
SS-Hauptsturmführer	Captain
SS-Sturmbannführer	Major
SS-Obersturmbannführer	Lieutenant-Colonel
SS-Standartenführer	Colonel
SS-Oberführer	Brigadier equivalent
SS-Brigadeführer	Major-General
SS-Gruppenführer	Lieutenant-General
SS-Obergruppenführer	General
SS-Oberstgruppenführer	Colonel-General (only Sepp Dietrich ever attained this rank)

Bibliography

Ailsby, Christopher, *Hell on the Eastern Front: The Waffen-SS War in Russia 1941–1945*, Spellmount, 1998

Ailsby, Christopher, *Waffen-SS The Unpublished Photographs 1923–1945*, Bookmart, 2000

Bauer, Eddy, Lt.Col, *World War II*, Orbis, 1972

Beevor, Antony, *Berlin: The Downfall 1945*, Penguin, 2002

Bellamy, Chris, *Absolute War: Soviet Russia in the Second World War*, Macmillan, 2007

Biddiscombe, Perry, *The SS Hunter Battalions, The Hidden History of the Nazi Resistance Movement 1944–45*, Tempus, 2006

Bishop, Chris, *Hitler's Foreign Divisions, Foreign Volunteers in the Waffen-SS 1940–1945*, Amber, 2005

Bishop, Chris, *Hell on the Western Front: The Waffen-SS War in Europe 1940–1945*, Spellmount, 2003

Bishop, Chris, *The Military Atlas of World War II*, Amber, 2005

Bishop, Chris, *The Essential Vehicle Identification Guide – Waffen-SS Divisions 1939–45*, Amber, 2007

Butler, Rupert, *Hitler's Jackals*, Leo Cooper, 1998

Butler, Rupert, *Legions of Death*, Hamlyn, 1983

Butler, Rupert, *SS-Wiking: The History of the Fifth SS Division 1941–45*, Spellmount, 2002

Butler, Rupert, *The Black Angels*, Arrow, 1989

Carell, Paul, *Hitler's War on Russia*, Volume 1, Corgi, 1966 (translated by Ewald Oser)

Carell, Paul, *Hitler's War on Russia*, Volume 2, Scorched Earth, Corgi, 1971 (translated by Ewald Oser)

Cornish, Nik, *Armageddon Ost: The German Defeat on the Eastern Front 1944–5*, Ian Allan, 2006

Davies, Norman, *Rising '44: The Battle for Warsaw*, Pan, 2004

Davies, Norman, *Europe At War 1939–1945: No Simple Victory*, Macmillan, 2006

Edwards, Robert, *White Death: Russia's War on Finland 1939–40*, Weidenfeld & Nicolson, 2006

Estes, Kenneth W, *A European Anabasis – Western European Volunteers in the German Army and SS 1940–1945*, Gutenberg, 2007

Forte, Angelo (and Richard Oram and Frederik Petersen), *Viking Empires*, Cambridge University Press, 2005

Glantz, David M., *The Battle for Leningrad 1941–1944*, University Press of Kansas, 2004

Graber, G.S., *History of the SS*, Diamond, 1994

Hausser, Paul, Wenn Alle Brüder Schweigen – Grosser Bildband über die Waffen-SS (When all our brothers are silent), Nation Europa, 1973

Healy, Mark, *Zitadelle: The German Offensive against the Kursk Salient 4–17 July 1943*, Spellmount, 2010

Hillblad, Thorolf (editor), *Twilight of the Gods: A Swedish Waffen-SS Volunteer's Experiences with the 11th SS-Panzergrenadier Division 'Nordland' Eastern Front 1944–45*, Helion, 2004

Jurado, Carlos Caballero, *Resistance Warfare 1940–45*, Osprey, 1985 (translated by Anunciacion Somavilla)

Kaltenegger, Roland, *Mountain Troops of the Waffen-SS 1941–1945*, Schiffer, 1995

Kurowski, Franz, *Bridgehead Kurland: The Six Epic Battles of Heeresgruppe Kurland*, J. J. Fedorowicz, 2002 (translated by Fred Steinhardt)

Landwehr, Richard, *Estonian Vikings: Estnisches SS-Freiwilligen Bataillon Narwa and Subsequent Units, Eastern Front, 1943–1944*, Shelf, 1998

Landwehr, Richard, 'The European Volunteer Movement of World War II', Journal of Historical Review

Landwehr, Richard, 'Siegrunen', Vol. IX, No.4, Whole Number 54 plus Volume number 41

Littlejohn, David, *Foreign Legions of the Third Reich* Vol. 1, R. James Bender, 1981

Littlejohn, David, *Foreign Legions of the Third Reich* Vol. 2, R. James Bender, 1981

Littlejohn, David, *Foreign Legions of the Third Reich* Vol. 3, R. James Bender, 1985

Littlejohn, David, *Foreign Legions of the Third Reich*, Vol. 4, R. James Bender, 1987

Littlejohn, David, *The Patriotic Traitors: A History of Collaboration in German-Occupied Europe 1940/1945*, William Heinemann, 1972

Michaelis, Rolf, *The 11th SS-Freiwilligen-Panzer-Grenadier-Division Nordland*, Schiffer, 2008 (translated by Dr Edward Force)

Munoz, Antonio J., *Forgotten Legions: Obscure Combat Formations of the Waffen-SS*, Axis Europa, 1991

Nash, Douglas, *Hell's Gate: The Battle of the Cherkassy Pocket January–February 1944*, RZM, 2002

Quarrie, Bruce, *Hitler's Samurai*, Patrick Stephens, 1983

Reitlinger, Gerald, *The SS: Alibi of a Nation, 1939–1945*, Heinemann, 1956

Rikmanspoel, Marc J., *Waffen-SS Encyclopedia*, Aberjona, 2004

Rogers, Duncan and Sarah Williams, *On the Bloody Road to Berlin: Frontline Accounts from North-West Europe and the Eastern Front, 1944–45*, Helion, 2005

Stein, George H., *Hitler's Elite Guard at War 1939–1945*, Cornell University Press, 1966

Taylor, Brian, *Barbarossa to Berlin Volume Two: The Defeat of Germany, 19 November 1942 to 15 May 1945*, Spellmount, 2004

Ungvary, Kristian, *Battle for Budapest: 100 Days in World War II*, I.B. Tauris, 2005

Williamson, Gordon, *Loyalty is my Honour: Personal Accounts from the Waffen-SS*, Motorbooks International, 1995

Williamson, Gordon, *The Blood Soaked Soil*, Blitz Editions, 1997

Williamson, Gordon, *The SS: Hitler's Instrument of Terror*, Sidgwick & Jackson, 1994

Williamson, Gordon, *The Waffen-SS – 11. to 23.* Divisions, Osprey Men-at-Arms series, 2004

Yerger, Mark C., *Waffen-SS Commanders: The Army, Corps and Divisional Commanders of a Legend – Augsberg to Kreutz*, Schiffer, 1997

Yerger, Mark C., *Waffen-SS Commanders: The Army, Corps and Divisional Commanders of a Legend – Krüger to Zimmermann*, Schiffer, 1999

www.axis101.bizland.com
www.ehistory.freeservers.com
www.fantompowa.net
www.feldgrau.com
www.feldpost.tv/forum
www.germanwarmachine.com
www.gutenberg-e.org
www.histclo.com
www.nuav.net

Index

DISCARD